D1070303

PMP Rapid Review

Sean Whitaker

WITHDRAWN

Published with the authorization of Microsoft Corporation by:
O'Reilly Media, Inc.
1005 Gravenstein Highway North
Sebastopol, California 95472

Copyright © 2013 by Sean Whitaker
All rights reserved. No part of the contents of this book may be reproduced or transmitted in any form or by any means without the written permission of the publisher.

ISBN: 978-0-7356-6440-1

1 2 3 4 5 6 7 8 9 LSI 8 7 6 5 4 3

Printed and bound in the United States of America.

Microsoft Press books are available through booksellers and distributors worldwide. If you need support related to this book, email Microsoft Press Book Support at mspinput@microsoft.com. Please tell us what you think of this book at *http://www.microsoft.com/learning/booksurvey.*

Microsoft and the trademarks listed at *http://www.microsoft.com/about/legal/en/us/IntellectualProperty/Trademarks/EN-US.aspx* are trademarks of the Microsoft group of companies. All other marks are property of their respective owners.

The example companies, organizations, products, domain names, email addresses, logos, people, places, and events depicted herein are fictitious. No association with any real company, organization, product, domain name, email address, logo, person, place, or event is intended or should be inferred.

This book expresses the author's views and opinions. The information contained in this book is provided without any express, statutory, or implied warranties. Neither the authors, O'Reilly Media, Inc., Microsoft Corporation, nor its resellers, or distributors will be held liable for any damages caused or alleged to be caused either directly or indirectly by this book.

Acquisitions and Developmental Editor: Kenyon Brown
Production Editor: Kara Ebrahim
Technical Reviewer: Dan Tuuri
Copyeditor: Box Twelve Communications
Indexer: Box Twelve Communications
Cover Design: Best & Company Design
Cover Composition: Ellie Volckhausen
Illustrator: Rebecca Demarest

Contents at a glance

Contents

What do you think of this book? We want to hear from you!

Microsoft is interested in hearing your feedback so we can continually improve our books and learning resources for you. To participate in a brief online survey, please visit:

microsoft.com/learning/booksurvey

What do you think of this book? We want to hear from you!

Microsoft is interested in hearing your feedback so we can continually improve our books and learning resources for you. To participate in a brief online survey, please visit:

microsoft.com/learning/booksurvey

Introduction

This Rapid Review is designed to assist you with studying for the Project Management Professional (PMP®) exam. The Rapid Review series is designed for exam candidates who already have a good grasp of the exam objectives through a combination of experience, skills, and study; and can use a concise review guide to help them assess their readiness for the exam.

The PMP® exam is aimed at a project management professional who has the following:

- A secondary degree (high school diploma, associate's degree, or the global equivalent) with at least 5 years of project management experience, with 7,500 hours of leading and directing projects and 35 hours of project management education.

  OR
- A 4-year degree (bachelor's degree or the global equivalent) and at least 3 years of project management experience, with 4,500 hours leading and directing projects and 35 hours of project management education.

Successful candidates who take this exam should have the knowledge and skills required to manage projects using processes, tools, and techniques that are generally considered to encompass "best practices" on a wide range of projects. It is important to note that real-world experience with managing projects is required prior to earning the PMP® certification, and that having practical knowledge is a key component to achieving a passing score.

This book reviews every concept described in the following performance domains:

- Initiating the project
- Planning the project
- Executing the project
- Monitoring and controlling the project
- Closing the project

This is a Rapid Review, not a comprehensive guide such as the PMP® Training Kit. The book covers every exam task on the PMP® exam, but does not necessarily cover every exam question. The Project Management Institute (PMI) regularly adds new questions to the exam, making it impossible for this (or any) book to provide every answer. Instead, this book is designed to supplement your existing independent study and real-world experience.

If you encounter a topic in this book that you do not feel completely comfortable with, you can visit the links described in the text. You can also research the topic further by using other websites, as well as consulting support forums. If you review a topic and find that you don't understand it, you should consider consulting the PMP® Training Kit from Microsoft Press. You can also purchase practice exams, or use the one available with the Training Kit, to further determine whether you need further study on particular topics.

> ***NOTE*** **The Rapid Review is designed to assess your readiness for the PMP® exam. It is not designed as a comprehensive exam preparation guide. If you need that level of training for any or all of the exam objectives covered in this book, we suggest the PMP® Training Kit (ISBN: 9780735657809). The Training Kit provides comprehensive coverage of each PMP® exam task, along with exercises, review questions, and practice tests.**

Project Management Institute Professional Certification program

The Project Management Institute (PMI) professional certifications cover the technical skills and knowledge you need to succeed as a project manager at different stages of your career and in a wide variety of industries. The PMP® exam is an internationally recognized validation of project management skills and knowledge and is used by organizations and professionals around the globe. The PMP® credential is ISO 17024 accredited (Personnel Certification Accreditation), so it undergoes regular reviews and updates to the exam tasks. PMP® exam tasks reflect the subject areas in an edition of an exam, and result from subject matter expert workshops and industry-wide survey results regarding the skills and knowledge required of a project management professional with a number of years of experience.

> ***MORE INFO*** **For a full list of Project Management Institute certifications, go to** ***http://www.pmi.org/Certification.aspx.***

Acknowledgments

Writing a book such as this requires the input of more than just me as the author. What you see before you is the end product of a dedicated team of professionals, without whom this book simply would not have been written. I'm extremely grateful for the help and support I received from multiple individuals at O'Reilly and Microsoft Press.

First of all, thanks to Kenyon Brown for allowing me to write this book. During the writing process, I also worked closely with Kara Ebrahim and Nancy Sixsmith, both of whom contributed in significant ways to making this a great book. Dan Tuuri was the technical reviewer, and he applied his expertise to the content. Each of these people contributed significantly to this book, and I look forward to working with them all in the future.

Support & feedback

The following sections provide information on errata, book support, feedback, and contact information.

Errata

We've made every effort to ensure the accuracy of this book and its companion content. Any errors that have been reported since this book was published are listed on our Microsoft Press site at oreilly.com:

http://aka.ms/PMPRR/errata

If you find an error that is not already listed, you can report it to us through the same page.

If you need additional support, email Microsoft Press Book Support at *mspinput@microsoft.com*.

Please note that product support for Microsoft software is not offered through the addresses above.

We want to hear from you

At Microsoft Press, your satisfaction is our top priority, and your feedback our most valuable asset. Please tell us what you think of this book at:

http://www.microsoft.com/learning/booksurvey

The survey is short, and we read every one of your comments and ideas. Thanks in advance for your input!

Stay in touch

Let's keep the conversation going! We're on Twitter: *http://twitter.com/MicrosoftPress*

Preparing for the exam

Certification exams are a great way to build your resume and let the world know about your level of expertise. Certification exams validate your on-the-job experience and product knowledge. Although there is no substitute for this experience, preparation through study and hands-on practice can help you prepare for the exam.

We recommend that you augment your exam preparation plan by using a combination of available study materials and courses. For example, you might use the Rapid Review and another training kit for your "at home" preparation, and take a PMP® professional certification course for the classroom experience. Choose the combination that you think works best for you.

CHAPTER 1

Initiating the project

The Initiating the Project performance domain covers approximately 13 percent of the Project Management Professional (PMP®) exam. It covers the processes involved in selecting, justifying, and approving a project; and creating the project charter. It also covers the identification and analysis of project stakeholders. The work performed during project initiation is used as a foundational input into the rest of the project management domains, so it is essential that it is carried out appropriately.

This chapter covers the following tasks:

- Task 1.1: Perform project assessment based on available information and meetings with the sponsor, customer, and other subject matter experts, in order to evaluate the feasibility of new products or services within the given assumptions and/or constraints.
- Task 1.2: Define the high-level scope of the project based on the business and compliance requirements, in order to meet the customer's project expectations.
- Task 1.3: Perform key stakeholder analysis using brainstorming, interviewing, and other data-gathering techniques, in order to ensure expectation alignment and gain support for the project.
- Task 1.4: Identify and document high-level risks, assumptions, and constraints based on current environment, historical data, and/or expert judgment, in order to identify project limitations and propose an implementation approach.
- Task 1.5: Develop the project charter by further gathering and analyzing stakeholder requirements, in order to document project scope, milestones, and deliverables.
- Task 1.6: Obtain approval for the project charter from the sponsor and customer (if required), in order to formalize the authority assigned to the project manager and gain commitment and acceptance for the project.

Task 1.1: Perform project assessment based upon available information and meetings with the sponsor, customer, and other subject matter experts, in order to evaluate the feasibility of new products or services within the given assumptions and/or constraints.

The first step in any project involves the tasks related to assessing the project feasibility and deciding whether the project will proceed. It is important during this process to assess the needs and requirements of the project sponsor, customer, and other significant stakeholders to determine whether the project is feasible with the knowledge and information available at that time.

> ***MORE INFO*** **You can find out more about this objective by reading the Develop Project Charter process in the PMBOK® Guide, 5th edition or Chapter 2 of the PMP® Training Kit.**

Exam need to know...

- Project selection

  For example: How are potential projects selected from all possible projects?
- Business case development

  For example: What is the business need or justification for the project?
- Project selection criteria

  For example: Does the project meet the required strategic, financial, and non-financial criteria?
- Project sponsor

  For example: What is the primary role of the project sponsor?
- Customer

  For example: What is the primary role of the customer?

Project selection

Project selection is the selection of projects via a defined process to select only those projects that meet the organization's strategic goals and any defined financial and non-financial criteria. Assessing all potential projects against these filters ensures that there is a greater chance of project success. The project selection process is the first task completed in the project lifecycle. The key purpose of a defined project selection process is to be able to assess all potential projects against a predetermined set of criteria; then after assessing each project, end up with an approved portfolio of projects, each of which might be given a score or priority assessment to determine the order in which the projects are completed. Figure 1-1 shows the process that a project should go through to make it into the portfolio of approved projects.

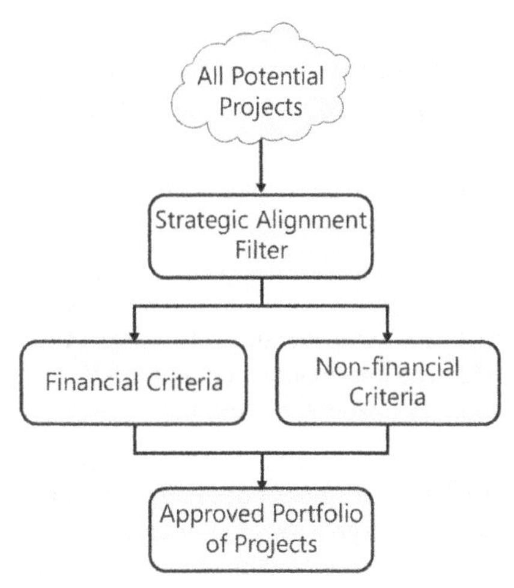

FIGURE 1-1 A diagram showing the process of assessing all potential projects against strategic, financial, and non-financial criteria

> ***NOTE*** **Each organization has its unique documented way of assessing a project's viability that reflects the things it considers most important. There are many different ways of assessing whether a project should make it through a selection process, but the most important aspect is that it is a documented process so that all projects are treated equally.**

True or false? All projects should be justified and selected on the basis of a predefined selection process.

Answer: *True.* All projects that an organization undertakes should have been through a defined process that assesses the strategic importance and alignment, and financial and non-financial criteria before being approved.

> ***EXAM TIP*** **In the exam, you should assume that all projects must go through an initial process that assesses them against predetermined criteria before they are authorized. You might be asked a question that indicates that a project is proceeding on the basis of its being a political or personal favorite. In that case, you should insist that it be subject to any documented organizational process assets relating to project selection.**

> ***MORE INFO*** **You can find out more about the project selection process in Chapter 2 of the PMP® Training Kit book and Chapter 4 of the PMBOK® Guide, 5th edition.**

Business case development

As part of the project-assessment and project-selection tasks, you should document the assessment process; assessment of financial and non-financial matters; and input from key stakeholders such as the sponsor, customer, and other subject matter experts (SMEs) in a business case. A business case can be a simple summary of relevant matters for small projects or an exhaustive document covering known risks, constraints, assumptions, and strategic financial and non-financial criteria for larger, more complex projects.

The development of a business case can be an initial phase of any project with an approval milestone required for proceeding to further planning.

True or false? The preparation of a business case authorizes a project to proceed.

Answer: *False.* The preparation of the business case does not authorize a project to proceed; it is authorized by the project charter. The information contained within the business case is considered by the appropriate stakeholders and then a decision is made.

The preparation of a business case is one of the first steps of deciding whether a project should go ahead. Projects are declined or given a lower priority based on the information contained in the business case, so the preparation of a business case is not a guarantee that the project will proceed.

> ***NOTE*** **A business case can contain a wide range of relevant and pertinent information reflecting what an individual organization requires to assess the viability of a project. The most typical information contained in a business case is the business need, issue, or opportunity; and a description of the financial benefits of completing the project. However, it is up to the organization to decide what information is contained within the business case.**

> ***EXAM TIP*** **In the exam, you should assume that all projects that have been authorized have had a business case developed and approved. If a question presents a scenario that indicates that your project has been formally approved, it already has a business case completed in some form.**

> ***MORE INFO*** **Chapter 2 of the PMP® Training Kit provides more information on project business case development.**

Project selection criteria

As part of performing project assessment and documenting the business need, financial and non-financial matters in a business case, you should have defined project selection criteria by which to measure whether a project should proceed. Project selection criteria are generally sorted into strategic, financial, and non-financial criteria.

Strategic criteria determine whether the proposed project will assist an organization in achieving its strategic goals. Any project that does not assist the organization in achieving strategic goals should not be selected.

Financial criteria for project selection include an analysis of whether the project will provide sufficient financial returns to enable it to be authorized. Typical measures of financial return include the following:

- **Present value (PV)** Calculates the value in today's dollars of future in coming cash flows generated by a project when a discount rate is applied. The formula for calculating a particular PV is

$$PV = \frac{C}{(1 + r)^n}$$

where C equals the future cash flow, r equals the discount rate, and n equals the time period.
- **Net present value (NPV)** Takes the total PV calculation for a given time period and subtracts it from the initial investment in the project to determine a net present value. The formula for calculating NPV is

$$NPV = Co + PV1 + PV2 + PV3 \text{ etc.}$$

where Co is the initial outlay represented as negative number; and PV1, PV2, PV3, and so on represent the PV calculations for the defined time period.
- **Return on investment (ROI)** Determines what the percentage financial return is on any investment in the project.
- **Internal rate of return (IRR)** Defines the expected percentage return on any project investment. Most organizations have a defined expectation of what this figure is and do not approve any projects that do not meet this requirement.
- **Payback period criteria** Determines how quickly an initial investment in the project is repaid.
- **Cost benefit analysis** Measures the costs of a project against the expected and forecast benefits.

Non-financial criteria for project selection include increased market share, environmental management, health and safety, and not-for-profit motivation.

The only projects that can bypass strategic, financial, or non-financial criteria are compliance or emergency projects.

True or false? Except for complaince and emergency projects, only projects that have been assessed against project selection criteria should be considered for formal approval.

Answer: *True.* Having a defined set of project selection criteria against which all potential projects are assessed ensures greater chances of project success.

The project selection criteria represent initial constraints imposed on a project because they must be met before a project can be approved to go any further.

EXAM TIP **You might be asked about some form of financial or mathematical calculation used to justify whether a project should proceed. You should know that it is a form of project selection criteria. The most likely one is focused on either present value (PV) or net present value (NPV).**

MORE INFO **You can find out more about project selection techniques in The Standard for Portfolio Management (Project Management Institute, 2013) and The Standard for Program Management (Project Management Institute, 2013).**

Project sponsor

As part of the tasks involved in initiating the project and assessing whether it should proceed, you will require the input and support of the project sponsor. The project sponsor is an internal stakeholder who provides financial and political support for the project and has ultimate accountability for its success. The project manager reports directly to the project sponsor, and it is important that the two have a good working relationship.

The sponsor provides the initial idea, opportunity, or issue that needs to be addressed by the project; and furnishes initial authorization for project assessment tasks to be completed before the sponsor takes responsibility for approving the project by authorizing the project charter.

True or false? The project sponsor manages the project.

Answer: *False.* The project sponsor provides financial and political support for the project and has ultimate accountability for the project, but does not actively manage it. It is the role of the project manager to take responsibility for managing the project and report to the project sponsor.

The project sponsor is part of the project steering committee that provides oversight, and governance and senior level advice to the project manager. The project manager reports regularly to the project steering committee on the project progress and any risks or issues.

True or false? The project manager is part of the project steering committee.

Answer: *False.* The project steering committee is composed of senior-level stakeholders and SMEs who provide oversight and governance to the project. The project manager reports to the project steering committee and is not part of it.

EXAM TIP **Ensure that you know the different roles of project manager, project sponsor, and project steering committee members. They all have distinct roles and responsibilities, and you should know who is responsible for the different parts of a project.**

MORE INFO **Chapter 1 of the PMBOK® Guide, 5th edition has more information about the role of the project manager.**

Customer

The customer is the stakeholder who is requesting the delivery of a unique product, service, or result from the performing organization. The customer can be either internal or external to the performing organization. If the customer is external to the performing organization, a contract can be used between the organizations to document roles and financial responsibility between the two organizations. The project manager liaises directly with customers and seeks to understand their requirements as part of this project assessment task.

True or false? The project sponsor and the customer are the same.

Answer: *False*. The project sponsor and customer are different roles, and they should be separate because they have different interests in the project. The project sponsor provides financial and political support for the project; the customer has expectations about and requirements for the project deliverable.

Successfully completing any project assessment relies heavily on evaluating and understanding what a customer requires of the project, so it is imperative that a project manager seek to understand the customer's requirements.

EXAM TIP **Ensure that you know the differences between the project sponsor and customer, and the respective roles of each. A key difference is that the project sponsor comes from within the performing organization, whereas the customer can be internal or external depending on the nature of the project.**

Can you answer these questions?

You can find the answers to these questions at the end of this chapter.

1. Why is important that all projects are subject to a defined project selection process?
2. What are typical financial criteria used to assess projects?
3. What is the present value of $50,000 in 2 years at a discount rate of 10 percent?
4. Your project will cost $30,000 and generate income in the first year of $7,000, $10,000 in the second year, and $15,000 in the third year. What is the net present value of your project at a discount rate of 8 percent?
5. What role does the project sponsor play in the project?

Task 1.2: Define the high-level scope of the project based on the business and compliance requirements, in order to meet the customer's project expectations.

This task is part of the iterative description of the scope of work of the project and is the first iteration of this process that focuses on the high-level scope of the project, mainly reflecting the customer's project expectations and requirements.

MORE INFO **You can find out more about this objective by reading the Develop Project Charter process in the PMBOK® Guide, 5th edition or Chapter 2 of the PMP® Training Kit.**

Exam need to know...

- Statement of work

  For example: What is the purpose of a statement of work?
- Project and product scope

  For example: What is the difference between the project scope and the product scope?
- Customer expectations

  For example: Why are customer expectations important when defining the project scope?

Statement of work

The project statement of work is a high-level narrative description of the product, service, or result to be delivered by a project. It is the first iteration of what will eventually become the complete project scope statement that contains only that information, which is known at this early initiation point in the project. It contains as much information about the business need for the project, the stakeholder requirements and expectations, and a product scope description; and how all of these contribute to, and align with, the organization's strategic goals. Additionally, the project statement of work will be used as an input into future scope, time, cost, quality, and risk tasks. During this iterative process, it will be further defined.

True or false? The project statement of work contains a complete description of all the work to be done as part of the project.

Answer: *False.* Given that the project statement of work is part of the initiating work on the project, it contains only as much information as is known at that time. Generally, a complete description of all the work to be done as part of the project is not known at this point in initiating a project, so the project statement of work contains a high-level narrative description of the product, service, or result delivered by a project.

The complete description of all the work to be done as part of the project is included in the project scope statement.

> ***EXAM TIP*** **If a question in the exam refers to a project statement of work, you should immediately know that the project is in the early initiating stages, and any information it contains will be high level and generally in narrative form only.**

> ***MORE INFO*** **You can find out more about the project statement of work in Chapter 4 of the PMBOK® Guide, 5th edition.**

Project and product scope

The project statement of work is a high-level narrative description of products and services, or a result to be delivered as part of the project, and refers to both project scope and product scope. The product scope is a subset of the project scope that focuses on the product, service, or result to be delivered to meet customer expectations as part of the project. The project scope refers to all work to be done as part of the project—including initiating, planning, executing, monitoring, and controlling—and closing project management tasks. Figure 1-2 shows the product scope as a subset of the total project scope.

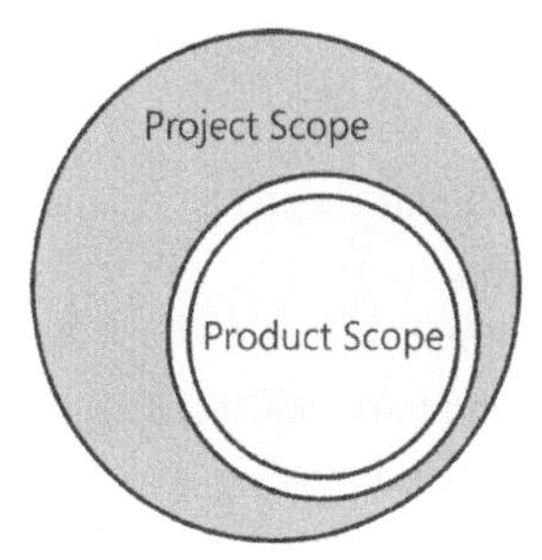

FIGURE 1-2 A diagram showing the product scope as a subset of the project scope

True or false? The work to be done as part of a project includes both the product and project scope.

Answer: *True.* In order to deliver the product, service, or result of the project, the work to be done refers to both the product and project scope.

> ***EXAM TIP*** **When reading questions in the exam, pay particular attention to whether the question is referencing the project or product scope. You might easily think the word says "project" because that is what you are looking for, when in fact it is referring to a "product" scope or "product" lifecycle.**

Customer expectations

The customer's expectations of the project are central to the very reason why the project exists. As such, it is very important that as part of the tasks involved in initiating the project that a project manager seeks to fully understand exactly what the customer's project expectations are in the initiating phase of a project. These expectations are captured in the project statement of work. The project manager might want to provide the customer with several drafts of the project statement of work and seek feedback, in order to ensure that the customer's project expectations are correctly and fully captured.

> ***NOTE*** **Some projects have external customers who have contracted the organization to complete the required work. In other instances, customers are internal to the organization.**

True or false? The customer's project expectations define the project scope of work.

Answer: *False.* The customer's project expectations are an important part of the project scope of work but do not represent the entire project scope.

EXAM TIP Given that most projects are undertaken in response to a customer's request, it is imperative that a project manager have a direct relationship with the customer. In the exam, you should assume that the project manager has direct access to the customer in order to define the customer's project expectations. Customer acceptance is a primary focus of any project that can be obtained only by first understating and documenting the conditions for acceptance at an early stage in the project.

Can you answer these questions?

You can find the answers to these questions at the end of this chapter.

1. What information does the project statement of work contain?
2. Why is the statement of work typically in narrative form only?
3. What is the difference between the project scope and the product scope?
4. Why is defining the customer's project expectations important?
5. Who takes responsibility for ensuring that the customer's project expectations are gathered and documented?

Task 1.3: Perform key stakeholder analysis using brainstorming, interviewing, and other data-gathering techniques, in order to ensure expectation alignment and gain support for the project.

To gain support for the project, a key means of discovering and documenting exactly what stakeholder expectations are is to use various data-gathering techniques. A project manager should always take responsibility for communicating with stakeholders. There are various ways to ensure that stakeholder expectations are aligned with the project goals and deliverables and that stakeholders support the project.

MORE INFO You can find out more about this objective by reading the Identify Stakeholders process in the PMBOK® Guide, 5th edition or Chapter 11 of the PMP® Training Kit..

Exam need to know...

- Stakeholders

  For example: What is any person or organization that can be affected by the project called?
- Stakeholder analysis

  For example: How does a project manager identify the stakeholders that must be monitored the most?
- Data-gathering techniques

  For example: How is information about stakeholders gathered?
- Stakeholder register

  For example: How does a project manager record individual stakeholder interests in the project?

Stakeholders

A stakeholder is defined as any person, group, or organization that can affect or be affected by the project. The primary goal that the project manager has in identifying stakeholders is to ensure their support for the project (or that they do not oppose the project). It is important to fully understand the stakeholder expectations and requirements of the project so they can be met, managed, or influenced.

True or false? Stakeholders on a project include only the project manager, project sponsor, customer, and project team members.

Answer: *False.* These are all excellent examples of some stakeholders that you might have on your project, but the definition of "stakeholders" is much broader than those people directly involved in the project. It includes any person, group, or organization that can affect or be affected by the project or any of its deliverables.

> ***EXAM TIP*** **You will find a great emphasis in the exam placed upon the identification and influencing of stakeholders. Influencing is the process of managing and changing stakeholder expectations and requirements of the project so that they support the project, or at least do not oppose it. A project manager uses a variety of interpersonal skills, management skills, and communications techniques to proactively carry out stakeholder influencing.**

> ***MORE INFO*** **Chapter 13 of the PMBOK® Guide, 5th edition has more information about the process of identifying stakeholders.**

Stakeholder analysis

After stakeholders have been identified, it is important to analyze their expectations, requirements, and the priority with which they should be looked after. This process of stakeholder analysis includes various techniques for gathering and analyzing quantitative and qualitative information about the stakeholders. The first step of stakeholder analysis is to identify all potential project stakeholders and relevant information about them. The second step is to analyze the potential impact, influence, or support that each stakeholder has or could generate for the project, and then use this information to classify and prioritize stakeholders to ensure an efficient use of stakeholder expectation management tasks and activities.

Note that although a lot of stakeholder analysis is done at the beginning of the project, new stakeholders can appear at any point during the project lifecycle, and stakeholder analysis has to be updated to reflect this.

True or false? The project manager should take ultimate responsibility for the identification and analysis of stakeholders.

Answer: *True.* The project manager takes responsibility for the identification and analysis of stakeholders, but they use the skills and experience of project team members and SMEs with experience in this particular area to do the work.

The result of the stakeholder analysis is a stakeholder register that contains all relevant information about the stakeholders and a prioritized list of stakeholders. Stakeholders can then be represented graphically on a classification model stakeholder analysis such as a grid that shows power/interest, power/influence, or influence/impact. Figure 1-3 shows an example of a power and interest grid that classifies how stakeholders should be managed.

		LEVEL OF INTEREST	
		Low	High
Power	Low	Monitor	Keep informed
	High	Keep satisfied	Key players, manage closely

FIGURE 1-3 A grid showing the classification of stakeholders according to the level of power and interest they have in the project

An additional stakeholder classification model is a salience model, which describes stakeholders based on their level of power, urgency, and legitimacy. Figure 1-4 shows an example of a salience model.

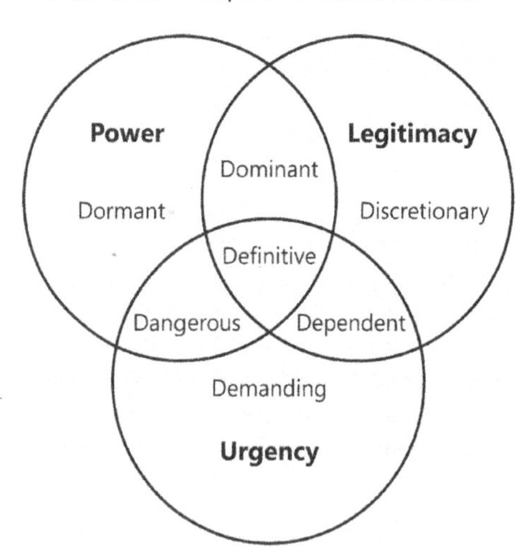

FIGURE 1-4 A diagram showing the intersection and overlap of stakeholder power, urgency, and legitimacy

Data-gathering techniques

In order to understand what stakeholder expectations are, a project manager uses a variety of data-gathering techniques. Each of these data-gathering techniques is focused on soliciting information from or about identified stakeholders. Data-gathering techniques can include any of the following:

- **Brainstorming** Gathering experts with particular information into a meeting and requesting that they began to think laterally in order to come up with as many different ideas as possible. This is an effective technique to identify a wide range of potential stakeholders.

- **Interviewing** This technique involves interviewing stakeholders directly and in formal or informal settings to determine their expectations of the project. It can also be used to gather information about stakeholders from people with experience in dealing with particular stakeholders.
- **Focus groups** A technique that can facilitate specific information about stakeholder expectations and how they can be managed and influenced.
- **Facilitated workshops** A technique that uses focused workshop sessions to bring together key stakeholders to more formally define the requirements and expectations of the project.
- **Questionnaires and surveys** A technique that can be used to solicit information from stakeholders who might not want to give it in person or are geographically isolated from the project.
- **Observations** A technique that can be used by the project manager and SMEs to observe and document stakeholders' expectations of the project.

True or false? The best method of gathering data about stakeholders is to ask the stakeholders directly.

Answer: *True.* Although there are many ways to gather information about stakeholder expectations, the best method is to communicate directly with them.

> ***EXAM TIP*** **Questions in the exam assume that you understand the importance of gathering data about stakeholder expectations because understanding them is seen as crucial to the success of the project. Failure to do so means that you could have a stakeholder or group of stakeholders actively opposing your project.**

Stakeholder register

As a result of carrying out stakeholder identification and analysis, you develop a stakeholder register that lists all relevant information about stakeholders, including their contact details, their interest in the project, an assessment of their ability to influence or affect the project, and your particular strategies for managing and influencing their expectations. The stakeholder register should be reviewed and updated on a regular basis because stakeholders and their expectations can change throughout the lifecycle of a project.

True or false? The stakeholder register can be used to understand stakeholder power and influence on the project.

Answer: *True.* The stakeholder register documents many things about individual stakeholders, including level of power, influence, impact, and interest in the project.

The stakeholder register is an important document used as a key input into tasks focused on collecting requirements, plan and quality management, planning communications management, planning risk management, identifying risks, and planning procurement management.

EXAM TIP **You should assume that you have a well-documented stakeholder register and that it is kept up to date. If you have need to communicate with any stakeholders and are unsure about their interest in the project or the best way to manage their expectations, the stakeholder register is the best place to look.**

Can you answer these questions?

You can find the answers to these questions at the end of this chapter.

1. What is the best definition of a stakeholder?
2. What is the key purpose of using data-gathering techniques during stakeholder analysis?
3. If you have gathered a group of stakeholders together in a meeting and are asking them to think creatively about potential project deliverables and ways of achieving them, what data-gathering technique are you using?
4. What information is contained in the stakeholder register?
5. If you have identified stakeholders on your project and classified them according to their power, legitimacy and urgency, what model are you using?

Task 1.4: Identify and document high-level risks, assumptions, and constraints based on current environment, historical data, and/or expert judgment, in order to identify project limitations and propose an implementation approach.

A key task performed during project initiation is the preliminary identification and documentation of high-level risks, assumptions and constraints that the project is subject to. This information is very useful in assessing the merits of whether the project should proceed, and if given approval to proceed with the project, this information also informs more detailed planning on how to deal with identified risks, assumptions, and constraints.

MORE INFO **You can find out more about this objective by reading the Develop Project Charter process in the PMBOK® Guide, 5th edition or Chapter 2 of the PMP® Training Kit.**

Exam need to know...

- High-level risks

  For example: What does an initial assessment of project risks reveal?
- Assumptions and constraints

  For example: What factors will play an important role in work involved in initiating a project?
- Historical data

  For example: When beginning work a new project, what resource should a project manager ensure they have access to in order to ensure they are able to leverage past experience?

- Implementation approach

  For example: What is the best implementation approach for your project?

High-level risks

During the initiating phase of any project, it is important to identify and document any known high-level risks that might negatively or positively affect the project. Given that this task is performed during initiating processes, it is possible to determine only high-level risks. A more detailed definition of risks is carried out in the risk management planning processes.

True or false? All high-level risks adversely affect the project.

Answer: *False.* A risk represents uncertainty and can be either positive or negative.

High-level risks can be identified via a variety of means, including an examination of archived historical data, lessons learned, and/or the use of experts.

> ***EXAM TIP*** **The questions in the exam assume that you have been through a thorough set of initiating tasks that have included a business assessment of the project and that you have carried out tasks associated with the identification and documentation of high-level risks.**

Assumptions and constraints

It is important to document any known assumptions and constraints that affect the project in order that they be included in any assessment of whether a project should go ahead, and it is also useful when you undertake more detailed planning of the project after it has approval to proceed. The assumptions that you make become foundational and instrumental when approving or declining the project, so it is important that they are documented carefully. For example, you can make assumptions about market conditions, availability of technology and resources, future state of financial markets, and demand for use of the project deliverable. Each of these assumptions is critical for approving and planning the project.

It is also important during the initiating tasks that any known constraints (such as time, cost, quality, or scope) are also documented so that they can be used to assess the viability of the project and as a basis of future more detailed planning.

True or false? Any assumptions made during initiating processes are not relevant to the future detailed planning processes.

Answer: *False.* Any assumptions made during initiating processes affect the project right from the beginning: whether it is approved and any subsequent more detailed planning.

> ***EXAM TIP*** **As you collect your assumptions and constraints, you should document and store them in a place in which they can be accessed easily, and you should refer to them regularly to a project to see whether they are changed.**

Historical data

A key element of any project is the historical data and information collected and made available to future projects so that mistakes are not repeated, and factors that contribute to success are identified and repeated. It is a very valuable resource that a project manager should have access to, particularly during the initiating work being completed. Additionally, a project manager should develop and document historical data future projects to use.

True or false? Historical data is limited to relating to cost and time of projects.

Answer: *False*. Historical data and information can include any documents and data about prior projects, including project files, project records, correspondence, contracts, post-implementation reviews, and lessons learned.

> ***EXAM TIP*** **The exam assumes that you have access to historical data from previous projects and that as part of your own project you collect, document, and store your own historical data. Historical data is one of the most important organizational process assets that a project manager should have access to.**

Implementation approach

After you have gathered enough preliminary information about your project—including the financial or non-financial viability, and any high-level risks, assumptions and constraints—you can decide on the best implementation approach to take to successfully deliver your project. The implementation approach that you select reflects the complexity, size, difficulty, and industry of your project. The implementation approach also helps you make decisions about particular project management methodologies to use to deliver your project. The particular implementation approach or project management methodology you choose to use is documented in your organizational process assets.

Typical implementation approaches reflect different project lifecycles and the speed of the project work. The following are the most common forms of implementation approach:

- **Phased** An implementation approach that sees the project broken down into phases of work to be completed with a significant milestone between each phase, which represents a stop/go point in the project.
- **Iterative or incremental** Used when a product of a project will be developed through a series of repeated cycles, each one incrementally adding to the understanding of the functionality of the product.
- **Adaptive** Used in projects with high levels of change and ongoing stakeholder involvement. These methods are often used in complex IT projects and usually referred to as change-driven or agile methods.
- **Predictive** Used when the scope of the project and product can be fully defined and broken down into a series of easy-to-find sequential steps.

True or false? Every project that you work on uses the same implementation approach.

Answer: *False.* Each project is different in relation to size, complexity, and difficulty, so the implementation approach for each project should reflect the unique aspects of the project.

> ***NOTE*** **Tailoring is the process of selecting which implementation approach and project methodology to use when completing a project. In addition to deciding which particular implementation approach best suits the project, a project manager should also select the particular methodology that best delivers the project and tailor it to suit.**

> ***EXAM TIP*** **Questions in the exam assume that you have a defined and documented implementation approach as part of your organizational process assets and use it.**

> ***MORE INFO*** **Chapter 1 of the PMP® Training Kit provides more information about implementation approaches and the project lifecycle.**

Can you answer these questions?

You can find the answers to these questions at the end of this chapter.

1. Why is it important to identify high-level risks as soon as possible in the project initiation processes?
2. What are the assumptions that you might make about the project?
3. What are examples of typical project constraints?
4. What is the best implementation approach to use for a project?
5. If you are first completing the process of developing a business case for a project, waiting for approval to proceed before moving on to design the deliverable, and then waiting for approval to start manufacturing, what sort of implementation approach should you use?

Task 1.5: Develop the project charter by further gathering and analyzing stakeholder requirements, in order to document project scope, milestones, and deliverables.

A fully developed project charter that reflects the information known about the project during the initiating phases, and enables senior stakeholders to make informed decisions about whether the project should proceed is central to every project no matter the size, complexity, or duration.

> ***MORE INFO*** **You can find out more about this objective by reading the Develop Project Charter process in the PMBOK® Guide, 5th edition**

Exam need to know...

- Project charter

  For example: What are the key elements of the project charter?
- Stakeholder requirements

  For example: What are stakeholder requirements?
- Milestone

  For example: What is the definition of a milestone?

Project charter

The project charter is the foundational document for the project that proves that it has political and financial support, and authorizes project work to formally begin. Each and every project undertaken must have an approved project charter. The project charter contains information such as the known statement of work, stakeholder requirements, milestones, and deliverables. Once approved, it also includes the signatures of significant stakeholders such as the project sponsor, project manager, and customer.

The tasks involved in further gathering and analyzing stakeholder requirements build on the work performed in the previous initiating tasks that gathered and defined preliminary information. This task takes the preliminary information and refines it in order to analyze stakeholder requirements about project scope, milestones, and deliverables more fully. This might involve an iterative process of presenting drafts of the project charter to stakeholders to get their feedback and to gauge support for developing the final project charter and presenting it for approval.

True or false? All projects, no matter how big or complex, must have a project charter.

Answer: *True.* One of the foundational concepts of project management is that each and every project has a project charter.

The size and complexity of the project charter reflects the size and complexity of the project being undertaken. A short and simple project might have a short and simple project charter; a complex project with a long duration might have an extensive project charter that is prepared as part of the initiating phase. In this case, the milestone between phases is the approval of the project charter.

EXAM TIP **When answering questions in the exam, be aware that the absence of certain things means you should stop the project and ensure that the missing document is created before proceeding. One of these essential elements is the project charter. If you discover that the project is proceeding without an approved project charter, your first course of action is to stop the project and develop a project charter to be approved by the appropriate stakeholders.**

MORE INFO **You can find out more about the project charter by reading Chapter 4 of the PMBOK® Guide, 5th edition.**

Stakeholder requirements

Stakeholder requirements define the expectations of the project and product for the stakeholders. The customer is one of your stakeholders, and the requirements will focus on the project deliverables. Other stakeholders might have requirements about other aspects of the project such as quality, communications, health and safety, and environmental management. It is the responsibility of the project manager to capture and document these requirements in the project charter.

True or false? Stakeholder requirements refer only to the technical specifications of the product of the project.

Answer: *False.* The requirements of the customer might focus on the technical specifications of the product of the project, but other stakeholders have other requirements for the project.

Milestone

The project charter is developed during the initiating phase of a project lifecycle, and at this point detailed information about the project schedule is not known. However, there should be enough information to define the major milestones that must be met. A milestone can be a normal part of the project schedule or it can be used as a point between phases that might require specific approval before proceeding to the next phase.

True or false? The project charter should contain detailed information about the project schedule.

Answer: *False.* The project charter generally does not contain detailed information about the project schedule, but does contain information about known milestones. Detailed information on the project schedule is completed as part of the planning activities carried out after the approval of the project charter.

> ***EXAM TIP*** **Remember in the exam that a milestone has a duration of zero days. This is particularly important during your project-scheduling work.**

Can you answer these questions?

You can find the answers to these questions at the end of this chapter.

1. At what point in a project should the project charter be developed?
2. What is the purpose of the project charter?
3. What sort of project should always have a project charter?
4. If you are working on a project and discover the project charter was never formally signed off on, what should you do?
5. What sort of information is captured as part of documenting stakeholder requirements?

Task 1.6: Obtain approval for the project charter from the sponsor and customer (if required), in order to formalize the authority assigned to the project manager and gain commitment and acceptance for the project.

This task builds on the work completed by the previous tasks and seeks to gain official approval for the project charter from the relevant stakeholders. Approval from the project sponsor is essential, and if there are internal or external customers, their approval is also required. Approving the project charter formally authorizes the project to proceed.

> ***MORE INFO*** **You can find out more about this objective by reading the Develop Project Charter process in the PMBOK® Guide, 5th edition or Chapter 2 of the PMP® Training Kit.**

Exam need to know...

- Project charter approval

  For example: What must occur in order to commence detailed planning and execution work on a project?

- Project managers authority

  For example: How does a project manager ensure they have the ability to make decisions to keep the project moving along?

Project charter approval

After gathering all the information that is known about the project at the initiating stage of the project and including it in the project charter, the next step is to get formal approval from the relevant stakeholders for the project charter. Internally, this should be done by the project sponsor on behalf of the performing organization. The customer might also approve the project charter. Approval for the project charter should be done formally and in writing, so that there is a clear record of the commitment given to the project. A project manager should not proceed on a project until formal approval has been given.

True or false? Project charter approval can be represented as a milestone in the project schedule.

Answer: *True.* Whether the project charter is approved can be displayed as a milestone in the project schedule and represent a stop/go point in the project.

> ***EXAM TIP*** **Remember that after the project charter is approved, it should not be changed except under exceptional circumstances that represent significant changes to the project. The project sponsor must be consulted about any potential changes to the project charter.**

Project manager authority

In addition to the information about the scope, milestones, deliverables, a high-level risks, assumptions, and constraints about the project, the project charter should identify the project manager and also clearly state the level of authority that project manager has. Ideally, the project manager has high levels of responsibility and authority, often documented as delegated authority levels in relation to ability to approve changes and control budget and resources on a project.

True or false? A project manager can have either high levels of both responsibility and authority, or low levels of both responsibility and authority. What is important is that they are equal.

Answer: *False.* A project manager has both high levels of responsibility and authority, which is documented in the project charter.

There are a number of other roles in the project such as project coordinator and project expeditor, which both have lower but always equal levels of responsibility and authority.

> ***EXAM TIP*** **If a question in the exam presents a scenario in which a project manager's authority is being questioned, the place to look for where this level authority is documented is the project charter.**

The biggest challenge to a project manager's authority generally comes from the type of organizational structure in which the project is being completed. Most organizations are arranged as functional structures, and it is the functional manager who has the most power and authority over resources in the organization. In this case, the project manager has little or no authority. In a matrix organization, the project manager uses resources from across the different functional areas of the organization. If it is a strong matrix, the project manager has been given more power and authority than the functional manager over resources. If it is a weak matrix, the functional manger has more power and authority over resources than the project manager. In a balanced matrix, they both have equal amounts of power.

Only in a projectized organizational structure, in which the company is organized along the projects it undertakes, does the project manager have full power and authority.

> ***MORE INFO*** **You can find out more about organization structures and a project manager's power in Chapter 2 of the PMBOK® Guide, 5th edition.**

Can you answer these questions?

You can find the answers to these questions at the end of this chapter.

1. Who should take responsibility for getting approval of the project charter?
2. What level of responsibility and authority should a project manager have?
3. In a weak matrix organization, who has the most power: the functional manager or the project manager?

4. At what point in the project lifecycle should the project manager be identified?
5. If you are a project manager in an organization, are utilizing staff from several different functional areas, and you are continually having to ask each of the functional managers to use staff you need on the project and they occasionally decline your requests, what sort of organizational structure are you working in?

Answers

This section contains the answers to the "Can you answer these questions?" sections in this chapter.

Task 1.1: Perform project assessment based upon available information and meetings with the sponsor, customer, and other subject matter experts, in order to evaluate the feasibility of new products or services within the given assumptions and/or constraints.

1. It is important that all projects are subject to a defined project selection process in order to standardize and provide a robust, defensible process for selecting projects from all the available projects that could be undertaken.
2. Difficult financial criteria for assessing whether or not the project should go ahead include payback period, present value, and net present value, return on investment, internal rate of return and cost benefit analysis.
3. The present value is $50,000/((1+ .1)2) = $41 322.31.
4. The net present value equals –$30,000 + ($7,000/((1+ .08)1)) + ($10,000/((1+ .08)2)) + ($15,000/((1+ .08)3)) = $3, 037.65.
5. The project sponsor is the person in the organization completing the project who takes ultimate accountability for the success of the project, and provides financial and political support as part of the project charter-approval process.

Task 1.2: Define the high-level scope of the project based on the business and compliance requirements, in order to meet the customer's project expectations.

1. The project statement of work contains as much information as is known and a narrative form about the work to be completed in the project. Given that it is developed during the initiating tasks, it does not contain as much information as a fully developed project scope.
2. The project statement of work is typically in narrative form because that is the easiest way to describe the level of detail that is known about the work to be done at that stage in the project. It is highly unlikely that you can produce

a detailed description using diagrams, plans, or drawings at this stage because it will be done at the planning stages.

3. The product scope refers to the deliverable of the project, and might include technical specifications and requirements about the deliverable. The project scope includes the product scope and all the other work to be done as part of managing the project.
4. It is important to define customer expectations of the project because they are the party that defines and ultimately pays the deliverable of the project. If you do not understand customer expectations, you will not satisfy them.
5. It is the responsibility of the project manager to ensure that the stakeholders' expectations are gathered and documented. He or she might not actually do the work, but must take responsibility for ensuring that it is done.

Task 1.3: Perform key stakeholder analysis using brainstorming, interviewing, and other data-gathering techniques, in order to ensure expectation alignment and gain support for the project.

1. A stakeholder is best defined as any person, group, or organization that can affect or be affected by your project.
2. Stakeholders provide expectations and requirements of the project; the best way to gather these expectations and requirements is to use data-gathering techniques to communicate with stakeholders.
3. This is an example of using brainstorming as a data-gathering technique.
4. The stakeholder register contains information about stakeholders: their contact details; a description of their interest, influence, or impact on the project; and a description of how their expectations will be managed.
5. This is an example of using the salience model to classify stakeholders.

Task 1.4: Identify and document high-level risks, assumptions, and constraints based on current environment, historical data, and/or expert judgment, in order to identify project limitations and propose an implementation approach.

1. It is important to identify the high-level risks as soon as possible because they might affect whether the project is given approval to proceed.
2. You will make several assumptions that influence whether or not the project is approved. These assumptions include future market conditions, demand for the product or deliverable, and quality of information used to approve a project.
3. Typical examples of project constraints include time, scope, cost, and quality. Other constraints include risk, health and safety, and customer satisfaction.

4. The type of project and its duration, complexity, and size dictate the best implementation approach to use. There is no one-size-fits-all solution.
5. This is an example of a phased implementation approach.

Task 1.5: Develop the project charter by further gathering and analyzing stakeholder requirements, in order to document project scope, milestones, and deliverables.

1. You should begin development of the project charter as soon as you begin assessing whether the project will be approved. The final form of the project charter contains all the information needed to approve it.
2. The purpose of the project charter is to document everything that is known about the project at the initiating stage and to provide enough information so the project has financial and political support to proceed to detailed planning.
3. All projects, no matter the size and complexity, should have a project charter.
4. If you are working on a project and discover the project charter was never formally signed off on, you should immediately discuss it with the project sponsor and stop work until it is signed.
5. The sort of information captured as part of documenting stakeholder requirements includes technical requirements and other non-technical requirements for the project.

Task 1.6: Obtain approval for the project charter from the sponsor and customer (if required), in order to formalize the authority assigned to the project manager and gain commitment and acceptance for the project.

1. The project manager should take responsibility for getting approval of the project charter, but it is the project sponsor and the customer who formally authorize the project charter.
2. A project manager should have high levels of both responsibility and authority, and this should be documented in the project charter.
3. In a weak matrix organization, the functional manager has more power than the project manager.
4. The project manager should be identified and authority given during the development of the project charter.
5. This is an example of the functional manager having the most power; it is a weak matrix organizational structure.

CHAPTER 2

Planning the project

The Planning the Project performance domain covers approximately 24 percent of the Project Management Professional (PMP®) exam. It includes the activities necessary to develop all the planning documents that when combined become the project management plan. There are plans and documents produced to assist and guide the project manager and project team in carrying out all the work associated with further planning, execution, monitoring and controlling; and closing work associated with scope, time, cost, quality, human resource, communications, risk, procurement, and stakeholder management throughout the project. Additionally, the planning work also produces the scope baseline, schedule baseline, and cost baseline. It is important that this planning work is done appropriately; and the amount of planning will reflect the size, complexity and duration of the project. Table 2-1 shows each of the primary planning documents created by each project management knowledge area.

TABLE 2-1 Primary planning documents

KNOWLEDGE AREA	PLANNING DOCUMENTS
Integration management	Project management plan Configuration management plan Change management plan
Scope management	Scope management plan Requirements management plan Requirements documentation Scope baseline
Time management	Schedule management plan Project schedule
Cost management	Cost management plan Cost baseline

KNOWLEDGE AREA	PLANNING DOCUMENTS
Quality management	Quality management plan Process improvement plan Quality metrics Quality checklists
Human resource management	Human resource management plan Staffing management plan
Communications management	Communications management plan
Risk management	Risk management plan Risk register
Procurement management	Procurement management plan Procurement statement of work Procurement documents
Stakeholder management	Stakeholder management plan Stakeholder register Issue log

This chapter covers the following tasks:

- Task 1: Assess detailed project requirements, constraints, and assumptions with stakeholders based on the project charter, lessons learned from previous projects, and the use of requirement gathering techniques (e.g., planning sessions, brainstorming, focus groups), in order to establish the project deliverables.
- Task 2: Create the work breakdown structure with the team by deconstructing the scope, in order to manage the scope of the project.
- Task 3: Develop a budget plan based on the project scope using estimating techniques, in order to manage project cost.
- Task 4: Develop a project schedule based on the project timeline, scope, and resource plan, in order to manage timely completion of the project.
- Task 5: Develop a human resource management plan by defining the roles and responsibilities of the project team members in order to create an effective project organization structure and provide guidance regarding how resources will be utilized and managed.
- Task 6: Develop a communication plan based on the project organization structure and external stakeholder requirements, in order to manage the flow of project information.

- Task 7: Develop a procurement plan based on the project scope and schedule, in order to ensure that the required project resources will be available.
- Task 8: Develop a quality management plan based on the project scope and requirements, in order to prevent the appearance of defects and reduce the cost of quality.
- Task 9: Develop the change management plan by defining how changes will be handled, in order to track and manage changes.
- Task 10: Plan risk management by developing a risk management plan, and identifying, analyzing, and prior to rising project risks in the risk register and defining risk response strategies, in order to manage uncertainty throughout the project lifecycle.
- Task 11: Present the project plan to the key stakeholders, (if required), in order to obtain approval to execute the project.
- Task 12: Conduct a kick-off meeting with all stakeholders, in order to announce the start of the project, to indicate the project milestones, and share other relevant information.

Task 1: Assess detailed project requirements, constraints, and assumptions with stakeholders based on the project charter, lessons learned from previous projects, and the use of requirement gathering techniques (e.g., planning sessions, brainstorming, focus groups), in order to establish the project deliverables.

One of the first tasks a project manager should complete after receiving a project charter is to communicate with the relevant stakeholders and to determine what the project requirements, constraints, and assumptions are. With this information, the project manager can produce a requirements documentation and requirements traceability matrix, which then go on to be used in the development of the project scope. There are many tools that a project manager can use to gather, analyze, and document project requirements, and the most appropriate one should be chosen.

MORE INFO You can find out more about the process of collecting project requirements by reading about the Collect Requirements process in the PMBOK® Guide, 5th edition, or Chapter 3 of the PMP® Training Kit.

Exam need to know...

- Scope management plan

  For example: What is the document that provides guidance to the project manager on how to carry out the work associated with collecting requirements, documenting the project and product scope, and assessing any scope change requests?

- Requirements management plan

  For example: What document guides the project manager and the project team as they seek, analyze, and document individual stakeholder requirements for the project?
- Stakeholder management plan

  For example: What document does the project manager refer to for guidance on how to manage stakeholder expectations?
- Stakeholder register

  For example: What document is used to record individual stakeholder contact details and an assessment of their expectations of and interest in the project?
- Requirements gathering tools

  For example: How do the project manager and project team collect requirements from project stakeholders?
- Requirements documentation

  For example: How does the project manager record individual stakeholder requirements?
- Requirements traceability matrix

  For example: What document is used to trace individual requirements and map the requirements to other aspects of the project such as work packages, activities, and resources?

Scope management plan

The scope management plan is the document that guides the project manager on how to complete all the work associated with the project scope. This work includes the work required to fully plan and document project requirements, and the project and product scope. The plan also provides guidance to the project manager on how to execute and deliver the project and product scope, how to monitor and control the project scope, and how to carry out appropriate closing activities. The scope management plan is a component of the project management plan.

NOTE **The project management plan can be a single document and plan or a collection of documents and plans. The exact nature of the project management plan depends on the size, complexity, and duration of the project being undertaken and the particular project management methodology being used to deliver the project. An important component of the project management plan is the configuration management plan that sets out how all aspects of the project will be tracked. For example, it can manifest as a document control system, a parts numbering system, unique numbers for each node of the work breakdown structure, or numbers allocated to each change request received.**

MORE INFO **You can find out more about the configuration management systems by reading ISO10007 Quality Management Systems: Guidelines for Configuration Management, available from *www.iso.org*.**

True or false? The scope management plan directs the project manager on how to assess and process change requests when potential changes to the project scope are received.

Answer: *True.* One of the roles of the scope management plan is to provide guidance on how any change requests affecting the project scope should be documented and evaluated, and how decisions are made.

> ***EXAM TIP*** **In the exam, you should always ensure that that you have an appropriate plan to guide any executing work before beginning the work. If you are presented with a scenario that suggests you do not have a planning document, your first step should be to ensure that you have a planning document developed as fast as possible.**

Requirements management plan

The requirements management plan is a specific management plan that focuses on how the project requirements will be captured, documented, and checked. It is an essential document for the project manager to have to be able to carry out the work associated with collecting requirements from relevant stakeholders. By following the requirements management plan, the project manager and project team can gather project requirements, assumptions, and constraints more easily.

True or false? The requirements management plan outlines how the project scope will be documented.

Answer: *False.* The requirements management plan guides the collection, documentation, and control of the project requirements. The scope management plan guides the work documenting the project scope.

> ***MORE INFO*** **Both the scope management plan and requirements management plan are outputs of the Plan Scope Management process described in the PMBOK® Guide, 5th edition.**

Stakeholder management plan

To successfully gather requirements from stakeholders the project manager requires the stakeholder management plan. The stakeholder management plan defines the processes, tools, and techniques to guide the project manager and project team in effectively engaging stakeholders and obtaining from their requirements for the project.

> ***MORE INFO*** **The stakeholder management plan is an output of the Plan Stakeholder Management process in the PMBOK® Guide, 5th edition.**

True or false? The stakeholder management plan provides a list of all the stakeholders and describes their interest in the project.

Answer: *False*. The stakeholder management plan describes the processes to gather information that can be included in the stakeholder register.

Stakeholder register

The stakeholder register is the result of following the stakeholder management plan to collect information about requirements from individual stakeholders.

> ***NOTE*** **A stakeholder is any person, group, or organization that can affect or be affected by your project. It is the job of the project manager to identify all these stakeholders and what their expectations are, keep them engaged, and ensure that stakeholder satisfaction becomes a key project deliverable to get stakeholders to support the project, or at least not oppose it. Stakeholder identification happens throughout the project, not just at the beginning.**

The stakeholder register records the results of stakeholder analysis, which begins with the use of information-gathering techniques such as brainstorming, interviewing, and other data-gathering techniques to identify stakeholders. The information gathered as part of carrying out stakeholder analysis enables you to clearly describe the power, interest, influence, impact, and engagement that stakeholders have. You can record this information in your stakeholder register and use it to develop a robust stakeholder management strategy.

After you gather data about stakeholders, there are a number of ways of presenting this data. The most popular way of recording this information is with a stakeholder register which contains information about stakeholders, an assessment of their interest, power or influence on the project, and a plan for how their expectations will be proactively influenced and managed. The stakeholder register probably contains information on the following:

- A classification of stakeholder categories so you can distinguish between different stakeholders and their expectations and engagement
- Information about individual stakeholders and their contact details
- A description of the interest that each stakeholder has in the project
- An assessment of the stakeholders' power, impact, influence, engagement, and interest in the project
- A description of the strategy to be employed to gain their support and keep them satisfied
- A description of the frequency and method by which you will revisit the stakeholder register

Figure 2-1 shows an example of a stallholder register.

Stakeholder	Contact details	Interest in project	Power	Influence	Strategy	Responsibility
Stakeholder A						
Stakeholder B						
Stakeholder C						
Stakeholder D						

FIGURE 2-1 An example of a stakeholder register

A key purpose of the information contained in the stakeholder register is to permit the project manager to proactively manage stakeholder's expectation to ensure their levels of engagement move to the defined optimal level of engagement. Figure 2-2 shows an assessment of both current and optimal levels of engagement for stakeholders. This information could be included in the stakeholder register if appropriate.

		Engagement				
		Leading	Supportive	Neutral	Resistant	Unaware
Stakeholder	Stakeholder A	CO				
	Stakeholder B		O		C	
	Stakeholder C		O	C		
	Stakeholder D				O	C

C = Current level of engagement
O = Optimal level of engagement

FIGURE 2-2 Measuring current and optimal levels of stakeholder engagement

The stakeholder register probably contains information on the following:

- A classification of stakeholder categories so you can distinguish between different stakeholders and their expectations and engagement
- Information about individual stakeholders and their contact details
- A description of the interest that each stakeholder has in the project
- An assessment of the stakeholders' power, impact, influence, engagement, and interest in the project

- A description of the strategy to be employed to gain their support and keep them satisfied
- A description of the frequency and method by which you will revisit the stakeholder register

True or false? The stakeholder register should be updated whenever new information about existing stakeholders becomes available or whenever new stakeholders are identified.

Answer: *True.* The stakeholder register is a live document that should be kept up to date at all times. If new information becomes available about already-identified stakeholders, it should be updated in the stakeholder register. As new stakeholders are identified throughout the project, this information should be added to the stakeholder register.

> ***NOTE*** **Be very careful with the information contained in the stakeholder register because some of the information contained in it can be very sensitive. You might not want to let stakeholders see your assessment of them.**

Requirements gathering tools

There is a wide variety of tools that can be used to gather requirements, assumptions, and constraints from stakeholders. What they all have in common is that they all gather or analyze information and data, and a project manager can use any one or more that provides assistance in gathering and documenting the project requirements. These tools include the following:

Interviews Can be formal or informal; they are focused on eliciting information from stakeholders.

Focus groups Use a trained moderator to bring stakeholders and subject matter experts together in an interactive setting to gather information about requirements, assumptions, and constraints.

Facilitated facilitated workshops Bring key stakeholders together to actively define product and project requirements. They are interactive in nature and lead by a trained facilitator.

> ***EXAM TIP*** **There are several specialized types of facilitated workshops, such as joint application design (JAD) and quality function deployment (QFD) workshops. If you see a reference to them, you should know they are forms of facilitated workshops.**

> ***NOTE*** **Focus groups tend to be for the purpose of learning about stakeholder expectations, whereas facilitated workshops tend to be more focused on addressing a particular solution.**

Group creativity techniques Methods used to get group members to think broadly about a particular issue. Common forms of group creativity techniques include brainstorming, nominal group technique, and mind-mapping.

Group decision-making techniques If using a group of stakeholders to gather requirements, techniques to make final decisions about which requirements should be recorded and which should be left out. Examples of group decision-making techniques include consensus, majority, plurality, and dictatorship.

Questionnaires and surveys Gather information quickly from stakeholders who might be not be able to be interviewed in person or attend focus groups. When using any form of questionnaire or survey, consider the language used to ensure that responses are as objective as possible.

Observations Provide a way for the project manager to observe stakeholders in their environment as a way to gain insight into what their requirements might be.

Prototypes A form of representation of the final deliverable that the customer can check. By presenting a stakeholder with a prototype showing requirements, the project manager can get feedback before producing the final versions.

Benchmarking Compares the planned requirements gathering processes against other similar projects to see whether they are appropriate.

Context diagrams Can be used to show how one setoff requirement interacts with another to demonstrate constraints and interdependencies.

Document analysis A project manager can review existing documents such as the business plan, historical information, contracts, and external regulatory documents to determine project requirements.

True or false? Requirements gathering tools are used by the project manager and project team members to gather information from relevant stakeholders to document project requirements.

Answer: *True*. The purpose of using requirements gathering tools is to get information from identified stakeholders to enable the project manager to document project requirements.

> ***MORE INFO*** **You can find out more about requirements gathering tools by reading about the Collect Requirements process in the PMBOK® Guide, 5th edition or Chapter 3 of the PMP Training Kit.**

Requirements documentation

The key output of this work to document requirements is the requirements documentation, which describes individual requirements and how they meet the business need for the project. Requirements documentation can include the following:

- Business requirements
- Stakeholder requirements
- Solution requirements
- Project requirements
- Transition requirements
- Assumptions, dependencies, and constraints

The requirements documentation is essential input for defining the scope of the project that is an iterative process of progressive elaboration that starts with the statement of work used as an input into the project charter and ends with the development of the work breakdown structure (WBS). Figure 2-3 shows the levels of documentation of the work to be done for the project and where requirements come in the process.

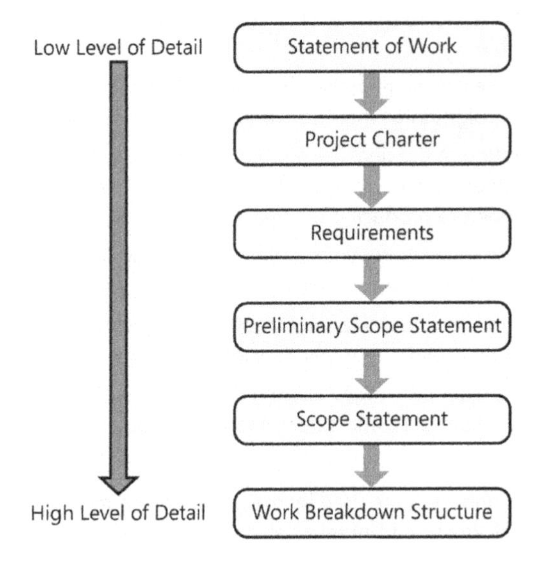

FIGURE 2-3 Descriptions of project work

True or false? The requirements documentation describes how individual project requirements will meet the business need of the project.

Answer: *True.* A key purpose of the requirements documentation is to describe how individual project requirements will meet the business need of the project.

> ***EXAM TIP*** **If you haven't taken the time to properly define the project requirements, you will have difficulty completing a project scope statement, so make sure that the requirements are fully defined and documented before attempting to define the scope.**

Requirements traceability matrix

The requirements traceability matrix maps and traces each documented project requirement to a particular business need, project task, deliverable, or test strategy. It is usually presented as a grid, with each requirement listed and an indication of how it maps back to other elements in the project so that required information about the purpose of the requirement can be quickly accessed.

True or false? The requirements traceability matrix can map individual requirements back to each unique node on the WBS.

Answer: *True*. Requirements represent work to be done on the project, so they should be captured in the WBS for the project, and the requirements traceability matrix should map the requirements to the respective WBS node.

MORE INFO **Throughout the PMBOK® Guide, 5th edition, there are a number of documents that are paired with ancillary documents that provide additional and more detailed information. For example, the requirements traceability matrix provides additional information about project requirements, the basis of estimates documents provide additional information about cost and time estimates, the activity attributes provide additional information about identified activities, and the WBS dictionary provides additional information about each node of the WBS.**

Can you answer these questions?

You can find the answers to these questions at the end of this chapter.

1. How does the scope management plan help a project manager and project team members gather project requirements?
2. What document provides information about individual stakeholders in the project?
3. If a project manager is trying to map individual project requirements to a particular business need that the project is attempting to satisfy, which document should be referred to?
4. Which has a more detailed description of the work to be done on a project—the project charter or preliminary scope statement?
5. What do all the requirements gathering tools and techniques have in common?

Task 2: Create the work breakdown structure with the team by deconstructing the scope, in order to manage the scope of the project.

This task takes the information gathered about the full scope of work to be done on a project and develops the WBS using decomposition to develop a graphical representation of the work to be done on the project. By completing a WBS for a project, a project manager can double-check that all the work required on the project scope has been captured and accounted for; and can also more accurately estimate time, cost, and resources required to complete work.

MORE INFO **You can find out more about the process of creating the WBS by reading the Create WBS Process in the PMBOK® Guide, 5th edition, or Chapter 3 of the PMP® Training Kit.**

Exam need to know...

- Scope management plan

  For example: What document guides the project manager and project team in defining, monitoring, and controlling the total project scope?

- Project scope statement

  For example: How will be work to be done by the project be documented?
- Requirements documentation

  For example: How are individual stakeholder requirements collected and recorded?
- Decomposition

  For example: What is the tool used to break the project scope down into its component parts?
- Work breakdown structure (WBS)

  For example: How is the total project scope represented graphically?
- Work breakdown structure dictionary (WBS dictionary)

  For example: What document provides additional detail about the information contained in each node of the work breakdown structure?
- Scope baseline

  For example: How is actual performance in relation to delivery of the project scope measured and evaluated to check for variance?

Scope management plan

The scope management plan, which is created during the plan scope management process, guides the project manager and project team members in all activities relating to defining the scope of the project, and describes how the scope will be monitored and controlled. As such, it is essential to have a scope management plan because it provides guidance on how the WBS is to be created. It includes information about the tools and techniques to be used to create and present the WBS, as well as how to make changes if necessary.

> ***EXAM TIP*** **The scope management plan is a subsidiary of the project management plan.**

True or false? The scope management plan provides detail on the scope of the project and product.

Answer: *False.* The scope management plan provides guidance on how the scope of the project and product is collected; it does not provide any detail on the scope of the project or product.

Project scope statement

The WBS is a graphical representation of the scope statement, so you should have the scope statement available to create the WBS. The project scope statement contains a full description of all the work to be done on the project and includes a thorough description of any deliverables.

The decomposition of the WBS happens to only those parts of the scope statement that can be fully defined. If the project is subject to progressive elaboration or rolling wave planning of the scope statement, the WBS reflects it and it is subject to progressive elaboration.

True or false? The project scope statement provides a full description of all the work to be done on the project, which includes work to produce the project deliverables and all other project-management-related work on the project.

Answer: *True.* Remember that the total project scope statement is broader than just a description of the deliverables to be produced by the project; it encompasses all the work to be done on the project.

> ***EXAM TIP*** **If you do not have a developed project scope statement, you cannot decompose it to develop WBS, so you should always ensure that you have a project scope statement before attempting to create the WBS.**

Requirements documentation

Having the requirements documentation available in addition to the project scope statement provides an additional level of detail to enable the project manager and project team members to double-check that they have captured all the work required to satisfy stakeholder requirements.

True or false? The requirements documentation provides details on individual stakeholders' requirements for the entire project, not just deliverables.

Answer: *True.* Many stakeholders have requirements relating solely to the project deliverables, but there will be some stakeholders whose requirements relate to other work to be done as part of the project. For example, some stakeholders might have requirements about working hours or noise levels for the project.

Decomposition

Decomposition is the main tool to be used to develop the WBS because it takes the higher-level description of the project and breaks it down into deliverables, then into subdeliverables, and finally into work packages. Work packages are the level at which decomposition of the WBS stops. Beneath this level, there is little benefit to be gained for the WBS. Further decomposition of work packages to activity level does occur during the development of the project schedule.

The exact definition of a work package can differ depending on the project size and complexity, but it is generally defined at the level at which both cost and duration can be reliably estimated and managed.

True or false? Decomposition for the creation of the WBS continues until a work package describes work that can reliably be estimated for both time and cost.

Answer: *True.* For the purposes of creating the WBS, it is necessary to decompose the project work down only to the work package level, which is the level at which both time and cost can reliably be estimated. This level will change depending on the complexity and size of the project.

EXAM TIP **Remember that for the creation of the WBS, decomposition goes down to the work package level; for development of the project schedule, it goes down farther to the activity level. Additionally, you should always ensure that you use the people responsible for the work to assist in the decomposition of the WBS because they know about the work to be done. By including them in this process, you create buy-in and commitment to the work. If you use the WBS as an estimating tool and you apportion cost or time from the highest level, you are using top-down estimating. If you instead assign individual cost or time estimates to the work package or activity level and then aggregate them upward, you are using bottom-up estimating.**

WBS

The WBS is often called the backbone of a project because it acts as an input into many other planning processes. Without a complete and accurate WBS, your efforts in cost estimating, budget estimating, activity definition, risk identification, and scope validation (and all the subsequent processes into which they provide inputs) will be extremely difficult.

A project manager should always involve members of the project team in the creation of the WBS for two main reasons. First, they are the ones expected to complete the work, so their experience and knowledge of the work to be done will be extremely useful in defining the work with the WBS. The second reason is that by involving them in the definition of the WBS, a project manager can create buy-in and commitment from team members.

EXAM TIP **If a question presents a scenario in which you discover that you do not have a WBS, the correct answer is always to stop work until you complete the WBS.**

Figure 2-4 shows a WBS for a new house project showing the breakdown of different work streams to the work package level. Note that all nodes in the WBS have a unique identifying number, as part of your project configuration management system, that enables you to track work being done and also to allocate costs to specific work packages for better cost reporting. The numbering system should clearly identify each node and relate to the node above so you can easily see related nodes and the way they are decomposed.

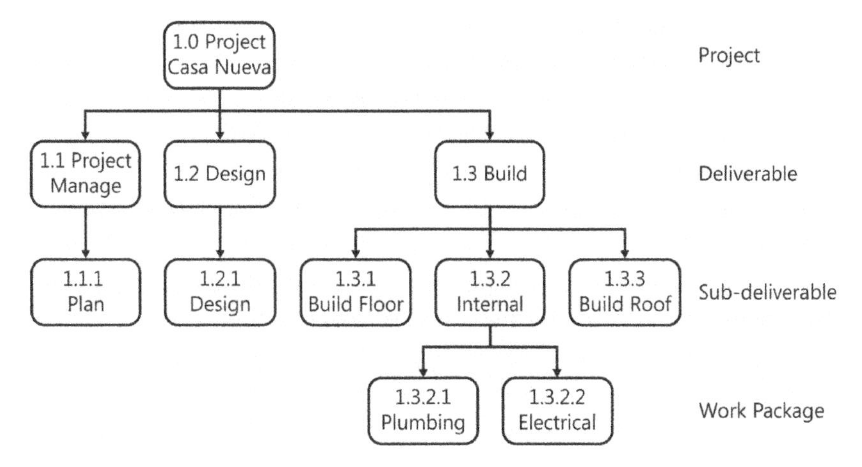

FIGURE 2-4 WBS showing the total project, deliverables, subdeliverables, and work packages

True or false? Any work that is not part of the WBS is not part of the work to be done on the project.

Answer: *True*. Because the WBS is a graphical representation of the total project scope, work that is not part of the WBS is not part of the work to be done on the project.

> ***EXAM TIP*** **There are four breakdown structures that can be useful to the project manager: the WBS, the organizational breakdown structure, the resource breakdown structure, and the risk breakdown structure. All look the same graphically and use decomposition to break down a higher-level concept into its constituent parts.**

> ***MORE INFO*** **You can find out more about the WBS by reading the Practice Standard for Work Breakdown Structures (Project Management Institute, 2nd edition, 2006).**

> ***NOTE*** **Remember to include all the project management work that has to be done on the project, not just the work associated with the product, so you can accurately represent the time and cost associated with the entire project. It is also a great way to communicate all the work to be done on the project to stakeholders.**

WBS dictionary

The WBS dictionary provides additional information about each of the nodes in the WBS. When presented graphically, each node on the WBS can contain only summary information, and the WBS dictionary provides more detail about each node. The types of information contained in the WBS dictionary include the following:

- Cost accounting code
- Detailed description of the work
- Assumptions or constraints

- Schedule milestones
- Description of the resources required
- Description of how cost estimates were developed
- Description of quality requirements for the work package
- Description of acceptance criteria

True or false? The WBS dictionary provides information on how each node of the WBS was developed.

Answer: *True.* The WBS dictionary provides a lot of additional information about each node of the WBS, including the techniques used to define the node.

> ***EXAM TIP*** **You should always assume that if you have a WBS, you also have a WBS dictionary.**

Scope baseline

The scope baseline includes the project scope statement, the WBS, and the WBS dictionary. Together, all three of these elements form the scope baseline for the project. The project manager will use the scope baseline to compare work that is actually being done to detect variance. A project manager detects variance between the work contained in the scope baseline and the work performance information about the work being done in relation to scope. Corrective or preventive actions are initiated and the project manager ensures that all changes to the scope baseline go through the approved change control process. If a change request is approved to the scope baseline, the approved change becomes part of the scope baseline.

True or false? The scope baseline includes the project scope statement, the requirements documentation, the WBS, and the WBS dictionary.

Answer: *False.* The scope baseline includes only the project scope statement, the WBS, and the WBS dictionary. The requirements documentation is used to develop the project scope statement, so it is captured there.

> ***EXAM TIP*** **The scope baseline is one of three major baselines used throughout the project to measure actual performance against. The other two baselines are the cost performance (budget) baseline and the time (schedule) baseline.**

Can you answer these questions?

You can find the answers to these questions at the end of this chapter.

1. What is the main tool or technique used to develop a WBS?
2. Why should a project manager involve team members in the creation of the WBS?
3. What is the relationship between the WBS and the WBS dictionary?
4. What is the lowest level of detail that a WBS goes to?
5. What are the three elements of the scope baseline?

Task 3: Develop a budget plan based on the project scope using estimating techniques, in order to manage project cost.

This task focuses on estimating individual work packages and activity costs, and then aggregating them over time to produce the cost performance baseline, or project budget. There are many reasons for producing a project budget, including being able to forecast a predicted total spend and also a forecast spend over time. Additionally, the project budget serves as a useful communications tool to manage stakeholder expectations about how much the project will cost. It is the responsibility of the project manager to develop the budget, track any variances, and manage any changes.

> ***MORE INFO*** **You can find out more about estimating costs and developing a project budget by reading Chapter 7 of the PMBOK® Guide, 5th edition, or Chapter 5 of the PMP® Training Kit.**

Exam need to know...

- Cost management plan

  For example: What document does the project manager use for guidance in developing both individual cost estimates and a project budget?
- Human resource management plan

  For example: What document provides guidance to the project manager on how the costs associated with the people working on the project will be accounted for in individual cost estimates and the project budget?
- Scope baseline

  For example: What is the combination of the project scope statement, WBS, and WBS dictionary more commonly known as?
- Project schedule

  For example: How are individual activity durations and the total project duration represented?
- Risk register

  For example: What document provides the project manager and project team members with information about uncertainty in the project relating to cost?
- Cost estimating techniques

  For example: How does the project manager estimate individual costs for identified activities?
- Reserve analysis

  For example: How is uncertainty within cost estimates incorporated into a project budget?

- Cost of quality

  For example: When considering individual cost estimates, which element of the project quality management needs to be taken into account?
- Project management software

  For example: What tool is useful to the project manager for quickly aggregating and analyzing individual cost estimates and a project budget?
- Vendor bid analysis

  For example: What tool should the project manager use to ensure that cost estimates provided by potential vendors to the project are within an expected range?
- Activity cost estimates

  For example: Where does information about the cost estimate for identified activities come from?
- Basis of estimates

  For example: What document provides additional information to the project manager about the assumptions made when estimating costs of individual activities?
- Agreements

  For example: What documents provide information to the project manager about legal obligations relating to timing of and amount of payments to be made to external vendors?
- Resource calendars

  For example: How are constraints upon human resources and the time periods they can work on the project documented?
- Cost aggregation

  For example: What is the technique called that adds up costs to get a total cost?
- Funding limit reconciliation

  For example: How does a project manager ensure that the funds requested to complete the project are available at the time they are requested?
- Cost baseline

  For example: What information does the project manager use to measure actual cost performance against to detect variance?
- Project funding requirements

  For example: How does a project manager describe the timing and cost of securing funding for the project?

Cost management plan

The cost management plan provides guidance to the project manager and project team members on how project cost will be estimated, aggregated, monitored, and controlled for individual cost estimates and the project budget. The cost management plan is produced as part of the initial cost management planning work and is a subsidiary of the project management plan.

Examples of the information that the cost management plan can include are these:

- The units of measure to be used when defining work to be done and resources to be used on the project
- The level of precision and whether estimates will be rounded up or down
- The level of accuracy expected for cost estimates
- Guidance on performance measurement, especially earned value management
- How contingency reserves will be developed and managed

The cost management plan is used to help develop individual cost estimates for work to be performed on the project; and how the project budget will be developed, approved, monitored, and controlled.

True or false? The cost management plan contains both the cost estimates for work packages and activities and the approved project budget.

Answer: *False.* The cost management plan provides guidance on how cost estimates of the work packages and activities will be developed. It also provides guidance on how an approved project budget will be created.

> ***EXAM TIP*** **As with all other areas of project management, you should always look to have some sort of document, in this case the cost management plan, to provide guidance on how work will be completed.**

Human resource management plan

After the cost management plan has been produced, it is the primary input used to guide the cost estimating work. There are also other important documents to be used when estimating cost; one of them is the human resource management plan because it provides information about project staffing attributes, reimbursement rates, project personnel, and other remuneration information that are required to develop accurate cost estimates.

True or false? The human resource management plan provides guidance to the project manager and project team members on what aspects of project personnel need to be taken into account when developing project cost estimates.

Answer: *True.* The human resource plan describes specific staffing attributes, personnel rates, and other remuneration information that can be used to improve the accuracy of cost estimates.

Scope baseline

The scope baseline is an essential input when attempting the estimate costs for a project. The scope baseline is composed of the project scope statement, WBS, and WBS dictionary. The project scope statement provides a description of all the work to be done on the project, and it is this work for which cost estimates will be developed.

The WBS provides a graphical decomposition of the project scope statement down to the work package level. By estimating the costs associated with individual work packages and then aggregating them with a bottom-up estimating technique, individual cost estimates and a total project cost estimate can be developed. The WBS dictionary provides additional and more detailed information about the work packages, assumptions made, and estimating techniques used to develop individual cost estimates.

True or false? Any cost estimates developed without reference to the scope baseline will be inaccurate.

Answer: *True.* All cost estimates should map back to the scope baseline; in turn, the scope baseline provides information to ensure that any cost estimates that are developed are as accurate as possible and reflect the work to be done on the project.

EXAM TIP **The more detailed and developed the scope baseline, the more detailed and developed your cost estimates will be.**

Project schedule

The development of an approved project budget requires taking individual cost estimates and aggregating them by the time period in which they are incurred, so the project schedule is an essential input into the development of the approved project budget. The project schedule is developed during the time management planning activities, so you can see the interdependencies between successful cost estimating and successful time estimating.

The project schedule also provides an indication of the time period over which the costs will be incurred. Depending on the link, this time period might well also have an impact on the cost estimates. For example, if you are working on a multiyear project, you have to take into account economic price adjustments to cost estimates to reflect such things as inflation and changes in prices caused by demand fluctuations of goods.

True or false? The project schedule provides information to the project manager and project team members about individual cost estimates and how those estimates relate to the project scope statement.

Answer: *False.* The project schedule provides information about the timing of work to be done on the project. By assigning cost estimates to the work to be done on the project and then aggregating it, a project budget can be developed.

EXAM TIP **In the exam, you need to use the words "costs" and "budget" correctly. In your job as a project manager, you might use the two terms interchangeably, but for the exam "cost" means the cost associated with an individual work package or activity, whereas "budget" refers to costs over time.**

MORE INFO **You can find out more about the project schedule by reading the Practice Standard for Scheduling, 2nd edition (Project Management Institute, 2011).**

Risk register

When developing individual cost estimates for the project budget, a risk register provides information about uncertainty related to costs of the project and of planned risk responses. It is important to have both of these elements of risk information to improve the level of cost estimates and the development of the project budget.

When using the risk register to perform quantitative risk analysis, you can develop a contingency reserve for the project based on quantifiable probability and impact assessment of identified risks. This contingency reserve should be included as part of an approved project budget.

> ***EXAM TIP*** **A contingency reserve should be approved as part of the project budget and should be under the delegated authority of the project manager. A management reserve, on the other hand, is under the control of senior management within the organization, and a project manager will apply to use funds from the management reserve if the project encounters "unknown unknowns."**

True or false? The risk register is an important input into any estimation of project costs because it outlines the planned risk responses, and some of these risk responses can have a cost associated with them.

Answer: *True.* Planned risk responses can have a cost associated with them and they also represent work to be done on the project. As such, any planned risk responses should be included in any work associated with estimating costs and in the project scope of work to be completed.

Cost estimating techniques

There are a number of cost estimating techniques that can be used to develop individual cost estimates for identified work packages and activities. Each estimating technique has different strengths and weaknesses and whether you use it depends on the level of detail of information about the work to be done, the urgency of the assessment, and the requirements of stakeholders.

The most common forms of cost estimating techniques include the following:

- **Expert judgment** expert judgment is one of the most important tools that can be used with estimating costs because not only does it provide information about individual cost estimates but also provides the experience to use other estimating techniques.

  > ***EXAM TIP*** **Keep in mind that you as project manager are an expert, your project team members are experts, and any other person you choose to consult should be seen as an expert**

- **Historical information** An important resource for any estimating technique because it collects and records information about estimates used in the past and any variances between what was estimated and the actual costs incurred. All this information can be used to improve the level of estimating and future projects.

- **Analogous estimating** Often used if only a limited amount of detail is available about the work to be done on the project. It can be used at the beginning of the project and also during the process of progressive elaboration for work not yet fully defined, so it might be less accurate than other forms of estimating. Analogous estimating compares a current description of work to actual work already performed on the project or previous projects and extrapolates a cost estimate. For example, you might have worked on a house six months ago that cost $20,000 to lay the floor slab, and the current floor slab is twice the size; therefore, your analogous cost estimate would be $40,000.
- **Parametric estimating** A technique that multiplies a known quantity by a known rate. Parametric estimation usually relies on well-developed historical information and published estimating data. It generally takes longer and costs more than analogous estimating techniques, but produces more accurate estimates. For example, you might know you need 10 m^3 of concrete that costs $100 per cubic meter, so your parametric cost estimate is $1,000.
- **Bottom-up estimating** Relies on estimating individual costs for work packages or activities and then aggregating, or rolling up, these costs upward to develop an overall cost estimate.
- **Three-point estimating** Part of the program and evaluation review technique (PERT), it aims to improve the accuracy of a cost estimate by considering the optimistic (O), most likely (M), and pessimistic (P) cost estimates and then obtaining a weighted average of all three. To get a simple average, take these three figures, add them together, and divide by 3. If you want to get a weighted average that gives greater weight to the most likely (cM) figure, the formula to use is shown in Figure 2-5.

$$\frac{cO + (4 \times cM) + cP}{6}$$

FIGURE 2-5 Three-point estimating formula

- **Top down estimating** A technique that sees costs apportioned to different project deliverables, usually on the basis of historical information.

For example, if you have an optimistic cost estimate of $10, a most likely cost estimate of $16, and a pessimistic cost estimate of $25, the weighted average using three-point estimating is $16.50.

EXAM TIP **This formula is also used for estimating duration of activities. The formula simply changes the letter "c," which represents cost, to the letter "t" to represent time.**

All estimates are simply a best guess at the future based on the information a project manager has available at the time. The better the information you have, the better the estimates will be. Thus, there is nearly always an element of uncertainty inherent in any estimate. It is often important to express this range of uncertainty, and the accuracy of cost estimates usually improves as the project progresses. As part of its organizational process assets, your organization might have guidelines for the necessary level of accuracy required before proceeding. Table 2-2 shows the typical description of a variety of estimate ranges.

TABLE 2-2 Range of estimates

ESTIMATE TYPE	ESTIMATE RANGE
Order of magnitude estimate	–50% to +100%
Rough order of magnitude estimate	–25% to +75%
Conceptual estimate	–30% to +50%
Preliminary estimate	–20% to +30%
Definitive estimate	–15% to +20%
Control estimate	–10% to +15%

> ***EXAM TIP*** **The best cost estimates are worked up and developed by the people performing the work. Therefore, any question in the exam assumes that you consult with your project team members and use their expertise.**

True or false? The information produced by a cost estimate reflects the level of information contained in the description of work to be done and the particular estimating technique used.

Answer: *True.* All cost estimates are dependent on the level of detail provided to describe the work to be estimated and the particular estimating technique used. The more detailed the description of the work to be done, the better the cost estimate can be. The type of estimating technique used also affects the accuracy of the estimate. For example, parametric estimating techniques produce a more accurate estimate than analogous estimating techniques.

> ***MORE INFO*** **You can find out more about cost estimating techniques by reading the Estimate Costs Process in the PMBOK® Guide, 5th edition or Chapter 5 of the PMP Training Kit.**

Reserve analysis

Most cost estimates that you produce include some sort of contingency reserve to reflect the level of cost uncertainty within them. The total contingency reserve for a project should be included as part of the approved cost baseline. A contingency reserve is developed for what is called "known unknowns" about the project, which is a rather complex way of describing the uncertainty you can identify. A contingency reserve should be under control of the project manager, and should be eliminated from the project budget if not used.

A management reserve is an amount identified as part of the project budget that is controlled by management and is generally reserved for unforeseen work, or unknown unknowns, that might arise

True or false? As more precise information about the project becomes available, any contingency reserve can be used, reduced, or eliminated.

Answer: *True.* A contingency reserve should be developed against specific cost items and the uncertainty around the estimates. If the uncertainty eventuates, the contingency reserve can be used to cover the additional costs. If it does not eventuate, however, the contingency reserve should be either reduced or eliminated from the project budget. It is not appropriate to keep unused contingency reserve to cover other areas of uncertainty in the project.

> ***EXAM TIP*** **You should always assume that your approved project budget has a contingency reserve that has been developed to reflect individual cost estimate uncertainty and work packages and activities. The contingency reserve is under the control of the project manager and is released back to the organization if not required.**

Cost of quality

As part of developing your individual cost estimates, you have to make assumptions about the cost of quality and how it will be incorporated into your particular cost estimates. This information will come out of your quality management planning work and will provide guidance on the level of quality expected of the project.

> ***NOTE*** **When pressed for project cost savings after initial cost estimating, a project team might decide to reduce the quality of deliverables on the project to lower the total spend on the project. This is generally not a good thing to do because all it does is transfer the cost of quality from the project to the owners, operators, or maintenance personnel; the reduced level of quality will result in higher costs over the entire product lifecycle.**

Project management software

Project management software is a useful tool to use in developing cost estimates because it can quickly and efficiently gather, analyze, record, and present the cost estimating data in a variety of ways.

Vendor bid analysis

It is important during the cost estimating process to have some sort of expected value that will arise from the cost estimates, particularly if using cost estimates from subcontractors or external parties. Vendor bid analysis ensures that all bids received are with in an expected range and the cost estimates provided are neither too high nor too low.

True or false? Vendor bid analysis should primarily be focused on ensuring that cost estimates are not too high because low cost estimates should always be accepted immediately to secure the low price.

Answer: *True*. Vendor bid analysis seeks to determine whether cost estimates being provided are either too high or too low. In both cases, it could indicate that the party providing the cost estimate has misunderstood the work to be done or that the description provided is not detailed enough. If a cost estimate received is too high, it could indicate an unscrupulous seller. If the cost estimate provided is too low, it could indicate that the person or organization providing a cost estimate does not have the required level of competency to do professional cost estimating and could go out of business during the project.

Activity cost estimates

As a result of carrying out cost estimating activities in accordance with your cost management plan, you will develop activity cost estimates that will include the probable cost estimate and an indication of the range of uncertainty. The activity cost estimates are quantitative assessments of the estimated costs to complete the project work. They can refer to direct or indirect costs, variable or fixed costs, and economic price adjustments or inflation; and include other elements such as the cost of financing and any cost contingency reserve developed.

The activity cost estimates are used to develop the project budget at overlaying the cost estimate with the time period in which the cost is expected to be incurred.

True or false? Activity cost estimates can be summary or detailed depending on the level of detail known about the activity.

Answer: *True*. All cost estimates directly reflect the level of detail known about the activity. If lots of detail is known, the activity cost estimate will also be detailed. If little is known about the activity, the cost estimate will be less accurate.

> ***EXAM TIP*** **Activity cost estimates are an essential input into the development of the project budget; you cannot develop a robust accurate project budget without the activity cost estimates.**

Basis of estimates

The basis of estimates document provides additional supporting detail for the activity costs estimates. The type of additional detail it provides can include the following:

- Estimating techniques used
- List of assumptions and constraints
- Range and confidence level of estimates

True or false? The basis of estimates document provides information to the project manager about the particular estimating technique that was used to develop an individual cost estimate.

Answer: *True*. The basis of estimate document provides ancillary and more detailed information of each of the activity cost estimates.

Agreements

Important inputs into the development of your approved project budget are any agreements or contracts you might have that have terms and conditions specifying the timing and frequency of payments to be made. These documents provide important information that needs to be taken into account when developing the project budget cost baseline because they specify when payments need to be made or when payments are to be received. It might not align with project funding, so the project manager might need to look at other ways of funding the project until the money becomes available.

Resource calendars

Resource calendars are an important for the budget because they document the constraints when particular project resources are available. These time constraints need to be taken into account when determining when work is going to be performed and the cost incurred for developing a project budget.

Funding limit reconciliation

It is important for both the project manager and performing organization to carry out a funding limit reconciliation to ensure that any discrepancy between when project funds are forecast to be paid or received is matched by the funds the organization has available.

If there is a discrepancy between the two it might be that the organization has to secure additional sources of funding, or delay work until funding becomes available.

Cost baseline

The simplest way to develop or determine the project budget is to take the cost estimates that have been developed and map them against the time period in which they are forecast to be incurred. This involves combining the activity cost estimates with the project schedule.

The project budget represents the cost baseline, which is one of the three main baselines you use to measure progress on the project. The others are the scope baseline, consisting of the project scope statement, WBS, and WBS dictionary; and the time baseline, or project schedule.

> ***EXAM TIP*** **The cost baseline is one of the three baselines used and project management. The other two are the scope baseline and the time baseline or project schedule. Some people also refer to a quality baseline as a fourth project baseline, which is used to compare forecast quality against actual quality to detect variance.**

The key element of the cost baseline is that it takes the aggregated individual estimates of cost for each activity and applies them to the time periods in which the costs will be accrued. This is the baseline against which you will measure project cost performance. Figure 2-6 shows an example of a cost baseline represented graphically. It shows the total amount of spend for each time period in months. It also shows the cumulative spend over the life of the project. This is represented by the line, which is often referred to as the "S-curve" because it is in the shape of the letter S (there is little spending at the beginning of a project, a lot of spending in the middle section of the project, and a decrease in spending toward the end of the project).

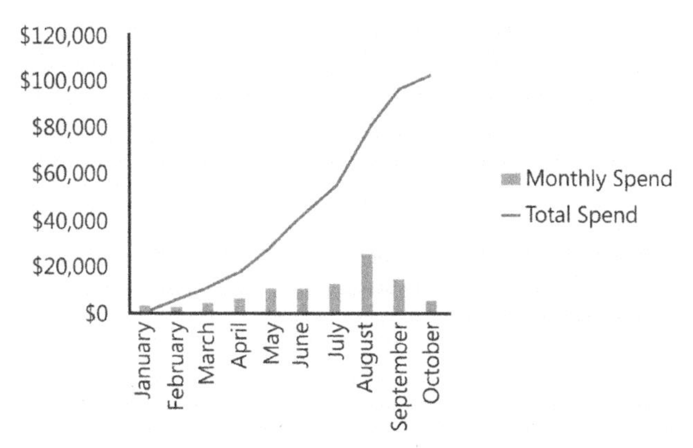

FIGURE 2-6 An example of a cost baseline showing individual monthly cost estimates and a cumulative total forecast spend

After the cost baseline or project budget has been developed, this information can then be used by the project manager and the performing organization to determine the project funding requirements.

True or false? The project cost baseline documents and aggregates individual cost estimates over time.

Answer: *True*. The project cost baseline, or budget, is the summary of all your individual activity cost estimates aggregated for the time period in which they are forecast to occur to get a forecast rate of project spend, which can then be aligned with any project funding requirements.

MORE INFO **You can find out more about the development of the project budget by reading the Determine Budget process in the PMBOK® Guide, 5th edition, or by reading Chapter 5 of the PMP® Training Kit, which also has exercises to complete.**

Can you answer these questions?

You can find the answers to these questions at the end of this chapter.

1. What is the difference between project costs and the project budget?
2. If you have an optimistic estimate of $100, a most likely estimate of $150, and a pessimistic estimate of $250, what is your three-point cost estimate?
3. What is the relationship between the activity cost estimates and the basis of estimates document?
4. Why is it important to have any agreements, or contracts, available when developing the project budget?
5. Why is it important to carry out vendor bid analysis for any cost estimates received?

Task 4: Develop project schedule based on the project timeline, scope, and resource plan, in order to manage timely completion of the project.

This task is focused on the work involved in developing the project schedule that becomes the baseline against which time performance on the project is measured. Development of the project schedule involves using the schedule management plan to guide work relating to defining activities, sequencing these activities, estimating both activity resources and activity durations, and then collating all this information into the project schedule.

> ***MORE INFO*** **You can find out more about developing a project schedule by reading the Time Management Planning processes in Chapter 6 of the PMBOK® Guide, 5th edition or Chapter 4 of the PMP Training Kit.**

Exam need to know...

- Schedule management plan

  For example: What document can the project manager turn to if there is confusion about how the work associated with the development of the project schedule is meant to be carried out?
- Defining activities

  For example: To successfully develop project schedule, a project manager must further decompose the work packages and the WBS into what?
- Sequencing activities

  For example: What is the work that involves linking individually identified activities as either predecessor or successor?
- Estimating activity resources

  For example: How does a project manager account for resource availability to complete work when developing the project schedule?
- Estimating activity durations

  For example: How does a project manager develop a time estimate for individually identified activities?
- Critical path method

  For example: What is the scheduling method that analyzes the different paths through a network diagram to determine which of them represents the greatest risk to the project duration?
- Critical chain method

  For example: If you have identified buffers to allow you to deal with time uncertainty on the project, which method are you using?

- Resource leveling

  For example: What are you doing if you are attempting to ensure that people assigned to your project are not sitting around with no work to do while others are having to work overtime to complete their assigned work?
- Schedule compression

  For example: If your customer requests that the project be completed more quickly, what techniques can you use to shorten the project duration?

Schedule management plan

The schedule management plan is invaluable to project managers as they seek to develop a project schedule because it provides guidance on how all the work associated with developing the project schedule is to be carried out. The schedule management plan might be unique for a project or it might be part of organizational process assets. The schedule management plan also sets how the project schedule, after it has been developed and approved, is to be monitored for any variance between the forecast schedule and the actual schedule, and how any changes to the project schedule will be assessed.

True or false? The schedule management plan provides guidance to the project manager and project team members on how project schedule will be monitored and controlled using earned value management techniques.

Answer: *True*. Earned value management techniques are just one of the many tools that can be used by a project manager to detect variance. In this instance, the most useful components of the earned value management are the schedule variance (SV) and schedule performance index equation (SPI).

> ***EXAM TIP*** **Before attempting to do any planning, executing, monitoring and controlling, or closing work, you should ensure that you have an appropriate planning document to provide guidance on how this work will be carried out.**

> ***MORE INFO*** **You can find out more about the schedule management plan by reading the Plan Schedule Management process in the PMBOK® Guide, 5th edition.**

Defining activities

There are a number of steps that a project manager should go through to develop an appropriate project schedule. The first of these steps is to take the work packages that have already been defined and documented in the WBS and decompose them further to the activity level.

Remember that a work package is defined as a piece of work broken down to the level at which it can be reliably estimated for time and cost. An activity is a piece of work at a more detailed level than a work package that is more distinct than a work package. For the purposes of building an accurate project schedule, it is better to have more detail than less detail, so it is better to use activities rather than work packages. The main tool used to define activities is decomposition, which takes the work packages that been identified and breaks them down a step or two further.

Keep in mind that this process might be iterative and subject to both progressive elaboration and rolling wave planning. This means that you might break down only the work packages in the next couple of months and not yet break down work packages in the future.

Figure 2-7 shows an example of a WBS broken down beyond the work package level to the activity level.

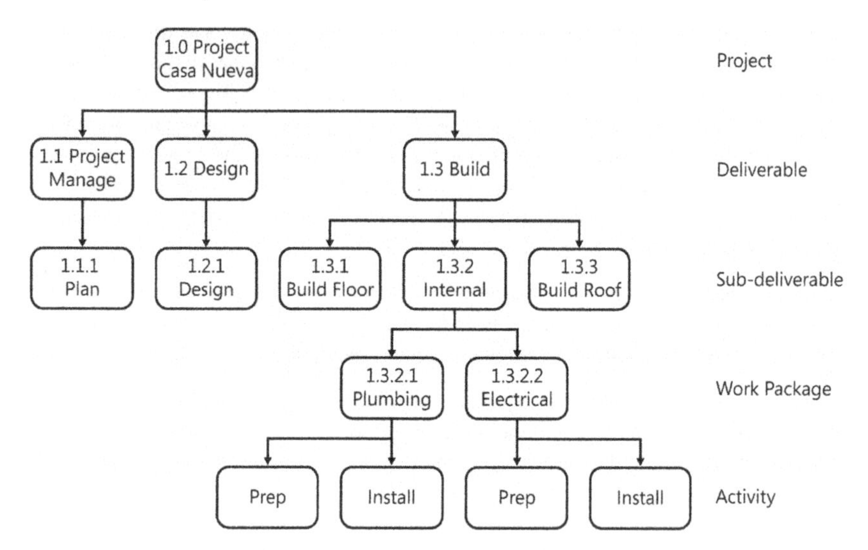

FIGURE 2-7 An example of decomposition of the work packages down to the activity level

True or false? A project manager should break down work packages to be decomposed to the activity level only if the project sponsor in the steering committee requests it.

Answer: *False.* By breaking down work packages to the activity level, a greater level of detail can be obtained and help develop a more accurate project schedule.

> ***MORE INFO*** **You can find out more about the process of defining activities by reading the Define Activities process in the PMBOK® Guide, 5th edition or Chapter 4 of the PMP Training Kit.**

Sequencing activities

After defining the activities. the next step in the process of developing a project schedule is to sequence the activities. Sequencing the activities means to put them in the order in which they will occur and to also indicate the relationships between them.

The best way to sequence activities is to use the precedence diagramming method (PDM), which is a graphical representation of activities in a project, represented on nodes, with the relationships between them indicated by arrows. It is more commonly called the activity-on-node (AON) diagram because the information about the activities is contained with them the rectangular node, and the relationship between individual nodes is represented by arrows. The arrows show a predecessor and successor relationship between activities. An activity can be a predecessor of other activities, meaning that it must be done before them. The same activity can also be a successor activity to one or more activities, meaning it must be done after them.

Figure 2-8 shows an example of Activity A as the predecessor activity, with Activities B and C as the successor activities. Activity A is also a burst activity because it is a predecessor to more than one successor activity.

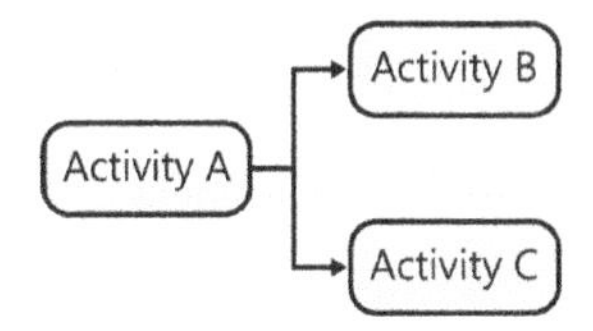

FIGURE 2-8 Predecessor and successors

There are four types of relationships that exist between predecessor and successor activities:

- **Finish-to-start (FS)** A finish-to-start relationship is one in which the successor activity cannot start until the predecessor activity has finished. Figure 2-9 depicts how this would be represented diagrammatically.

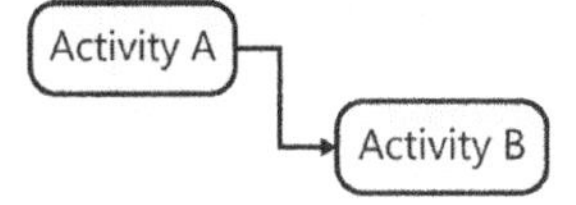

FIGURE 2-9 Finish-to-start relationship

- **Finish-to-finish (FF)** A finish-to-finish relationship is one in which the successor activity cannot finish until the predecessor activity has finished. Figure 2-10 depicts this diagrammatically.

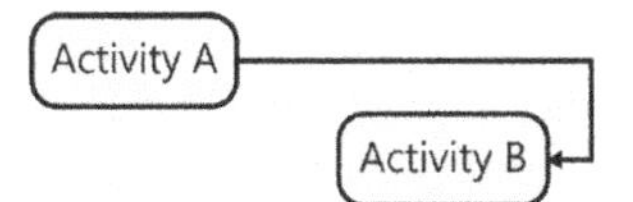

FIGURE 2-10 Finish-to-finish relationship

- **Start-to-start (SS)** A start-to-start relationship is one in which the successor activity cannot start until the predecessor activity starts. Figure 2-11 depicts this diagrammatically.

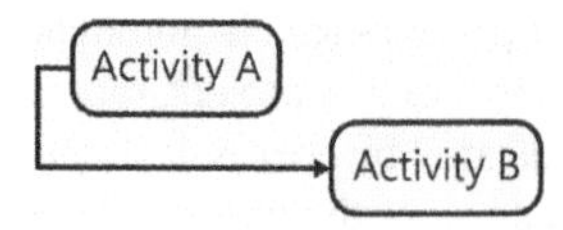

FIGURE 2-11 Start-to-start relationship.

- **Start-to-finish (SF)** A start-to-finish relationship indicates that the successor cannot finish until predecessor starts. Figure 2-12 depicts how this would be represented diagrammatically.

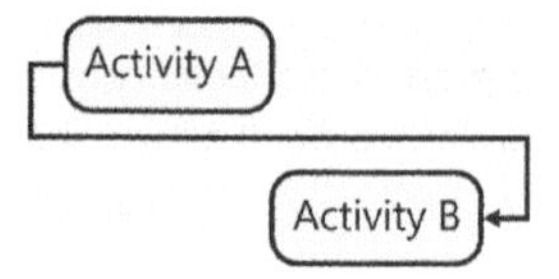

FIGURE 2-12 Start-to-finish relationship

True or false? If Activity B cannot start until Activity A finishes, it is an example of an SF relationship.

Answer: *False.* If Activity B cannot start until its predecessor activity finishes, it is an example of a FS relationship.

Figure 2-13 shows what an AON network diagram might look like at the end of the sequencing process. Information about each activity is represented in the nodes on the diagram, and the arrows indicate the relationship between the activities.

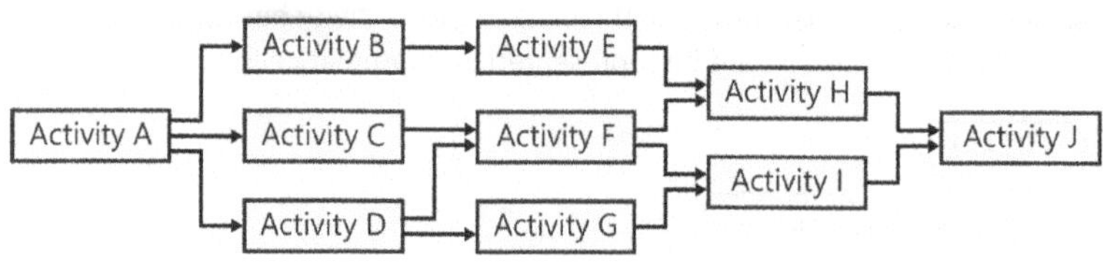

FIGURE 2-13 AON network diagram

In addition to documenting the relationships between activities using the precedence diagram method, you might also want to determine and document the type of dependencies that exist between activities. There are three main types of dependencies that can exist between activities: mandatory, discretionary, and external dependencies. A mandatory dependency means that the successor activity cannot start until the predecessor is finished. A discretionary activity means that the successor activity should not start until the predecessor activity is finished, but there can be some discretion. An external dependency means that the activity is waiting for another activity that is outside of your control and external to the project.

As part of your sequencing, you might want to consider the use of leads and lags. A lead indicates that a successor activity in an FS relationship can start prior to the finish of its predecessor. A lag indicates that a successor activity must wait for a defined period of time after the completion of its predecessor activity before it can start.

MORE INFO **You can find out more about sequencing activities by reading the Sequence Activities process in the PMBOK® Guide, 5th edition.**

Estimating activity resources

After activities have been defined and sequenced, the next step in building a project schedule, particularly a project constrained by resources rather than time, is to estimate the activities required in the activities that are available to complete the work.

NOTE **Whether you estimate activity resources first and use this information to estimate activity durations, or whether you estimate activity durations and then use that information to estimate resources will depend on whether your project is resource-constrained or time-constrained. If resources are constrained and time is flexible, your activity resource estimates can dictate the duration of the project. If time is the major constraint, activity durations dictate what resources must be obtained to complete the work within the time allocated.**

To accurately estimate activity resources, a project manager should use the schedule management plan, the activity list, and activity attributes developed during the work of defining activities; and other elements such as the resource calendar, risk register, and activity cost estimates because they all have some sort of impact on the activity resource requirements that are developed.

Useful tools for the project manager to use include expert judgment, published estimating data, and project management software. With these tools, the project manager can produce the activity resource requirements that identify which resources are available to be used to complete the work.

This work also produces a resource breakdown structure that is a graphical decomposition of the resources required on the project. The resource breakdown structure, like other breakdown structures, is used to decompose the categories of resource required and the specific resources required for the project. Figure 2-14 shows an example of a resource breakdown structure.

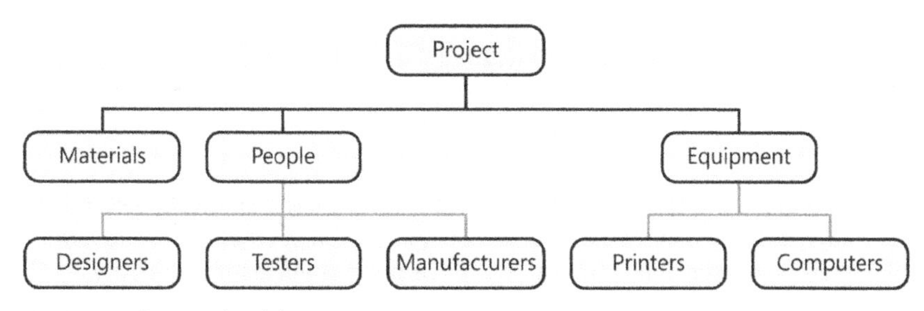

FIGURE 2-14 Resource breakdown structure

True or false? Resources that can be used on a project include both people and machinery.

Answer: *True*. Resources refer to any person or machine that can be used to complete the work required on the project.

MORE INFO **You can find out more about estimating activity resources by reading the Estimate Activity Resources process in the PMBOK® Guide, 5th edition.**

Estimating activity durations

A further step toward completing an approved project schedule is to estimate the time duration of each of the activities that have been identified. The work involved in estimating activity durations uses the list of activities and the defined activity resource requirements, along with the resource calendars that describe constraints on when resources are available to do work, to develop individual activity duration estimates.

The types of tools and techniques used to estimate activity durations are very similar to the ones used to estimate costs. They include the following:

Analogous estimating A technique that uses a similar situation from the past and extrapolates from that a time estimate for current work.

Parametric estimating A technique that takes an unknown unit and multiplies it by a known time period. For example, you might know that a software developer can test three software modules per day, and you have nine modules to test, so the activity duration estimate is nine days.

Group decision-making techniques If consulting groups of people for their opinion and experience to develop activity duration estimates, you might need to use some techniques to enable the group to make decisions. You can use techniques such as brainstorming or the Delphi technique to solicit information from the people, and use decision-making techniques such as consensus or majority rules to make decisions.

Three-point estimating Part of the PERT suite of tools and techniques that can be used in the profession project management. It uses three estimates, an optimistic, most likely, and pessimistic estimate, to develop a weighted average of the three.

The formula for calculating the three-point estimate is this:

$$\frac{tO + (tM \times 4) + tP}{6}$$

For example, if you have an optimistic estimate of 4 days, a most likely estimate of 7 days, and a pessimistic estimate of 12 days, and you put these estimates into the three-point estimating formula, your three-point estimate for this activity is 7.33 days:

$$\frac{4 + (7 \times 4) + 12}{6}$$

$$= \frac{4 + 28 + 12}{6}$$

$$= \frac{44}{6}$$

$$= 7.33$$

In addition to calculating the expected duration, you can also calculate the standard deviation and variance. The standard deviation (SD) is a calculation of how far away from the average duration, or the expected duration using the three-point estimating formula, your data is spread. A smaller SD means that the data is tightly grouped, whereas a larger SD means that the data is more widely spread.

The SD calculation used in the three-point estimating technique is essentially a heuristic, or rule-of-thumb, way of calculating SD rather than the full formula used by statisticians. The formula subtracts the optimistic from the pessimistic, and divides the result by 6. So, using the previous example, the SD is 8 divided by 6, which equals 1.33 days.

$$\text{Standard deviation} = \frac{P - O}{6}$$

A benefit of calculating the SD is that you can then estimate the confidence interval for a range of estimates. The confidence interval states the amount of the data that you expect to fall between the number of SDs above and below the mean. An SD of 1 either side of the mean represents a confidence interval of 68 percent, an SD of 2 either side of the mean gives a confidence interval of 95 percent, and an SD of 3 either side of the mean gives a confidence interval of 99.7 percent.

EXAM TIP **An SD of 6 either side of the mean contains 99.999 percent of the population. More commonly known as Six Sigma, it is used as a quality management tool in the project quality management knowledge area.**

Figure 2-15 shows a normal distribution and the range of a population you would expect to find with 1, 2, or 3 SDs either side of the mean.

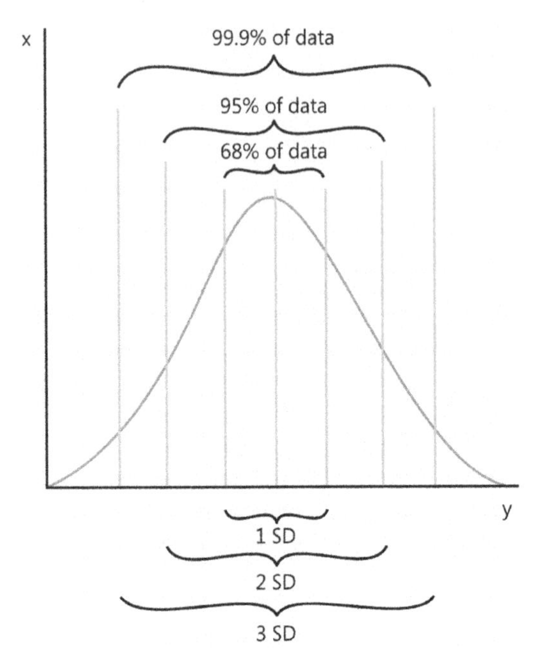

FIGURE 2-15 Standard deviations

True or false? The best estimating technique to use is parametric estimating.

Answer: *False.* The best estimating technique to use is the one that reflects the level of detail available to the project manager. If you are in early stages of progressive elaboration, you might find it best to use analogous forms of estimating. If you have a lot of detailed information available about exact units of work, you might find it better to use parametric estimating. Keep in mind that even if a large amount of data might exist, there might be times when the process of reviewing the data and developing exact figures is not a good use of time and resources.

Critical path method

The critical path method focuses on identifying all the paths through a project and, with the aid of a network diagram, determines which of these paths presents the shortest duration and also the least amount of scheduling flexibility, as indicated by the length of slack or float. The path with the shortest duration and the least slack or float through the project represents the path of most risk to the project, hence the name critical path.

There can be many paths through a project, as Figure 2-16 shows.

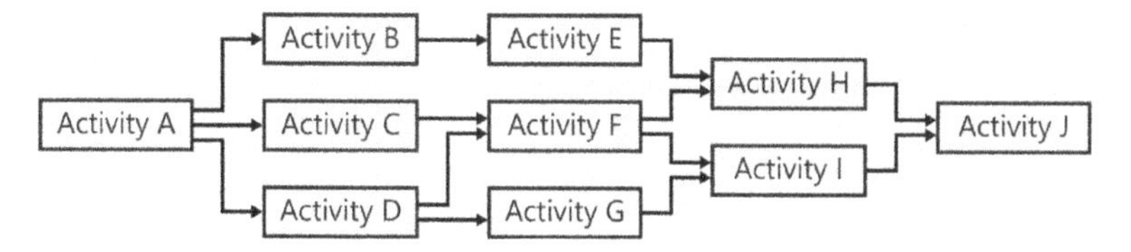

FIGURE 2-16 Network paths

Here are the following paths through this network diagram:

- A-B-E-H-J
- A-C-F-H-J
- A-C-F-I-J
- A-D-F-H-J
- A-D-F-I-J
- A-D-G-I-J

You cannot determine which path or paths are the critical paths until you complete a full schedule network analysis.

To calculate the critical path in an AON diagram, you can use a node to represent the information about the activity. The information contained in the node includes the Task ID, the duration of the activity, the Early Start (ES), the Early Finish (EF), the Late Start (LS), the Late Finish (LF), and the amount of Total Float in the activity. Figure 2-17 represents a node.

<table>
<tr><td>Early Start
(ES)</td><td rowspan="3">Activity
ID</td><td>Early Finish
(EF)</td></tr>
<tr><td>Total Float</td><td>Duration</td></tr>
<tr><td>Late Start
(LS)</td><td>Late Finish
(LF)</td></tr>
</table>

FIGURE 2-17 The activity node

> ***NOTE*** **Be aware that in the real world and in the exam, many different forms of nodes can be used with information displayed differently, yet they all display the same information, just in different ways.**

Now if you take the information contained in Table 2-3 and map it over an entire network diagram, you can calculate the total project duration, and the critical path or paths.

TABLE 2-3 Activity information

ACTIVITY ID	DURATION (DAYS)	PREDECESSOR
A	3	-
B	5	A
C	4	A
D	2	B, C
E	6	C
F	5	D, E
G	4	E
H	7	F, G

The first step in the process is to construct a network diagram showing the relationships between the activities. In this instance, assume that all activities have a FS relationship, and there are no leads and lags. Figure 2-18 shows the network diagram.

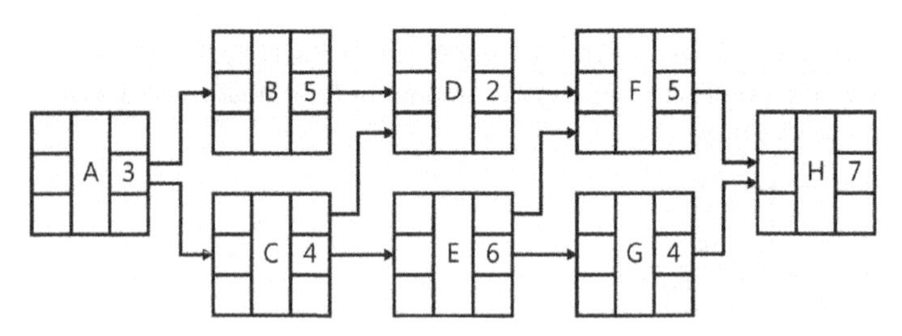

FIGURE 2-18 Network diagram example

By examining this network diagram, you can now write the paths through the diagram as follows:

- A-B-D-F-H
- A-C-D-F-H
- A-C-E-F-H
- A-C-E-G-H

The next step in the process is to complete a forward pass by working from left to right and calculating the ES and EF for each task. The earliest a task can start is immediately after the latest EF of all its predecessor activities. For example, if Activity A has an EF of day 3 (which means it finishes at the end of day 3), Activity B has an ES of day 4 (which means it starts at the beginning of day 4). If an activity has more than one predecessor, the earliest it can start is immediately after the latest early finish of all its predecessors. Figure 2-19 shows the network diagram with the forward pass completed. You can now determine that the project duration is 25 days.

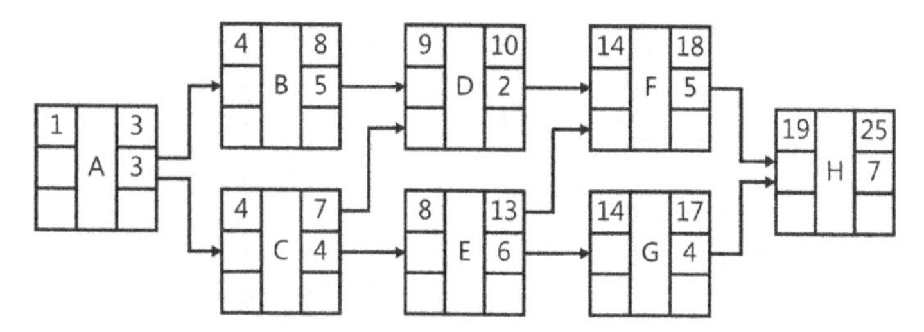

FIGURE 2-19 Forward pass is complete

The next step in the process is to complete a backward pass, in which you work from right to left, and you calculate the LF and LS for each activity. This time, when calculating the LF for an activity, you must look to its successor activities; the LF for an activity is immediately prior to the earliest of all successor LS dates. For example, if Activity D is the successor to Activity B, and Activity D has an LS of day 12, Activity B has a LF of day 11. As you complete the backward pass, you can also calculate the total slack for each task by subtracting the LS from the LF. Figure 2-20 shows a completed backward pass.

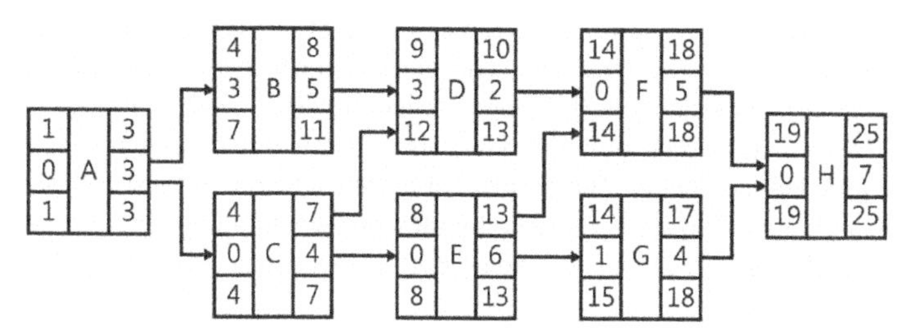

FIGURE 2-20 Backward pass is complete

To calculate which path through the network diagram is the critical one, you simply look at all the activities that have zero total float because they represent activities that, if delayed, will affect the total project duration. If you do this, you can determine that the critical path in this network diagram is A-C-E-F-H.

The project schedule can also be represented by a milestone chart or, less commonly, by the project schedule network diagram. Figure 2-21 shows an example of a Gantt chart.

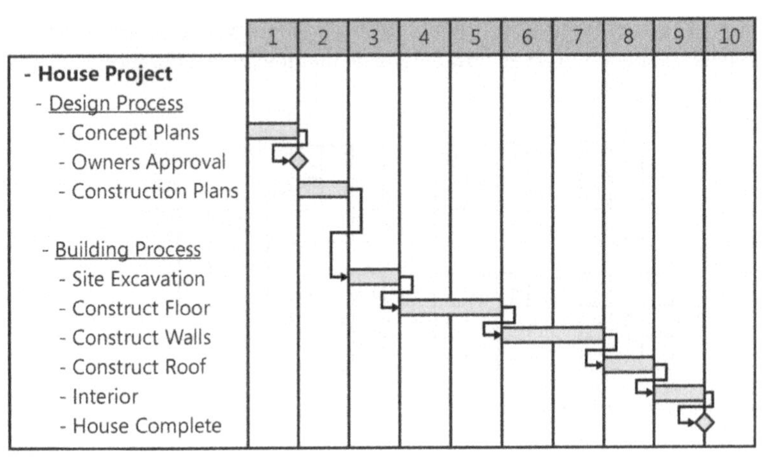

FIGURE 2-21 Gantt chart

Critical chain method

The critical chain method, which was developed by Eli Goldratt, is a scheduling method that allows for the provision of time buffers to account for project uncertainties or identified points of limited resource causing bottlenecks. Buffers can be developed using a variety of methods, including historical information, expert judgment, and statistical analysis. The buffer can be in one of two forms. The first is a total project buffer, which is used like a bank account from which time withdrawals can be made when any uncertainty in the project schedule causes delays. The other type of buffer is known as feeding buffer and it is associated with a specific point in the chain of dependent activities. The purpose of buffers is to protect the critical chain of activities from causing an increase in the total project duration. Figure 2-22 shows an example of project buffers and feeding buffers in a critical chain method schedule analysis.

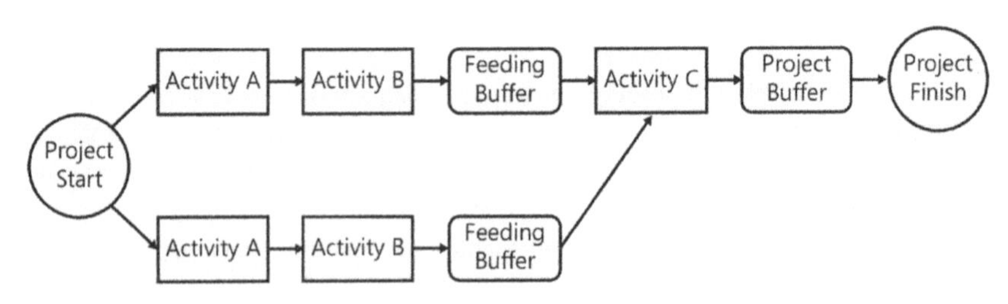

FIGURE 2-22 An example of a critical chain method

True or false? The critical chain method and the critical path method are just two different names for the same schedule analysis technique.

Answer: *False*. The critical path method analyzes the different paths through a network diagram to determine which of them presents the most risk to the project duration, whereas the critical chain method analyzes the work flow through a series of activities and allocates either project or feeding buffer to ensure that uncertainty that arises does not affect the forecast project duration.

Resource leveling

As part of the development of your project schedule you might need to take into account the effects of resource leveling. Resource leveling is the process of optimizing resource usage throughout the life of the project to get the most efficient allocation of resources. There are two major reasons for undertaking resource leveling. The first reason is to deal with an inefficient allocation of resources that sees resources sitting idle at certain points on the project while other times they might be overallocated. The second reason is in response to resource constraints imposed on the project.

Your first attempted resource leveling usually results in an increase of the project duration that might require you to look at schedule compression techniques.

Schedule compression

After you complete your initial project schedule, you might find that you are required to reduce the duration of the project. If so, you have a number of options available to you. These options include reducing the project scope or reducing the project quality, but the two most popular forms of reducing a project duration are crashing and fast-tracking.

Crashing as a schedule compression technique involves allocating greater resources to activities to have them completed in a shorter time. Because crashing involves an extra allocation of resources, it usually involves an extra cost.

> ***EXAM TIP*** **If a question in the exam presents a scenario in which you are required to reduce shall project duration, but you have no additional budget to do it, you cannot choose crashing because it usually requires extra costs.**

Fast-tracking is a schedule compression technique that takes activities that are normally done in sequence and does them in parallel. This can result in increased risk to the project and needs to be applied only where fast-tracking activities would result in a decrease in the project duration.

True or false? If you are required to reduce project duration, the best option is to crash certain activities on the project schedule.

Answer: *False.* There is no single best answer for how to reduce a project duration using schedule compression techniques. The best answer reflects your particular approaches to risk, costs, and quality on the project, and you might select several different schedule compression techniques to reduce the project duration.

> ***MORE INFO*** **You can find out more about the work involved in developing a project schedule by reading Practice Standard for Scheduling, 2nd edition (Project Management Institute, 2011).**

Can you answer these questions?

You can find the answers to these questions at the end of this chapter.

1. If you are adding up a most likely time estimate, a pessimistic time estimate, and an optimistic time estimate to determine a weighted average to include in your activity duration estimates, what tool or technique are you using?
2. If you have decided to ask your project team to work overtime to complete work faster, which schedule compression technique have you chosen to use?
3. After you complete a forward pass through a network diagram, what information about the project duration do you have?
4. What is the difference between project work packages and project activities?
5. If you are working on a project that is resource constrained, should you estimate activity resources or activity durations first?

Task 5: Develop a human resource management plan by defining the roles and responsibilities of the project team members in order to create an effective project organization structure and provide guidance regarding how resources will be utilized and managed.

The key purpose of this task is to develop a human resource management plan that will then assist the project manager and project team members in identifying which personnel they need, the level of skills those personnel need, how the personnel are going to be obtained to work on the project, and how the project manager will develop and lead individuals and team.

> ***MORE INFO*** **You can find out more about the managing human resources on a project by reading the Plan Human Resource Management process in Chapter 9 of the PMBOK® Guide, 5th edition or Chapter 7 of the PMP Training Kit.**

Exam need to know...

- Human resource management plan

  For example: What document provides guidance to the project manager on how the entire human resource management activities for the project will be carried out?
- Staffing management plan

  For example: Where will the project manager turn to find out when specific staff are required for a project?
- Roles and responsibilities

  For example: How do different organizational structures affect the power a project manager has over project personnel?
- Interpersonal skills

For example: What skills must the project manager have to successfully lead, develop, and manage a project team?

- Ethics and professional conduct

  For example: When confronted with a potentially unethical or illegal situation, how must a professional project manager act?

Human resource management plan

The ultimate aim of the work involved with this task is to produce the human resource management plan, which is a component of the overall project management plan. The human resource management plan provides guidance to the project manager on how project personnel will be identified, recruited, developed, managed, and eventually released from the project.

The contents of the human resource management plan can include the following:

A clear and concise description of individual project team members' experience, authority, roles, and responsibilities

A project organization chart providing a graphical display of project team members and where they fit within the project organization structure

A staffing management plan, which is a component of the overall human resource management plan and describes how and when personnel will be recruited and for how long

True or false? The human resource management plan provides guidance to the project manager on how all resources for the project will be obtained.

Answer: *False.* The human resource management plan focuses on the human resources, not all resources. Remember that the definition of resources includes both people and machinery.

Staffing management plan

The staffing management plan is an important component of the human resource plan. Depending on the size, complexity, and duration of the project the staffing management plan can include lots of detail or little detail. The staffing management plan is constantly updated as human resource needs are identified and changed throughout the project. It is important that the project manager has a staffing management plan to ensure that project personnel are acquired at the time they are needed on the project.

The staffing management plan can have a variety of information and reflects the size and complexity of the project; some of the things it can refer to are these:

- Clarification on whether project personnel will come from within the organization or be recruited externally
- Whether the project team members will be co-located or work remotely as a virtual team
- Interactions between the project and the organization's human resource department

- Roles and power that functional managers have over project personnel
- Any constraints on when project personnel can work
- A plan for how and when team members will be released from the project
- Both individual and team training needs
- How individuals in the team will be rewarded
- Any relevant health and safety matters

True or false? A staffing management plan provides guidance to the project manager on who has the most power in a matrix organization in relation to project personnel.

Answer: *True*. The staffing management plan contains a lot of information about how the project will be staffed, including an analysis and description of the distribution of power between the project manager and the functional manager in a matrix organization.

> ***EXAM TIP*** **In the exam, remember that whenever and wherever possible, it is better to get team members to sit in a face-to-face format to enhance the chances of building a highly productive team. If a virtual team is to be formed, explicit strategies should be put in place to deal with some of the issues that virtual teams can experience.**

Roles and responsibilities

It is important to ensure throughout the life of the project that each and every project team member understands the roles and responsibilities clearly. If members do not understand the roles and responsibilities clearly, there might be some ambiguity or disagreements that could lead to inefficiencies in completing the project work. There are several ways to demonstrate to team members their role and responsibility; the most common ways are by using organizational charts, responsibility assignment matrices, or text-based descriptions of roles and responsibilities.

Organizational charts are an effective way to demonstrate graphically how the organization is structured. They can also be used to demonstrate how the project team is structured. When the organizational chart is used, it clearly identifies individual personnel and their reporting lines. When used to demonstrate the entire organizational structure, an organizational chart will first outline the type of organizational structure within which the project is being carried out which will have a direct effect on the chances of the project success.

> ***NOTE*** **The organizational chart is another example of a breakdown structure such as the WBS. It takes a high-level concept, in this case the organization, and breaks it down into its component roles. It starts at the top with the chief executive officer (CEO) or general manager, and breaks it down into lower-level roles such as line manager, team leader, team member, and specific technical roles. You can also use it to break down project roles, in which case you would have the project manager at the top and lower-level project roles beneath.**

There are three main types of organizational structure:

- **Functional organization** The organization is divided along functional lines, with a general manager of each functional area controlling the staff. The power of a project manager is extremely weak in this type of organizational structure because personnel report directly to the functional manager. Figure 2-23 shows an example of a typical functional organizational structure.

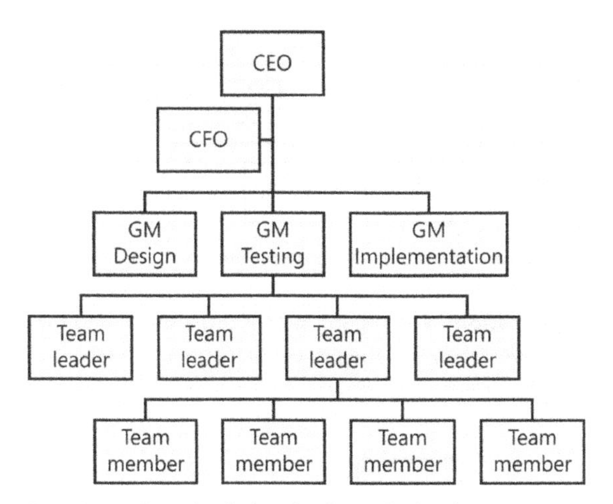

FIGURE 2-23 Example of a functional organizational structure

- **Matrix organization** The organization retains its functional demarcation, but allows the project manager to work across functional areas and draw staff from different areas when their skills and expertise are required for the project. There are three distinct forms of matrix organization that reflect the amount of power and authority that a project manager has over such things as personnel and budget. In a strong form of matrix organization, the project manager, not the functional manager, has the most power over personnel and project budgets. In a balanced form of matrix organization, power between the project manager and functional manager is equally shared. In a weak matrix organization, it is the functional manager, not the project manager, who has most power over project personnel in the project budget. Figure 2-24 shows an example of a matrix organizational structure.

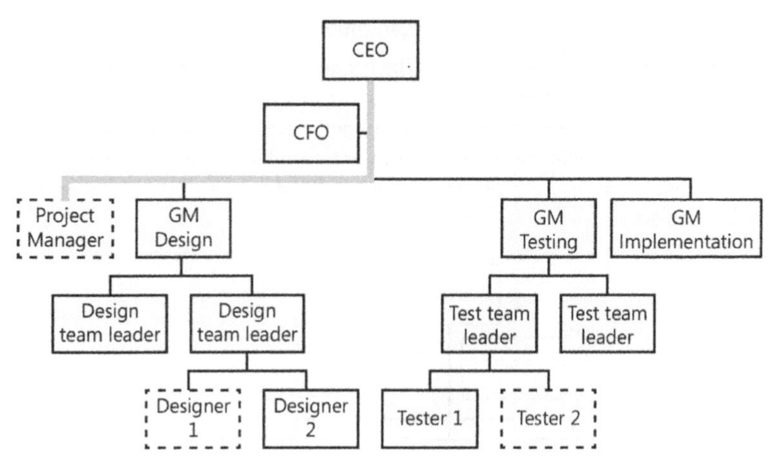

FIGURE 2-24 An example of a matrix organizational structure

- **Projectized organization** The organization is organized along the lines of the projects it undertakes, and the project manager is directly in charge of personnel. Figure 2-25 shows an example of a projectized organizational structure.

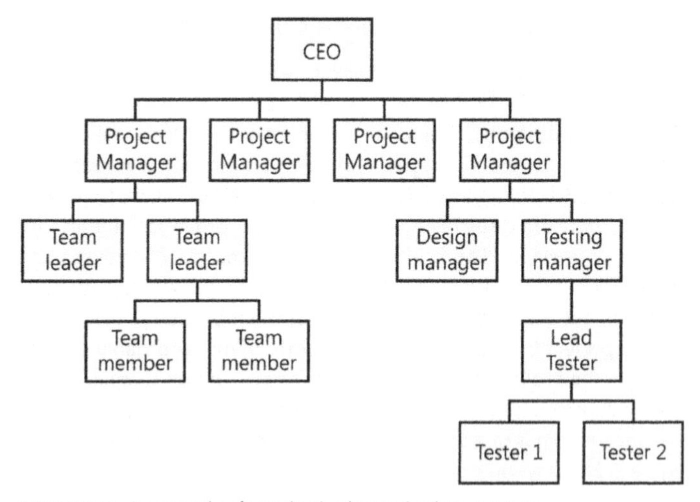

FIGURE 2-25 An example of a projectized organization structure

True or false? In a strong matrix organization, it is the project manager who has the most power to determine when staff from functional areas will work on the project.

Answer: *True.* A strong matrix organization indicates that with the distribution of power and authority between the functional manager and the project manager, it is the project manager who has the most power and authority over project personnel in the project budget.

MORE INFO For more information about project organizational structures, read Organizing Projects for Success by V. K. Verma (Project Management Institute, 1995).

Table 2-4 sums up how power and authority is distributed between functional managers and project managers in different organizational structures.

TABLE 2-4 Organizational structures, authority, and power

FUNCTIONAL	WEAK MATRIX	BALANCED MATRIX	STRONG MATRIX	PROJECTIZED
Project manager might be part-time and has very little power and authority Functional manager has most authority over people and budget	Project manager might be part-time and has low levels of power and authority Functional manager has most authority over people and budget	Project manager might be part- or full-time and has equal levels of power and authority with the functional manager Functional manager has equal levels of authority with the project manager over people and budget	Project manager is full-time and has more power and authority than the functional manager Functional manager has less authority over people and budget than the project manager	Project manager is full-time and has high to almost total power and authority Functional manager has very little, if any, authority over people and budget

Another way to demonstrate roles and responsibilities to project team members is to use a responsibility assignment matrix that clearly shows which team member has responsibility for which role on the project. The most common form of responsibility assignment matrix is the RACI diagram. Figure 2-26 shows an example of a RACI chart. The letter "R" identifies who is responsible, "A" identifies who is accountable, "C" identifies who will be consulted, and "I" identifies who will be informed.

	Team Member			
Activity	David	Thomas	Jayne	Mark
Collect requirements	R/A	C	C	I
Design prototype	C	A	R	
Test		I	R	A

FIGURE 2-26 An example of a responsibility assignment matrix, specifically a RACI chart

NOTE **There are many different forms of responsibility assignment matrices. The RACI chart is the most popular, but there are also charts that use different letters. What they all have in common is that they clearly identify the roles and responsibilities of the project team members.**

True or false? The responsibility assignment matrix shows who must take responsibility for completing the work and who will be held accountable for the work.

Answer: *True*. There are many forms of responsibility assignment matrices, but the most common is the RACI chart, which clearly shows which team members have responsibility and accountability for work being completed on the project.

A third way to clearly indicate roles and responsibilities to project team members is with a text-based description. The most common form of text-based description of roles and responsibilities is a job description, which delineates the role, expected experience and capability to complete the role, level of responsibility and delegated authority the team member has, and any other factors that need to be documented to ensure that the project team member has a clear outline of their role in the project.

Interpersonal skills

One of the key indicators of whether a project manager can successfully lead and develop individuals and project team is the use of interpersonal skills.

NOTE **Although there are times when it seems that a project manager's technical skills (such as time and cost estimating, variance analysis, reporting and scope definition of a key indicating a project success), it is in fact the ability of a project manager to use interpersonal skills that is the greater indicator a project success. Keep in mind that it is the people on the project who complete the project, and leading these people is essential for project success. In relation to your own professional development, you should ensure that you make a commitment to the ongoing development of your interpersonal skills.**

There are 11 key interpersonal skills that a project manager must develop and learn to use appropriately to get the best from individuals and the project team:

- Leadership
- Team building
- Motivation
- Communication
- Influencing
- Decision making
- Political and cultural awareness
- Negotiation
- Trust building
- Conflict management
- Coaching

MORE INFO **You can find out more about these 11 key interpersonal skills by reading Appendix X3 of the *PMBOK® Guide*, 5th edition. Other valuable resources you might want to read include these:**

- ***Seven Habits of Highly Effective People*, by S. R Covey (Free Press, 2004)**
- ***Human Factors and Project Management*, by P. C. Dinsmore (Amacom Books, 1984)**
- ***Essential People Skills for Project Managers*, by G. Levin & S. Flannes (Management Concepts, 2005)**
- ***Human Resource Skills for the Project Manager*, by V. K. Verma (Project Management Institute, 1996)**

True or false? A project manager must display both leadership and management skills at the correct time to increase the chances of developing a high-performing project team.

Answer: *True*. The range of skills the project manager must display is wide and varied. These skills include all the technical or hard skills around scope definition, cost and time estimating, schedule development, budget development, risk management, quality management, and other areas of the profession of project management. Perhaps more importantly are the development and display of soft skills that include both leadership and management to develop a high-performing project team.

MORE INFO **You can find out more about the interpersonal skills a project manager should have and seek to develop by reading Appendix G of the PMBOK® Guide, 5th edition.**

Ethics and professional conduct

Underpinning everything that a project manager does must be a high standard of ethical and professional behavior. Nowhere is this more apparent or necessary than when dealing with people on the project, particularly human resources. It is also important to display a high standard of ethical and professional conduct when dealing with any stakeholder on the project.

The four key principles of ethical and professional conduct are as follows:

- **Respect** Having appropriate regard for yourself and also regard for others personally and professionally. It requires you to negotiate agreements and contracts in good faith and not exercise the power of your expertise or position to influence the decisions or actions of others to benefit personally at their expense. Respect also means not acting in an abusive manner toward any other person. You respect the property rights of others, meaning that you must protect the intellectual property rights, copyright, and confidential information of any person or body. Demonstrating respect also means being aware of the norms and customs of others and avoid engaging in behaviors they might consider disrespectful.
- **Responsibility** Being personally and professionally accountable for your own actions, being accountable for acting ethically and professionally at all

times, and ensuring that others do the same. Responsibility also means that you as the project manager are responsible for the actions of those in your team. Furthermore, you must always report unethical or illegal conduct to the appropriate people or body. This means that whenever you discover or observe unethical or illegal behavior, you must report it to the appropriate authorities.

- **Honesty** Not engaging in or condoning behavior in others that is designed to deceive anyone. This includes making misleading or false statements; telling half-truths; providing information out of context; or omitting information that, if known, would make your statements misleading or incomplete.
- **Fairness** Avoiding conflicts of interest, favoritism and discrimination, which means that you do not hire or fire, reward or punish, or award or deny contracts based on your own personal considerations, bias, or benefit. You should treat everyone equally and fairly, regardless of gender, ethnicity, age, religion, disability, nationality, or sexual orientation.

NOTE **If you are a PMI member, credential holder, or volunteer and you breach the code of ethics and professional conduct, there is a range of disciplinary measures that PMI can take against you. You should be aware of the expected standard of ethical and professional behavior, display it consistently, expect it in others, and report any violations or breaches.**

True or false? The PMI code of ethics and professional conduct should be followed only if it agrees with organizational processes and policies.

Answer: *False.* If you are a PMI member, credential holder, or volunteer, or even if you are simply an aspiring professional project manager, you should always abide by the PMI code of ethics and professional conduct, even when it contradicts and contravenes your own organizational processes and policies. If you find yourself in this situation, you should attempt to change your organizational process and policies to align them with the PMI code of ethics and professional conduct.

EXAM TIP **In the exam, you might be presented with a scenario that outlines a situation that might be potentially unethical or illegal and asks you how to act. You must always act strictly according to the PMI code of ethics and professional conduct. This is true even when a potential answer describes something you might currently do and be encouraged to do by your organization. You are also required to follow these standards even if they are different from expected and accepted cultural practices.**

MORE INFO **You can find out more about the ethical and professional standards a project manager should display by reading the *PMI Code of Ethics and Professional Conduct* available from the Project Management Institute website: *www.pmi.org*.**

Can you answer these questions?

You can find the answers to these questions at the end of this chapter.

1. What is the difference between the human resource management plan and staffing management plan?

2. If you constantly have to negotiate with different functional managers across your organization to get project personnel allocated to your project, what sort of organizational structure are you working in?
3. What does a RACI chart show?
4. Why is important to clearly define individual roles and responsibilities on a project?
5. What role does the human resource management plan play in the execution stage of the project?

Task 6: Develop a communication plan based on the project organization structure and external stakeholder requirements, in order to manage the flow of project information.

This task addresses the need to develop an effective project communications management plan that reflects the organizational structure and existing process assets, and takes into account the communications requirements of all project stakeholders. The key purpose of developing a communications plan for the project is to ensure that a project manager can use effective communications to increase the chances of project success. Successful communications directly contribute to successful stakeholder expectation management in the two areas that are closely interlinked.

MORE INFO **You can find out more about developing a communications management plan by reading the Plan Communications Management process in the PMBOK® Guide, 5th edition, or Chapter 8 of the PMP® Training Kit.**

Exam need to know...

- Communications management plan

  For example: What document determines the frequency, content, and style of project communications between the project team and important stakeholders?

- Stakeholder management plan

  For example: How does a project manager proactively document the strategy for managing stakeholder expectations?

- Communications requirements analysis

  For example: How does a project manager determine the individual communications requirements for the project stakeholders?

- Communications models

  For example: What are some of the issues that can occur between a sender and receiver of communications?

- Communications methods

  For example: What is the best communication method to use to ensure that stakeholders receive information in a timely and effective manner?

Communications management plan

To complete the work associated with carrying out this task, a project manager needs to oversee development of an effective communications management plan. The communications management plan is part of the overall project management plan. It focuses on how all project communications will be planned, carried out, monitored, and controlled. There are many things that the communications management plan can include, but ultimately the format and content will reflect the size and complexity of the project being undertaken and also the organizational process assets that the company might have. The types of information that communications management plan might contain can include the following:

- Key messages
- Overall approach to communications (open or closed)
- Individual stakeholder communication requirements
- Language, format, content, and level of detail of communications
- Identification of those responsible for communicating, authorizing, and receiving information
- Communications methods
- Feedback and escalation processes
- Method for monitoring the effectiveness and updating the communications management plan
- Guidelines and ground rules for project status meetings
- Any known communications constraints

The communications management plan is developed by the project manager in conjunction with project team members using a variety of tools and techniques that include communications requirements analysis, a review of appropriate communications technology, and awareness of communications models and decisions about the particular communications methods to be used. These are discussed in more detail in the following sections.

True or false? The communications management plan identifies each of the stakeholders on the project and the requirements they have of the project.

Answer: *False*. The communications management plan might set out how to identify stakeholders, but it does not identify them. Identification of individual stakeholders is in the stakeholder register.

> ***EXAM TIP*** **There is a great deal of importance placed on effective project communications. It is often said that 90 percent of a project manager's time is spent communicating, and 50 percent of this time is spent communicating with the project team members. If presented with a scenario in the exam where the root cause might be poor communication, your best answer is to look at how you can improve communication.**

NOTE You might be surprised to realize the breadth and depth of effective communications on a project. Communications are not limited to just verbal conversations or project reports. Effective communication on the project includes the following:

- Internal and external communications
- Formal and informal forms of communications
- Vertical and horizontal communications
- Official and unofficial communications
- Push, pull and interactive forms of communication
- Written, oral, verbal and non-verbal forms of communication

Additionally, the range of communication skills the project manager should be aware of and demonstrate appropriately includes the following:

- Active and effective listening
- Providing feedback
- Fact-finding before making decisions
- Expectation management
- Influence through relationship building
- Coaching of team members
- Negotiation skills
- Conflict resolution skills

Stakeholder management plan

Closely interlinked with the communications management plan is the stakeholder management plan. The stakeholder management plan, like other plans, is a component of the overall project management plan. It specifically addresses and identifies stakeholder management strategies that will be used to record, analyze, engage, and influence stakeholders and their expectations throughout the project. The types of information that the stakeholder management plan might contain include the following:

- Methods for identifying and prioritizing stakeholders
- Reference to organizational process assets for stakeholder expectation management
- Description of roles and responsibilities for stakeholder expectation management
- Escalation path for stakeholder issues
- Recommended time frames, frequency, content, and format of the distribution of information to stakeholders
- Guidance on how to manage changes to stakeholder management strategies

The ultimate goal of stakeholder expectation management activities is to get stakeholders to support your project or at least not to oppose it.

True or false? The communications management plan and the stakeholder management plan are tightly interlinked because successful stakeholder expectation management relies on successful communications.

Answer: *True.* There is a large degree of overlap between communications management and stakeholder management on a project. Managing stakeholder expectations relies on many things such as relationship building, influencing, and effective communications. As such, it is important that your communications management plan and stakeholder management plan recognize the importance of each other.

Communications requirements analysis

A key step in the development of the communications management plan is an analysis of individual stakeholders' communications requirements. Each stakeholder has individual communications requirements, and is important that the project manager recognize both the particular interests that stakeholders have in the project, the frequency with which they want to be communicated, and the method of communication they prefer. To determine stakeholder requirements, the project manager can refer to historical information, project team members, data-gathering techniques to get information directly from the stakeholders, and communications management professionals. This communications requirements analysis can be captured in the stakeholder register.

As part of determining stakeholder communication requirements, the project manager should be aware of the number of potential communication channels. The exact number is not as important as realizing the magnitude of communications channels on the project. A project manager cannot hope to control every communication on the project, but should attempt to set the tone, style, and content of project communications.

> ***NOTE*** **It is extremely important that you undertake proactive and effective communications with all stakeholders. If you think that not communicating with the stakeholder means they are not receiving a message, you are incorrect. By not communicating with stakeholders, you are communicating to them that you do not value their requirements or expectations. Additionally in the absence of effective communications, rumor, gossip, innuendo, and assumption might take hold. So it is more effective to be proactive, not reactive, with your communications to try and remedy or change these misconceptions.**

The formula for calculating the number of communications channels on the project is this, where n equals the number of stakeholders on a project:

$$\frac{n(n-1)}{2}$$

So if you have 10 stakeholders on a project, you will have 45 potential communications channels. If you have 30 stakeholders on a project, you will have 435 potential communications channels.

True or false? The technique of communications requirements analysis involves assessing the individual communications requirements for each stakeholder in the project.

Answer: *True.* Communications requirements analysis is an important technique to use to understand and document how each stakeholder want to be communicated with, the frequency of communications, and the format and content of the communications.

Communications models

When determining how best to communicate on the project, a project manager should be aware of communications models that describe how communications move between the person who sends the message and the person who receives it. Figure 2-27 shows a standard communications model describing how a sender encodes a message and the receiver decodes the message.

First, the sender encodes a message according to preferences, prejudices, and particular world view. The sender then transmits this message via whichever communications technology or medium is selected. As the message is transmitted, it must pass through a particular medium; in doing so, it encounters noise. Noise includes any aspects present in the selected medium that might interfere with or change the message being transmitted.

Then the receiver receives the message and decodes it according to preferences and prejudices. If the receiver then attempts to send the message on to another person or back to the original sender, it must go through the same obstacles again.

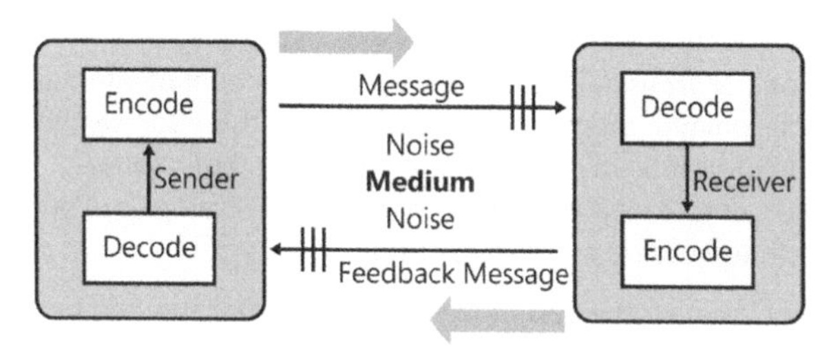

FIGURE 2-27 A communications model showing how a sender encodes and sends a message through a medium to a receiver

There are some communication skills that a project manager can practice to improve project communications between senders and receivers, including the following:

- **Active listening** Requires the listener to take active steps to ensure that the message was understood correctly. The result of this is that the listener is more engaged and there is a much better transfer of information between sender and receiver.
- **Effective listening** Similar to active listening, but requires the listener or receiver to also monitor nonverbal and physical communication.

- **Feedback** Relies on cues from the receiver back to the sender that indicate whether the message has been understood.
- **Nonverbal** Occurs in the form of body language, posture, and similar. Most human communication is nonverbal; people are very skilled at picking up nonverbal communication.
- **Paralingual** Vocal, not verbal; it includes tone of voice, inflections, and volume.

True or false? It is the responsibility of the receiver to decode the message.

Answer: *True.* The receiver takes responsibility for decoding a message that has been encoded by a sender and transmitted via a particular medium.

Communications methods

As part of the communications requirements analysis a project manager will determine which communication method is best to use to ensure effective communications. There are three general methods of communications, as follows:

- **Interactive communication** Occurs between two or more parties who carry out a multidirectional exchange of information between them. It is the most common form of communication and includes verbal conversations, meetings, phone calls, and web-based video conferencing.
- **Push communication** Occurs when a sender sends information to specific recipients. An advantage of push communication is that there is proof that the information is sent; a disadvantage is that there is no confirmation that it has been received. Common forms of push communications include email, reports, voice mail, and press releases.
- **Pull communication** Most useful when there is a large amount of information that needs to be communicated to a wide audience. In this instance, the project manager and project team members store the information somewhere and invite recipients to view it at their own discretion. Examples of pull communications include websites and intranet sites.

True or false? Push communication is the best form of communication method to use because you can prove that you have sent the message.

Answer: *False.* The best form of communication method depends on your communications requirements analysis of stakeholders and the tasks contained in your communications management plan. There are times when interactive communication is the best form of communication method; other times, either push or pull methods of communication are best.

Can you answer these questions?

You can find the answers to these questions at the end of this chapter.

1. What is the relationship between communications management planning and stakeholder expectation management planning?

2. If you currently have 20 stakeholders identified on your project, and another 5 stakeholders are identified, how many more communications channels are there?
3. In the standard communications model, what is the best definition of noise?
4. If you are studying another person's body language to understand them better, which communication skill are you using?
5. Who should take responsibility for controlling the communications process on the project?

Task 7: Develop a procurement plan based on the project scope and schedule, in order to ensure that the required project resources will be available.

The purpose of this task is to develop a procurement management plan to assist in the delivery of the project scope. Many projects use a procurement process to negotiate contracts for the supply of goods and services, and some projects are initiated with the successful negotiation of a contract. As such, the issue of project procurements is an important one that is made more important by the fact that any contracts signed are legally enforceable agreements; if the process is not done correctly, there could be severe legal repercussions.

> ***MORE INFO*** **You can find out more about the development of a procurement management plan by reading the Plan Procurement Management process in the PMBOK® Guide, 5th edition or Chapter 10 of the PMP Training Kit.**

Exam need to know...

- Procurement management plan

  For example: Where does the project manager turn for guidance on whether they should procure goods from external providers?
- Contract types

  For example: How does the choice of contract type affect the allocation of risk between buyer and seller?
- Procurement statement of work

  For example: What is the best way to describe the work to be done as part of the negotiated contract?
- Procurement documents

  For example: What documents can a project manager and project team use to solicit information from prospective sellers?
- Make-or-buy decisions

  For example: How does a project manager decide whether to get the project team to make a particular product or choose to procure it from an external provider?

- Source selection criteria

  For example: What information should be taken into account when deciding which of the potential sellers should be awarded a contract?

Procurement management plan

The purpose of the procurement management plan is to guide the project manager and project team on how the entire procurement process will be carried out. It should reference the following:

- Types of contracts to be used
- Types of procurement documents to be used
- Process for selecting successful sellers
- Management of all vendors and suppliers
- Assessment of how procurement activities interact with other activities
- Process of make-or-buy decisions
- Development of procurement metrics to be used to assess both the procurement process and products
- Assessment of the enterprise environmental factors affecting procurement decisions (legislative requirements and market conditions)
- Description of the organizational process assets that can be used to assist the procurement process (existing procurement policies and templates)

The development of the procurement management plan will take into account all other aspects of the project, including identified requirements, the project scope, risks relating to procurement, identified activity resource requirements, the project schedule, and activity cost estimates.

True or false? The procurement management plan will specify the process by which the project manager advertises the procurement statement of work to potential sellers and how the successful seller will be selected.

Answer: *True*. Selecting a seller to provide goods and services is a process that should be guided by a procurement management plan.

> ***EXAM TIP*** **If you are presented with any procurement scenarios in the exam, you should always first look for your own procurement management plan and the organizational process assets relating to procurement that your organization has. Exactly how you carry out procurement on your project will be guided by both of these sources of information.**

Contract types

As part of procurement management planning work, you will make an assessment and decision about the type of contract you might want to use to procure goods or services described in the procurement statement of work. There are three main types of contracts you might want to consider using:

- **Fixed price contract** Seeks to get a fixed price from a seller for a defined procurement statement of work. There are some variations to fixed-price contracts, including the basic fixed price contract, financial incentives, and economic price adjustments for contracts that run over a long period of time. These are generally referred to as firm fixed-price contracts (FFPs), fixed-price incentive fee contracts (FPIFs), and fixed-price with economic price adjustment contracts (FP-EPAs). In an FFP, the risk is with the sellers because they must deliver the work for the agreed price. Because it is a fixed-price form of contract, the buyer has little price risk.
- **Cost reimbursable contract** Reimburses the seller for all legitimate costs incurred in completing the procurement statement of will plus some form of fee. The three types of fee that can be added to the actual costs incurred produce a cost plus fixed fee (CPFF) form of contract, a cost plus incentive fee (CPIF) form of contract, or a cost plus award fee (CPAF) form of contract. The cost reimbursable formal contract is best used when there is a great deal of flexibility required in the delivery of the procurement statement of work. With this contract, the risk is shared between buyer and seller.
- **Time and materials contracts** An agreement to reimburse the seller for whatever time and materials are used in the contract. In its simplest form, the risk is all with the buyer. There are some forms of time and materials contracts that put in place maximum amounts in an effort to reduce the risk to the buyer. It is recommended that time and materials contracts be used only for simple straightforward work or for emergency work.

EXAM TIP **When reading a question in the exam, you should first determine whether your position in the scenario is one of buyer or seller. In the procurement process, you can be either the buyer or seller; in some projects you might be both buyer and seller of goods and services. Your position as buyer or seller will influence your preferred choice of contract type.**

Procurement statement of work

The procurement statement of work is the written description of the work to be done as part of any contracts negotiated. The work described in the procurement statement of work will be taken from the project scope baseline, and the level of detail in the procurement statement of work will directly affect the type of contract selected. For example, if the procurement statement of work lacks detail, the procurement process might begin by asking prospective sellers for the proposed solutions to define the details. If the procurement statement of work contains a lot of detail and plans, prospective sellers will be asked to provide firm prices to complete the work. The procurement statement of work can be modified during the process of selecting and negotiating with sellers, but after the contract is signed, it should be modified only via the approved procurement change control system.

True or false? The procurement statement of work should be written to be as clear, complete, and concise as possible to get a thorough response from prospective sellers.

Answer: *True*. If possible, the procurement statement of work should contain as much detail as possible. It might be better to delay procurement activities until the procurement statement of work can be adequately defined to remove uncertainty in the seller selection process.

> ***EXAM TIP*** **Always make sure that you have a procurement statement of work that is as detailed as possible if you are completing any form of procurement process. The level of detail in the procurement statement of work will have a direct impact on the type of contract used, the range of potential sellers interested, and the pricing of the work.**

Procurement documents

There is a range of procurement documents that accompany the procurement management plan. The procurement documents are used to give information to prospective sellers and to solicit information and responses from them. It is highly likely that your organizational process assets will include a procurement process with a range of approved procurement documents to be used. The most common forms of procurement documents used include the following:

- Request for information (RFI)
- Expression of interest (EOI)
- Invitation for bid (IFB)
- Tender notice
- Request for proposal (RFP)
- Request for quotation (RFQ)

The particular form of procurement document chosen will reflect the level of detail contained in the procurement statement of work and the complexity of the work to be carried out.

True or false? When preparing procurement documents, care should be taken to ensure accuracy because they might end up as part of a legally enforceable agreement.

Answer: *True*. Although a contract is usually legally enforceable only after it has been signed by all parties, the documents used that led to the contractual negotiations and agreements could become part of the contract and as such care should be taken when preparing procurement documents. A project manager might want to draw on the expertise of procurement or legal specialists to assist with the production of procurement documents.

> ***MORE INFO*** **You can find out more about contract forms and procurement documents by reading the Plan Procurement Management process in the PMBOK® Guide, 5th edition.**

Make-or-buy decisions

As an initial part of your procurement planning activities, you will carry out the make-or-buy analysis, which is a technique to determine whether you should make the goods and services you require or buy them from external providers. Make-or-buy analysis leads to make-or-buy decisions that need to take into account a range of factors that can influence whether you decide to make or buy the product, goods, or services you require.

The types of matters you will consider as part of your make-or-buy analysis can include the following:

- Capacity, experience and capability of your project personnel to complete the work
- Risks associated with doing the work
- Intellectual property issues
- Costs of completing the work
- Time required to complete the work
- Available contract types
- Market conditions procuring the goods or services you require

It is responsibility of the project manager to take into account all the relevant information before making a make-or-buy decision.

True or false? Regardless of whether you have the skills and experience to complete the work, a make-or-buy analysis should take into account whether it is the cheapest and least risky way to deliver the work.

Answer: *True.* There are many factors to consider when deciding whether to make the goods and services yourself or buy them from external sources. For example, you might have the capability and experience to complete the work, but you can procure it at less cost and with less risk using external providers.

Source selection criteria

Another important aspect of your procurement planning processes is the development of source selection criteria that are used by the buyer of goods and services to assess, evaluate, and make decisions about which potential sellers and vendors will be successful. These criteria are developed as part of your procurement planning activities because they need to be developed early on so that they can be taken into account in all procurement work.

It is not uncommon for the primary source selection criterion to be the price submitted in response to procurement documents, but in addition to the price there are a number of other potential source selection criteria that can be taken into account, including the following:

- Product life cycle cost
- Health and safety record
- Technical capability
- Management approach

- Financial stability of the organization
- Capacity
- Intellectual property rights
- Environmental record
- Complete life cycle cost
- Past performance
- Relevant experience

True or false? Source selection criteria should be used to choose the external sellers or vendors that best meet the procurement needs of the project.

Answer: *True.* A key purpose of deciding source selection criteria early on is to give consideration to the factors that will influence your decision about how you choose successful sellers or vendors. As such, your source selection criteria should contribute to choosing the most appropriate seller or vendor.

Can you answer these questions?

You can find the answers to these questions at the end of this chapter.

1. If you have provided all potential sellers with a detailed description of the procurement statement of work as part of your procurement negotiations and want a fixed price from the sellers to complete the work, what form of contract should you use?
2. If you are the seller responding to an RFP with a loosely defined procurement statement of work, what form of contract is better to enter into?
3. Why are any existing organizational process assets important considerations in the procurement planning work?
4. What are you doing if you carry out an assessment of whether your project team members should complete the required work or you should outsource it to another company?
5. Why should a project manager consider involving procurement specialists and legal specialists in the development of the procurement management plan?

Task 8: Develop a quality management plan based on the project scope and requirements, in order to prevent the appearance of defects and reduce the cost of quality.

This task focuses on the development of a project quality management plan that will assist the project manager and project team members in ensuring that the processes and product of the project meet the requirements. A key element of the work involved in satisfying this task includes the development of a comprehensive approach to quality management throughout the whole project.

Quality is defined as the degree to which a set of characteristics fulfills requirements. Therefore, to determine whether quality standards are being met, you first require a defined and documented set of requirements and some way of observing and measuring characteristics. There are several foundational concepts that define the expected approach to quality management on a project that should be reflected in the quality management plan. These foundational concepts include the following:

- **Prevention over inspection** Requires that quality should be proactively built into all aspects of your project instead of reactively inspected into the processes or deliverables. This is because the cost of preventing quality errors is usually less than the cost of fixing quality errors.
- **Continuous improvement** Also known as kaizen, a commitment to continuous quality improvement throughout the life of the project in relation to both process and product.
- **Total quality management (TQM)** A whole-organization approach to quality management as opposed to a management directive to employees. It seeks to embed within the entire organizational culture the importance of quality, prevention over inspection, and continuous improvement.
- **Cost of quality** An assessment of the total cost of quality work and the cost of low quality. The cost of quality should be assessed not just within the project but also over the entire product life cycle because quality decisions made during the production of the product will have an impact far beyond the life of the project.

NOTE **There are a couple of other quality management terms that you need to understand. "Quality" and "grade" do not mean the same thing: "quality" refers to the degree to which a set of characteristics fulfills requirements; while "grade" refers to the features or technical characteristics of a product. "Low grade" simply means that a product has fewer features or a lower range of technical characteristics. If the requirements specify "low grade," this is fine, but "low quality" is not fine. "Precision" refers to how tightly clustered a group of results is. A group of results that is tightly clustered demonstrates a high degree of precision. "Accuracy" refers to how close to the expected results the observed data points are. Figure 2-28 shows examples of both accuracy and precision using a bull's-eye target.**

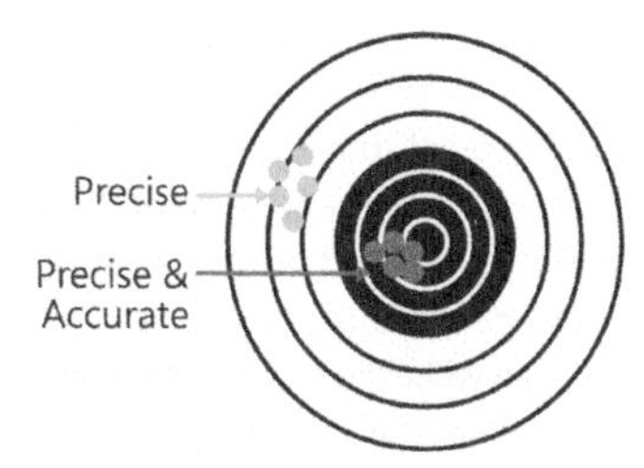

FIGURE 2-28 A diagram showing precision and accuracy

MORE INFO **You can find out more about quality management planning processes by reading the Plan Quality Management process in the *PMBOK® Guide*, 5th edition. Further information can also be obtained by reading the following ISO standards:**

- **ISO9000 Quality management systems: Fundamentals and vocabulary**
- **ISO9001 Quality management systems: Requirements**
- **ISO10006 Quality management systems: Guidelines for the quality management in projects**

Exam need to know...

- Quality management plan

  For example: What document provides guidance to the project manager on how quality assurance and quality control activities on the project will be carried out?

- Process improvement plan

  For example: How will the effectiveness of processes being used on the project be measured and continuously improved?

- Quality metrics and checklists

  For example: What values and attributes are used to measure whether quality is being achieved on the project?

- Benchmarking

  For example: How can a project manager compare their particular approach to quality against the approach to quality taken on other projects carried out by the organization?

- Design of experiments

  For example: What factors need to be taken into account when considering whether experiments to obtain quality measurements provide valid information?

- Statistical sampling

  For example: What data-collection technique can be used when the population size is extremely large and testing the entire population would not be feasible?

Quality management plan

The quality management plan provides guidance to the project manager on how all aspects of quality will be managed on the project. The quality management plan will provide guidance on quality assurance, which relates to how the processes are being implemented, and quality control, which relates to how the product complies with quality standards. The quality management plan will be developed using information from the stakeholder register, the scope baseline, the risk register, the schedule baseline, the cost baseline, and any relevant enterprise environmental factors and organizational process assets.

The quality management plan can contain a lot of detail or a little detail, and it will reflect the size and complexity of the project. Regardless of the size or complexity of the project, every project should have some form of quality management plan relating to both quality assurance and quality control. Project quality should be a standard item for consideration and discussion on all project status meetings.

True or false? The quality management plan provides guidance to the project manager and project team members on how all aspects of project quality will be developed and maintained, including both quality assurance and quality control.

Answer: *True*. The quality management plan provides guidance for all aspects of quality on the project. It should be detailed enough and broad enough to enable the project manager and project team members to assess all aspects of quality assurance and quality control on the project.

EXAM TIP **Quality management is seen as an extremely important aspect of professional project management. For any question in the exam, you should assume that you do have a quality management plan and that you will follow it, check that you are following it, and are always seeking to continuously improve your approach to quality management.**

NOTE **You can find out more about modern quality management by reading the work of or about William Edwards Deming, Walter Shewart, Joseph Juran, or Kaoru Ishikawa—each of whom has contributed significantly to the profession of quality management and thus the profession of project management. Deming is seen as the founder of modern quality management and his Plan-Do-Check-Act (PDCA) cycle forms the basis of the profession of project management. The PDCA cycle recognizes that any effort starts with appropriate planning (the planning process group). By using the plans, you can then do the work (the executing process group), check what you are doing against what you planned to do (the monitoring and controlling process group), and act if you find a variance and begin the planning process again.**

Figure 2-29 shows the Plan-Do-Check-Act cycle.

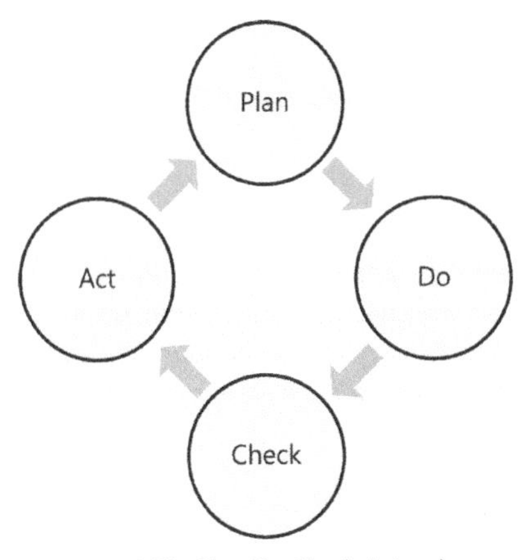

FIGURE 2-29 The Plan-Do-Check-Act cycle

Process improvement plan

The process improvement plan is a part of the quality management plan that is focused on the processes being used and is used to determine quality assurance on the project. A key focus of the process improvement plan is a commitment to continuous improvement of all processes on the project. This includes an assessment of whether they provide value and ways in which they can enhance the value of the project.

True or false? The process improvement plan provides guidance on how the product will be inspected to ensure conformance to quality requirements.

Answer: *False*. The process improvement plan is not focused on the product at all; instead, it is focused on the processes being used to achieve quality on the project.

> ***EXAM TIP*** **Make sure you understand the difference between quality assurance, which is focused on the processes, and quality control, which is focused on the product and deliverables.**

Quality metrics and checklists

The quality management plan will outline a lot of different information about how all aspects of quality will be managed on the project. Included with this information will be both predetermined quality metrics and quality checklists.

Quality metrics is an actual value that is used to describe an expected project or product attribute and the means by which this value will be measured, usually some form of inspection or audit.

A quality checklist is a document that outlines a set of steps to be performed to ensure that quality is being measured and achieved on the project. As part of its organizational process assets, the performing organization most likely has some form of standardized quality checklists or the project manager can develop checklists just for the project.

True or false? Quality metrics can provide detail on expected attributes for both quality assurance and quality control processes.

Answer: *True*. There is a wide range of quality metrics or values, and they can relate to both quality assurance and quality control processes.

Seven basic quality tools

As part of developing the quality management plan in giving consideration to quality issues project manager can use and refer to Ishikawa's seven basic quality tools as effective ways of documenting and displaying quality information for easy interpretation. Each of the seven basic quality tools is a graphical representation of data. They include the following:

- Cause and effect diagram
- Flowchart

- Check sheets
- Pareto diagrams
- Histograms
- Control charts
- Scatter diagrams

MORE INFO You can find out more about the seven basic quality tools by reading Chapter 3 of this book and the Plan Quality Management process in the PMBOK® Guide, 5th edition.

NOTE There is a wide range of quality planning tools available to a project manager to assist in all aspects of quality management on the project. Ishikawa's seven quality tools are most often used, but there are also additional tools such as the following:

- **Affinity diagrams**
- **Process decision program charts**
- **Interrelationship digraphs**
- **Tree diagrams**
- **Prioritization matrices**
- **Activity network diagrams**
- **Matrix diagrams**
- **Brainstorming**
- **Force field analysis**
- **Nominal group technique**

Benchmarking

As part of the development of the particular approach to quality on a project, a project manager might want to benchmark the selected approached quality against other projects or organizations to identify best practices and provide a basis of measuring quality performance. To benchmark successfully, the project manager needs to have access to information about other projects the organization is undertaken (this is normally kept in the historical information database for the organization). Alternatively, a project manager can seek information from other organizations or from relevant industry standards.

Design of experiments

An important part of planning quality management is to consider the design of experiments, which will ensure that any experiments carried out to determine quality on the project are valid and give useful data. When considering how different experiments will be designed, it is important to keep in mind factors such as how the experiment will affect the data collected, the cost of carrying out the experiment versus the data gathered, and how the results of one experiment will affect other quality factors. The quality management plan should contain guidance on how the design of experiments will be carried out.

Statistical sampling

Whether statistical sampling will be used on the project should be decided during quality management planning. The quality management plan should outline whether statistical sampling will be used on the project after giving consideration to the costs involved in testing an entire population. If sampling the entire population would not be feasible due to the large size or if testing involves destructive testing, statistical sampling would be more beneficial. Statistical sampling involves testing a smaller portion of the total population and extrapolating the results from this sample to the entire population.

Can you answer these questions?

You can find the answers to these questions at the end of this chapter.

1. What document describe how audits of the quality processes will be carried out?
2. What is the difference between quality assurance and quality control activities?
3. If you are using a graphical tool to determine the root cause of a known quality issue, what is the name of this tool?
4. Under what circumstances should you plan to use statistical sampling to gather data about quality on the project?
5. What is the difference between quality and grade?

Task 9: Develop the change management plan by defining how changes will be handled, in order to track and manage changes.

The focus of this task is to ensure that all changes to any part of the project are managed in a coherent manner; and that they are documented, evaluated, tracked, and incorporated into the relevant parts of the project management plan. The development of a comprehensive and appropriate change management plan to guide this work is an essential part of the development of the overall project management plan.

MORE INFO **You can find out more about managing change on a project by reading the Perform Integrated Change Control process in the PMBOK® Guide, 5th edition or Chapter 2 of the PMP Training Kit.**

Exam need to know...

- Change management plan

  For example: What document provides guidance on how changes received from stakeholders will be documented and evaluated?
- Change control meetings

  For example: How are significant requested changes assessed and evaluated?

- Change control board

  For example: What group of people takes responsibility for assessing changes and has the authority to approve or decline changes?
- Delegated authority

  For example: How does a project manager gain the ability to make decisions about whether to approve or decline minor change requests?
- Change log

  For example: How should all change requests that are received be documented and tracked?
- Configuration management system

  For example: How should any change requests be identified on the change log?

Change management plan

Like every other aspect of project management, it is important to have a plan to guide activities before embarking on them. This is true for change management activities, and the change management plan is the guide on how all changes to the project are documented, evaluated, and tracked; and how decisions are made and communicated.

Change can happen at any time during a project, from the moment it is conceived right through to the time it is closed. It is important that one of the first plans developed is the change management plan, which can manage and control change on the project immediately.

The change management plan will rely heavily on any existing organizational process assets that the organization has and can include any of the following:

- Text-based description, or flowchart, of the change control process
- Individual or group that has responsibility for receiving, recording, and making decisions about change
- Levels of delegated authority
- Examples of change control templates
- Change control board members
- Agenda of change control meetings
- Guidance on how integrated changes will be assessed
- Time frames for evaluating changes
- Description of how approved changes will be communicated and incorporated into the project

An effective and appropriate change management plan helps minimize the risk of either scope creep or gold plating occurring. Scope creep occurs when undocumented changes are allowed on the project. Gold plating occurs when the opportunity is seen to deliver more than what is required and is done without documentation. In both cases, the issue is not that change is occurring; it is that the changes are undocumented. At any time in your project, what you are delivering must equal what is documented and approved.

True or false? The change management plan will provide guidance to the project manager and project team on how changes requested by stakeholders will be documented, assessed, and evaluated.

Answer: *True*. The purpose of the change management plan is to provide guidance to the project manager and project team members on how all changes, in a matter from which they originate, are to be recorded and evaluated, and how decisions will be made and communicated.

> ***EXAM TIP*** **In the exam, you should assume that all change, without exception, is subject to the agreed-upon change control process. Furthermore all change, no matter how it starts, should eventually be documented and recorded, and it should be incorporated into the relevant baselines if it is approved. Remember that any changes that are approved represent additional work on the project, and this work should be immediately incorporated into the scope baseline, including the WBS, so the time and cost associated with it can be accurately estimated. Any approved changes should also be subject to monitoring and control to ensure that the approved work is carried out in accordance with the documented change control.**

Change control meetings

Change control meetings are meetings specifically held to consider, evaluate, and make decisions about change requests that are being received. They can be held regularly or convened by special change requests.

Change control board

The change control board will consider any change requests outside of the levels of delegated authority of the project manager. The change control board will be made up of people with the experience, responsibility, and authority to be able to consider any change requests and make decisions about them. The change control board should also be able to consult with any subject matter experts who have the experience needed to enable them to make decisions about change requests.

True or false? A change control board should meet only at regularly scheduled intervals.

Answer: *False*. A change control board should have a regular schedule of meetings set, but be prepared to meet at any time to ensure that change requests do not unnecessarily hold up the project.

Delegated authority

An important means of ensuring that requested changes do not hold progress up to give the project manager delegated authority to make decisions about whether a change request has merit, and also whether minor changes should be approved or declined. It is common for project managers to have a level of delegated authority that enables them to make decisions about change requests on the spot and keep the project moving along. If the change request is outside the levels of the project manager's delegated authority, there should be a clear process for how the change request will be considered and then approved or declined. The level of a project manager's delegated authority can often be determined and documented in the project charter.

True or false? A project manager should have the delegated authority to approve or decline any and all changes to a project.

Answer: *False.* Although you might think that a project manager should have complete authority to decide whether to approve or decline all changes to a project, it is better in terms of oversight and governance that the project manager be given a certain level of delegated authority to make decisions about minor change requests. Any large change requests should be considered by the change control board.

> ***EXAM TIP*** **In the exam, you should assume that a project manager has some level of delegated authority to approve or decline minor change requests, and to assess whether any change request has merit.**

Change log

All change requests that are received should be recorded on a change log that can then be used to track all changes, the status of the change request, who has responsibility for the change request, and whether the change request as approved or declined. The change log can be a useful communications tool to let stakeholders know which change requests have been received and their status.

Configuration management system

The configuration management system is a subsystem of the overall project management system that provides guidance on how different iterations of project documents, plans, parts, products, results, or components will be tracked and monitored. Common forms of configuration management systems include version control for documents and plans, a parts numbering system, unique identifiers on the WBS that match to cost accounts, and numbering of change requests on the change log.

By providing a means to track all these elements of the project, at any point in the project a project manager and project team members know exactly which document, part, product or version is the most recent, and its location and status.

> ***MORE INFO*** **To find out more about configuration management systems, see ISO10007, *Quality Management Systems: Guidelines for Configuration Management* from the International Organization for Standards website (*www.iso.org*).**

Can you answer these questions?

You can find the answers to these questions at the end of this chapter.

1. If a project team members are confused about how change requests are to be recorded and considered, what document should you refer them to?
2. What is the name of the group that meets regularly to consider whether to approve or decline change requests?
3. Why is important that all change requests received, no matter how small, be formally documented?
4. Why is it important that a project manager be given a level of delegated authority to make decisions about whether to approve or decline change requests received?
5. What is the process of allocating a unique number to each change request on a change log an example of?

Task 10: Plan risk management by developing a risk management plan, and identifying, analyzing, and prior to rising project risks in the risk register and defining risk response strategies, in order to manage uncertainty throughout the project life cycle.

This task is focused on both the development of a risk management plan and the ongoing iterative development of a risk register. The risk management plan is used to provide guidance to the project manager and project team members on how the overall approach to risk will be implemented in the project; and more specifically how the risk register will be developed, managed, and monitored. The development of the risk register is a highly iterative process, and a key purpose of this task is to ensure that it is carried out appropriately and reflects the risk tolerance levels of the project team and organization, and the complexity of the project work.

MORE INFO **You can find out more about the development of a risk management plan in the risk register by reading the project risk management knowledge area in the PMBOK® Guide, 5th edition, or Chapter 9 of the PMP® Training Kit. You can also find out more about risk management processes from the International Organization for Standards website (*www.iso.org*) particularly the following standards:**

- **ISO 31000:2009 *Risk Management: Principles and Guidelines***
- **ISO Guide 73:2009 *Risk Management: Vocabulary***
- **IEC 31010:2009 *Risk Management: Risk Assessment Techniques***

Exam need to know...

- Risk management plan

  For example: What document provides guidance on how risk identification and risk reassessment will be carried out?
- Risk identification

For example: How does the project manager gather information about potential risks that might affect the project?

- Qualitative risk analysis

  For example: What risk analysis technique uses subjective risk analysis to prioritize project risks?

- Quantitative risk analysis

  For example: What risk analysis method are you using if you are assessing a known and measurable risk probability assessment against a known quantifiable risk impact assessment to develop a contingency reserve for the project budget?

- Risk response planning

  For example: What is a key component of proactive risk management?

Risk management plan

A key first step in any risk-related work is the development of a risk management plan that provides guidance on how the development of a risk register will be carried out and how it will be monitored and controlled. The risk management plan should reflect the organization's risk appetite, risk tolerance, and risk thresholds. The risk management plan will also draw heavily on existing organizational process assets, such as policies and templates that the organization has. The risk management plan should also be consistent with all other aspects of the project management plan and baselines.

The development of an appropriate risk management plan will involve the use of a variety of analytical techniques and expert judgment from subject matter experts with specialized training or knowledge and the particular subject area being reviewed.

The risk management plan will include a variety of information that does provide guidance to the project manager and project team members on how all risk management activities will be carried out. Depending on the complexity of the project and the risk tolerance level of the organization, the risk management plan can include any of the following:

- Description of the risk management methodology to be used
- Description of roles and responsibilities
- Standardized definition of risk probability and impact assessment
- Assessment of both the organizational and individual stakeholder risk tolerances
- Description of how the risk register will be monitored and communicated
- Description of the risk categories, usually with the development of a risk breakdown structure

The risk breakdown structure, like other breakdown structures used in project management (organizational breakdown structure, WBS, and resource breakdown structure), provides a graphical decomposition of a higher-level concept into its component parts. In this case, the component parts are the risk categories and subcategories. They then become an initial input into the development of the risk register and help define specific risk events. Figure 2-30 shows an example of a risk breakdown structure.

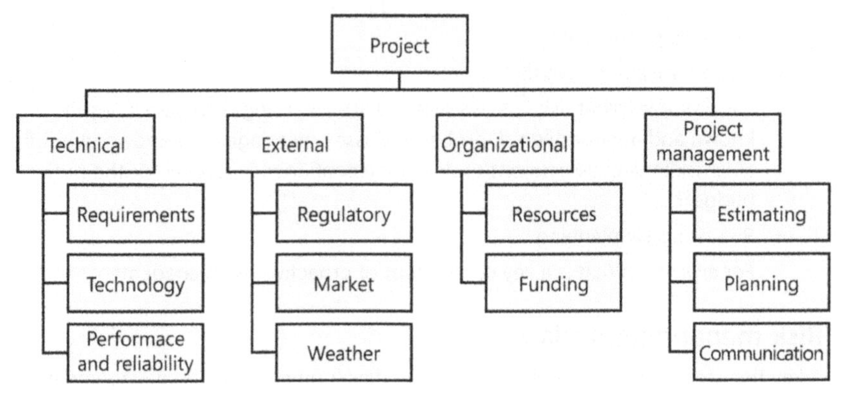

FIGURE 2-30 Risk breakdown structure

True or false? The risk management plan provides guidance to the project manager and project team members on how the risk register will be put together and monitored.

Answer: *True*. Like all other management plans in the project management profession, the key purpose of the risk management plan is to provide guidance on how risk management activities will be carried out throughout the life of the project.

> ***EXAM TIP*** **In any meetings held to review project status, it is advisable that risk management be a constant item on the agenda. So if you are presented with any scenario questioning how often you should review and re-evaluate the risk register, you should assume that you do it at all project status meetings.**

> ***MORE INFO*** **You can find out more about the development of a risk management plan by reading the Plan Risk Management process in the PMBOK® Guide, 5th edition or Chapter 9 of the PMP Training Kit.**

Risk identification

The first step of putting together a risk register is to complete an identification of the risks. Using the risk management plan and the information from the risk breakdown structure, a project manager can then draw on any information from any other part of the project in which there might be uncertainty to develop the risk register. There are several tools and techniques the project manager can use to assist with the development of the risk register:

- Review of other project documents, including other subsidiary plans and historical information

- Information-gathering techniques such as brainstorming, the Delphi technique, and interviewing
- Using the lowest level of the risk breakdown structure as a risk checklist
- Diagramming techniques such as a cause-and-effect diagram, flowchart, or influence diagram
- Strengths and weaknesses, opportunities, threats (SWOT) analysis

The specific tools and techniques selected by the project manager will reflect existing organizational process assets, enterprise environmental factors, and complexity of the project.

Risk identification includes a description of the risk event, the consequence, whether the risk is positive or negative, and an assessment of the urgency of the risk. During the process of risk identification, it is always a good idea to document the assumptions made so they can be revisited in the future to see whether there are changes that need to be made to the identified risks.

Risk identification is a continuous process to check whether the current identification is accurate and appropriate, whether the assumptions made about the risks are still accurate, and whether the risks have now passed and need to be removed from the risk register. At the completion of the project, all potential risks that have been identified should be closed

> ***EXAM TIP*** **Remember that risk simply means uncertainty, and it can be either positive or negative. If the uncertainty or risk is negative, you should attempt to minimize both the probability and impact of this negative risk. If the uncertainty or risk is positive, you should seek to maximize the probability and impact.**

True or false? The work involved in identifying risks is best lead by the project manager and should involve project team members.

Answer: *True*. Project managers should take responsibility for ensuring that risk identification is completed appropriately. They might choose to draw on a number of specialists but should always draw on the project team members for the input because project team members have experience in doing the work and the risks associated with it. Furthermore, by involving the project team members in the process of risk identification, it creates a commitment to risk management on the project.

> ***MORE INFO*** **You can find out more about the risk identification activities by reading the Identify Risks process in the PMBOK® Guide, 5th edition.**

> ***NOTE*** **In addition to a risk register for a project, you might want to develop a watch list for risks that don't necessarily warrant inclusion on the risk register at this point. These low-priority risks will be put on the watch list and periodically monitored to see whether the assessment or assumptions made about them have changed and need escalation to the risk register.**

Qualitative risk analysis

After the risk identification is complete, the next step in the ongoing iterative development of the risk register is to perform an analysis of the risks. This analysis can either be qualitative or quantitative, depending on the risks. Qualitative risk analysis has the goal of assessing the probability and impact of all the risks to develop a prioritized list of the risks so that the project manager and project team can assess which risks are the most important. Being able to develop a prioritized list of risks is also useful for deciding which risks should have qualitative risk analysis performed on them.

Qualitative risk analysis can be performed quickly, so it should be performed on all risks on the risk register. What it seeks to do is gather information about the probability of a risk event occurring and the impact should the risk event occur.

The assessment of probability and impact can be on a numerical scale (1 to 5), in which 1 equals no probability of the risk occurring at all, and 5 indicates a definite certainty of the risk occurring. It can also be a text-based assessment such as Highly likely, Likely, Neither likely or unlikely, Unlikely, and Highly unlikely. The analysis is performed by multiplying the probability and impact assessment together. For example, you could decide that the probability of a risk event occurring on a scale of 1 to 5 is a 3, and the impact of the risk event occurring is a 4. By multiplying the 2 numbers together, you get a qualitative risk assessment of 12 out of 25.

Given that there is an element of subjectivity in qualitative risk assessment, it is important to keep a record of the assumptions made and the quality of the data used to complete the assessment. There are also some useful tools to assist with standardization of qualitative risk analysis; they include the probability and impact matrix, and a predefined definition of qualitative impact scales. Figure 2-31 shows an example of a text-based definition of qualitative impact scales that attempts to bring a degree of standardization to a subjective analysis.

	Very low or 1	Low or 2	Moderate or 3	High or 4	Very High or 5
Scope	No noticeable change to scope	Minor changes to scope	Significant change to scope	Changes to scope unacceptable to sponsor or client	Changes the complete purpose of the project
Time	No noticeable change to time	Less than 10% increase in time	10-20% increase in time	20-30% increase in time	Greater than 30% increase in time
Cost	No noticeable change to cost	Less than 10% increase in cost	10-20% increase in cost	20-30% increase in cost	Greater than 30% increase in cost

FIGURE 2-31 Standardized description of qualitative risk assessment

True or false? In addition to individual assessment of probability and impact, one of the main benefits of completing qualitative risk analysis is a development of a prioritized list of risks.

Answer: *True.* Because qualitative risk analysis can be performed relatively quickly and easily, it should be performed on all risks in the risk register. It provides both an individual assessment of probability and impact from identified risks, and also a prioritized list of risks. With this prioritized list of risks, the project manager can then choose to complete quantitative risk analysis on only those most important risks.

> ***EXAM TIP*** **Make sure you understand the difference between qualitative and quantitative risk analysis. Qualitative risk analysis is subjective and prioritizes the risks; quantitative risk analysis is more objective and assigns a financial or time value to the risk.**

> ***MORE INFO*** **You can find out more about qualitative risk analysis by reading the Perform Qualitative Risk Analysis process in the PMBOK® Guide, 5th edition.**

Quantitative risk analysis

As part of the development of a risk register, a project manager might choose to perform quantitative risk assessment on those risks deemed to be the highest priority. Quantitative risk assessment provides a numerical analysis of an identified risk probability and impact. This numerical analysis can generate information about financial and schedule risk to the project. Quantitative risk analysis usually involves mathematical models and statistical analysis of risk probability and impact. Given that it is usually highly mathematical in nature, it often uses purpose-built project management risk analysis software. There are a number of tools and techniques that can be used to analyze and model quantitative risk analysis; the following are the most popular and useful:

- **Sensitivity analysis** A technique that looks at different aspects of the project and how they have an impact upon project risk to determine which parts of the project are most sensitive to risk. Sensitivity analysis is a highly complex set of calculations using software, so it usually requires specialized knowledge and expertise to carry out.
- **Tornado diagrams** Used to present the results of sensitivity analysis in different areas of the project. Figure 2-32 shows an example of a tornado diagram.

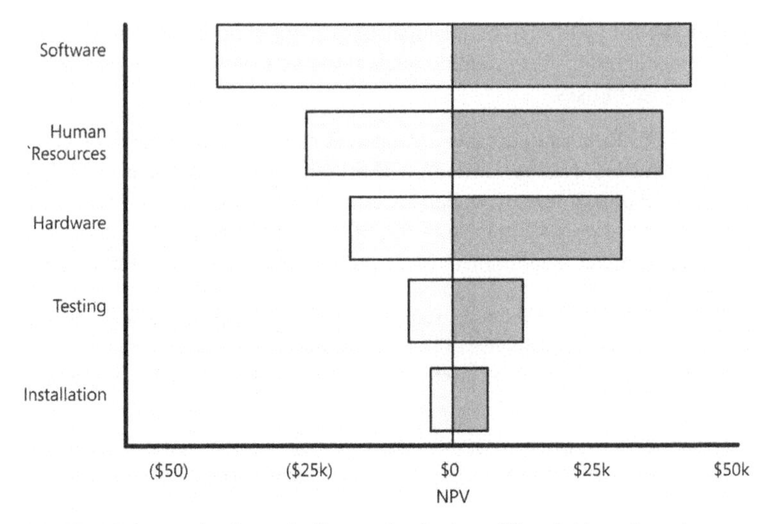

FIGURE 2-32 A example of tornado diagram showing how different risk can impact upon project net present value

- **Expected monetary value analysis (EMV)** A way to assess and allocate quantitative numerical probability and impact to particular options, and to arrive at the expected monetary value (EMV) of each option. The usual way of graphically representing the EMV is with decision trees.

  In Figure 2-33, a decision tree shows the calculation of expected monetary value regarding whether to upgrade existing customer ordering software or to develop a completely new piece of software.

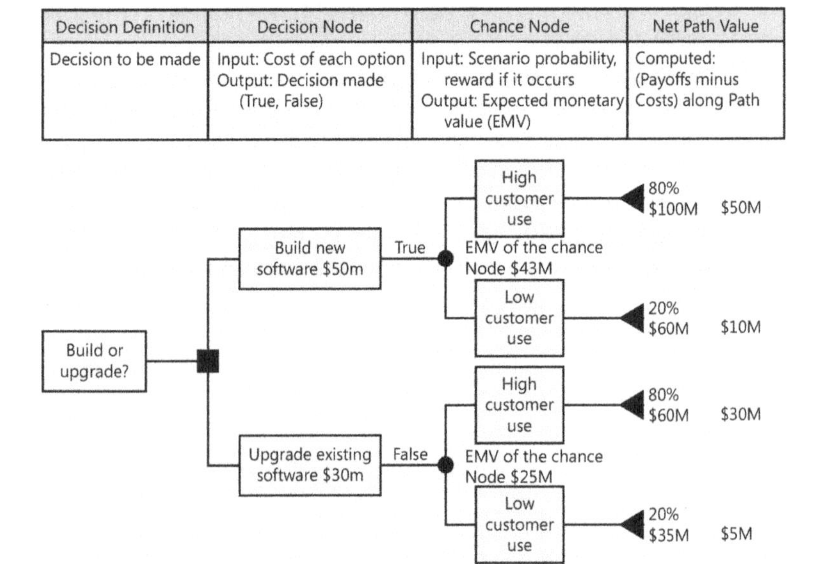

FIGURE 2-33 A decision tree analysis for assessing the EMV of building new software or upgrading existing software

Figure 2-33 shows that for either decision, there is an 80 percent chance of high customer use and a 20 percent chance of low customer use. If you decide to build new software, it will cost $50 million, and if there is high customer use, you will make $100 million, so there is an 80 percent chance of making a net figure of $50 million. By the same token, if you decide to build new software at a cost of $50 million, and there is low customer use, you will only make $60 million, so there is a 20 percent chance of making a net figure of $10 million. You would then add these two calculations together to get an expected monetary value (EMV) of $42 million:

(0.8 × $50m) + (0.2 × $10m)

The other option is to upgrade the existing software, which will cost $30 million and has an 80 percent chance of making a net figure of $30 million and a 20 percent chance of making a net figure of $5 million. Therefore, the expected monetary value for this decision is the following:

(0.8 × $30m) + (0.2 × $5m) = $25m

By using this form of quantitative risk analysis, you can recognize that the best decision is to take the option with the greater expected monetary value, which is to build new software. What is also apparent in this example is that the quality of the calculated outcome is only as good as the quality of the information going into the model. Here is another example of why it is important to document the assumptions that you've made, so that if any of this changes in the future you can quickly recalculate.

- **Modeling and simulation** Includes Monte Carlo analysis, which assesses all the potential outcomes of schedule or financial probability and impact is over multiple paths to determine those outcomes with the highest probability. You then come up with a probability distribution (normal, uniform, or beta) associated with each of these outcomes.

True or false? Quantitative risk analysis can be used to determine either financial or schedule contingency reserves for the project.

Answer: *True.* If you are using quantitative risk analysis to assess known and objective probability and impact, you can use this assessment to develop a contingency reserve for your project. For example, you might know that there is a 17 percent chance of a risk occurring that will have a $10,000 impact on your project, so you might choose to allow $1,700 as part of your contingency reserve.

EXAM TIP **If a question in the exam refers to any sort of mathematical analysis of risk event probability or impact, it is referring to quantitative risk analysis.**

MORE INFO **You can find out more about quantitative risk analysis by reading the Perform Quantitative Risk Analysis process in the PMBOK® Guide, 5th edition.**

Risk response planning

After risks have been identified, and either a qualitative or quantitative assessment has performed on the probability and impact, a key component of proactive risk management is the development of risk response strategies. A risk response strategy can either be proactive, in an attempt to deal with the risk before it occurs, or reactive, ready to be put in place after the risk occurs. There are four key strategies for either positive or negative risks or threats in relation to the development of appropriate risk responses:

- **Avoid** Making plans to avoid the risk occurring
- **Transfer** Making the responsibility and ultimately the consequences of the risk somebody else's responsibility
- **Mitigate** Accepting that the risk might occur, but attempting to put in place a risk response that minimizes the negative effects of the risk
- **Accept** Accepting the consequence of the risk occurring

You can have multiple strategies for each risk, and you should choose the most appropriate risk strategy or strategies for your particular risk and risk tolerance.

There are four key strategies for positive risks or opportunities that seek to maximize the chance of the positive risk occurring, and if it does occur, to maximize the positive impact upon the project:

- **Exploit** Seeking to ensure that the positive risk has the maximum chance of occurring
- **Share** Taking on board a third party with particular skills and experience to help maximize the occurrence and the impact of a positive risk
- **Enhance** Being prepared to increase the chances of the positive risk occurring, and if it does occur, increase its positive impact
- **Accept** Accepting that no changes will be made to the project management plan and accepting the chances of the positive risk occurring and its impact

It is highly likely that despite your best efforts you will end up identifying all the risks that can occur on a project, so it is prudent to have contingent response strategies in place, which are your planned responses to unplanned risk. The contingent response strategies outline the actions your project team will take if a set of predefined conditions occurs. A further means of dealing with unplanned risks occurring is a workaround. The difference between a workaround and contingent response strategies is that a workaround is an unplanned and reactive response to an unplanned risk occurring; a contingent response strategy is a planned and prepared response to an unplanned risk occurring. A workaround is a plan to get around a problem or risk that has arisen, not necessarily to fix it.

True or false? If a completely unforeseen risk occurs on your project, you should immediately consult your risk register for what actions to take.

Answer: *False.* The risk register documents identified risks and lists any proactive and reactive risk responses for them. If a completely unforeseen risk occurs, there will be no information on your risk register about it, so you should consult your risk management plan for how to carry out a workaround.

MORE INFO **You can find out more about risk response planning by reading the Plan Risk Responses process in the PMBOK® Guide, 5th edition.**

Can you answer these questions?

You can find the answers to these questions at the end of this chapter.

1. What document includes an analysis of the organization's risk tolerance and will does it affect the particular project's approach to risk?
2. What is the relationship between the risk register, the watch list, and the issues log?
3. What type of analysis seeks to evaluate risks and assign a financial or time figure to this assessment?
4. Who should take responsibility for ensuring that the risk register is regularly monitored and updated?
5. If you have decided to take out insurance to deal with an identified negative risk, what sort of risk response strategy does this represent?

Task 11: Present the project plan to the key stakeholders (if required), in order to obtain approval to execute the project.

This task is focused on the work of presenting the project plan to the key stakeholders to communicate with them that the project plan is complete and execution is about to begin, and to manage their expectations of the project.

Exam need to know...

- Key stakeholders

  For example: Who should the project manager consult with before moving on the project execution?
- Project lifecycle

  For example: How does a project move from planning work to executing work?

Key stakeholders

As part of the work to identify stakeholders on the project, key stakeholders would be identified as those who should be communicated with prior to executing the work. Some of the stakeholders will have formal power to approve or decline your project execution work; others will have informal forms of power. Although they might not be able to directly approve or decline your project, they should be communicated with to manage their expectations of the project. The project manager will take responsibility for ensuring that the correct stakeholders are informed and give their approval for the project to proceed.

To ensure communication with the relevant stakeholders, a project manager should consult with the stakeholder management plan, the communications management plan, any relevant organizational process assets, and enterprise environmental factors.

The stakeholders that have the power to approve whether the project moves to the executing phase are the project sponsor, the client or customer, and any governance or steering group. Of these, the project sponsor has responsibility for obtaining the financial resources for the project, approving the project charter, and appointing the project manager. As such, the sponsor's approval will definitely be needed.

There might also be a project governance group, such as the project steering committee, that must give approval for the project to move on to executing activities. In an organization with a high level of organizational project management maturity, the responsibility of providing project governance might rest with the project management office (PMO).

> ***NOTE*** **The format and role of a project management office (PMO) will vary considerably and reflect the level of organizational project management maturity of the organization. In its broadest sense, the project management office is defined as the center of excellence for project management in the organization. For an organization with a low level of project management maturity, this could simply mean a single repository of project management templates. For an organization with a high level of project management maturity, the project management office could be a place where all project managers are located; where all project management training is completed; or where project selection, prioritization, and potential conflicts are managed. Organizational project management maturity is a means of assessing what level of professional project management practices an organization currently has, and the model can also be used to determine where an organization should be. Many models are available for processing organizational project management maturity, such as the organizational project management maturity model (OPM3) from the Project Management Institute.**

True or false? The project sponsor provides financial and political support for the project.

Answer: *True.* The role of the project sponsor is to ensure that the project has the financial resources to be completed, to provide political support, and assist with managing stakeholders on the project if necessary.

> ***EXAM TIP*** **For the exam, you should have a clear understanding of the different roles and responsibilities of the project manager and project sponsor. The two roles need to work closely together, but the project manager has responsibility of the carrying out the project, whereas the project sponsor provides financial and political support for the project.**

MORE INFO **You can find out more about the role of key stakeholders in a project by reading Chapter 2 of the PMBOK® Guide, 5th edition.**

Project life cycle

A project moves through different stages as it moves from the initial idea, opportunity, or issue that initiated the project through to the production of an accepted deliverable and project closure. The generally accepted sequence of project management is initiating, planning, executing, monitoring and controlling, and closing activities. This is based on the Deming Plan-Do-Check-Act (PDCA) cycle already mentioned in this chapter.

These processes can be organized sequentially with a clear decision point, milestone, or stage gate between each piece of work, or they can more commonly be overlapping. In the first instance, approval from stakeholders to proceed to execution is sought after all planning work has been completed, which is an example of a phased approach. In the second instance, the approval sought from stakeholders to proceed with executing activities is done after enough planning has been completed to begin executing.

MORE INFO **You can learn more about the project lifecycle processes by reading ISO 21500:2012:** ***Guidance on Project Management.***

Can you answer these questions?

You can find the answers to these questions at the end of this chapter.

1. What is the role of the project sponsor?
2. Who should take responsibility for ensuring that the correct approval to proceed to project execution is obtained?
3. What are the five process groups of project management?
4. What role might a PMO play in approving a project plan?
5. What does the OPM3 model measure?

Task 12: Conduct a kick-off meeting with all stakeholders, in order to announce the start of the project, to indicate the project milestones, and share other relevant information.

This task is focused upon carrying out a kick-off meeting with stakeholders after enough planning has been done to begin execution on the project to communicate to stakeholders that the project is progressing as planned.

Exam need to know...

- Kick-off meeting

  For example: What meeting is held with stakeholders after enough project planning work has been completed to begin project execution?

Kick-off meeting

The kick-off meeting is a special meeting held right before project execution begins. It is either held at the end of planning activities in a phased project or after enough planning activity has been completed to begin execution in a project with process groups overlapping. The kick-off meeting has several purposes and tasks apart from announcing the beginning of executing work. It is also a planning, team building, communication, and expectation management exercise.

Information gathered from stakeholders attending the kick-off meeting can be used to confirm and add to project planning work already done. It can also serve as a team building exercise because it involves the project team in key stakeholders. It serves as an excellent communications device to let all stakeholders know that the project is about to begin execution and that their input and support is valuable. Finally, it serves as an expectation management exercise because it enables the project manager to exercise influence over stakeholder expectations of the project.

The project manager takes responsibility for organizing a kick-off meeting and deciding who should attend. It is up to the project manager to decide which stakeholders should attend, but at a minimum the meeting should include project team members, client, and sponsor. There might be other stakeholders who get value from the kick-off meeting; if so, they should also be invited to it.

A kick-off meeting, which is often held on site, presents an opportunity for stakeholders to meet each other and understand individual roles and responsibilities. It is also an opportunity for the project manager to communicate and allow discussion about the project goals, deliverables, and milestones. The project manager can also take the opportunity to explain the next steps in the project.

Like any other meeting, the kick-off meeting has a clear purpose and has an agenda sent out beforehand. It should set the tone for how all meetings on the project will be run. In addition to a defined agenda that should have a start and finish time, and a description of the purpose and tasks to be achieved, define the ground rules for participation and allow time for stakeholder questions and feedback. Somebody should be appointed to take meeting minutes, and the project manager should follow up on any agreed-upon actions.

True or false? In addition to giving key stakeholders an opportunity to meet each other, the kick-off meeting provides an opportunity for stakeholder expectation management.

Answer: *True.* The kick-off meeting has several purposes, including announcing the beginning of project execution, enabling stakeholders to meet each other and understand each other's roles and responsibilities, and also enable the project manager to communicate project progress to date, delineate planned progress going forward, and begin to influence stakeholder expectations of the project.

EXAM TIP **If a question in the exam refers to a scenario in which a kick-off meeting is to be held or has just been held, you should immediately know that project execution is about to begin. Furthermore, in order for project execution to begin, you must have completed enough planning work for this to happen. Therefore, the kick-off meeting provides a clear indication of your progress through the project.**

MORE INFO **You can find out more about project kick-off meetings by using an Internet search engine such as Bing.**

Can you answer these questions?

You can find the answers to these questions at the end of this chapter.

1. What role does the project manager have in the kick-off meeting?
2. Who should be invited to participate in the kick-off meeting?
3. Where should the kick-off meeting be held?
4. What should occur after the completion of the kick-off meeting?
5. At what point in the project should a kick-off meeting be scheduled?

Answers

This section contains the answers to the "Can you answer these questions?" sections in this chapter.

Task 1: Assess detailed project requirements, constraints, and assumptions with stakeholders based on the project charter, lessons learned from previous projects, and the use of requirement gathering techniques (e.g., planning sessions, brainstorming, focus groups), in order to establish the project deliverables.

1. The scope management plan provides guidance to the project manager and project team members on how all aspects of the project scope will be defined, and this begins with the process of gathering project requirements. The scope management plan will provide detail on the processes, tools, and techniques that can be used to gather project requirements from stakeholders.
2. The stakeholder register will provide information about individual stakeholders in the project.
3. The requirements traceability matrix maps individual project requirements to business needs and a project.
4. Of these two choices, it is the preliminary scope statement that will have more detail about the work to be done on the project because it is an iteration of the scope statement generally performed after requirements have been gathered and provided to stakeholders for their feedback.
5. All the requirements-gathering tools and techniques are ways to gather information from stakeholders.

Task 2: Create the work breakdown structure with the team by deconstructing the scope, in order to manage the scope of the project.

1. The main tool or technique used to develop WBS is decomposition.
2. The project manager should involve project team members in the creation of a WBS because they will be responsible for performing the work that is identified and will have experience of the work to be performed.
3. The WBS dictionary provides additional information about each identified work package in the WBS.
4. The lowest level of detail that a WBS goes to is the work package.
5. The three elements of the scope baseline are the scope statement, the WBS, and the WBS dictionary.

Task 3: Develop a budget plan based on the project scope using estimating techniques, in order to manage project cost.

1. Project costs are individual or aggregated cost estimates for work to be done on the project, on the project; budget represents these costs over time.
2. If you have an optimistic estimate of $100, a most likely estimate of $150, and a pessimistic estimate of $250, your three-point cost estimate will be the result of ((100 + (4 x 150) + 250)/6), which equals $158.33.
3. The basis of estimates document provides additional information about the assumptions made and the estimating techniques used to develop the activity cost estimates.
4. It is important to have any agreements, or contracts, available when developing the project budget because they will most likely spell out when payments are to be made. This information needs to be included in your project budget.
5. It is important to carry out vendor bid analysis for any cost estimates received to ensure that the estimate received is with in an expected range, neither too high nor too low.

Task 4: Develop a project schedule based on the project timeline, scope, and resource plan, in order to manage timely completion of the project.

1. If you are adding up a most likely time estimate, a pessimistic time estimate, and an optimistic time estimate to determine a weighted average to include in your activity duration estimates, you are using the three-point estimating technique.
2. If you have decided to ask your project team to work overtime to complete work more quickly, you are choosing to use the crashing schedule compression technique.
3. After you have completed a forward pass through a network diagram, you will have the total project duration.
4. The difference between project work packages and project activities is that project activities are decomposed work packages and used in developing the project schedule.
5. If you are working on a project that is resource constrained, you should estimate activity resources first because they represent a constraint on the project, and you will have to make project durations fit the available resources.

Task 5: Develop a human resource management plan by defining the roles and responsibilities of the project team members in order to create an effective project organization structure and provide guidance regarding how resources will be utilized and managed.

1. The difference between the human resource management plan and staffing management plan is that the human resource management plan is the broader of the two documents that provides guidance on how all aspects of human resources on your project will be carried out. The staffing management plan provides specific information about the roles and responsibilities, experience, and timings that project personnel are required on the project.
2. If you constantly have to negotiate with different functional managers across your organization to get project personnel allocated to your project you are most likely working in a weak matrix organization.
3. A RACI chart is a form of responsibility assignment matrix that shows which personnel are responsible, accountable, consulted, and informed about project work.
4. It is important to clearly define individual roles and responsibilities on the project so that there is no misunderstanding between team members that might cause conflict and inefficiency.
5. The human resource management plan provides guidance on how project personnel will be acquired, developed, and managed during the executing phase of the project.

Task 6: Develop a communication plan based on the project organization structure and external stakeholder requirements, in order to manage the flow of project information.

1. Both communications management planning and stakeholder expectation management planning are tightly interlinked. To effectively influence stakeholder expectations on the project, it is essential that project communications are carried out effectively and appropriately.
2. If you currently have 20 stakeholders identified on your project, and another 5 stakeholders are identified, there is now a total of 25 stakeholders. You must work out the difference between 20 stakeholders and 25 stakeholders by using the formula (n(n-1)/2). Twenty stakeholders represent 190 communications channels; 25 stakeholders represent 300 communications channels. Therefore, the difference between the two is an additional 110 communications channels.
3. In the standard communications model, the best definition of noise is anything that can interrupt the message sent by the sender to the receiver through the chosen medium.

4. If you are studying another person's body language to understand them better, you are using the effective listening skill.
5. The project manager should take responsibility for controlling the communications process on the project.

Task 7: Develop a procurement plan based on the project scope and schedule, in order to ensure that the required project resources will be available.

1. If, as part of your procurement negotiations, you have provided all potential sellers with a detailed description of the procurement statement of work and are seeking to get a fixed price from them to complete the work, you would prefer a fixed-price form of contract that allocates more risk to the seller than the buyer.
2. If you are the seller in negotiations, you would probably prefer a time and materials form of contract or a cost reimbursable form of contract.
3. Any existing organizational process assets that exist are an important consideration in the procurement planning work because they will outline the organization's procurement policies, which must be followed at all times.
4. If you are carrying out an assessment of whether your project team members should complete the required work or whether you should outsource it to another company, you are carrying out the make-or-buy analysis.
5. A project manager should consider involving procurement specialists and legal specialists in the development of the procurement management plan because the results of project procurement are legally binding and enforceable in court.

Task 8: Develop a quality management plan based on the project scope and requirements, in order to prevent the appearance of defects and reduce the cost of quality.

1. The document that describes how audits of quality processes are to be carried out is the process improvement plan. If there is no process improvement plan, the quality management plan is used.
2. Quality assurance is focused on ensuring that relevant policies and processes are in place and that they are being followed. Quality control is focused on checking the correctness of the project deliverables.
3. If you are using a graphical tool to determine the root cause of a known quality issue, you are using a cause and effect, fishbone, or Ishikawa diagram.
4. You use statistical sampling to gather data about quality on the project when the population size is too large or the testing involves destructive testing.
5. Quality refers to whether defined characteristics meet requirements; grade refers to the number of features a product or deliverable has. Low grade is acceptable if that is what is defined; low quality is not acceptable.

Task 9: Develop the change management plan by defining how changes will be handled, in order to track and manage changes.

1. If a project team member is confused about how change requests are to be recorded and considered, you should refer them to the change management plan.
2. The name of the group that meets regularly to consider whether to approve or decline change requests is typically called the change control board.
3. It is important that all change requests received, no matter how small, are formally documented to ensure that any and all changes on the project are properly documented so that they are incorporated into the relevant parts of the project management plan, and that at any time in the project what you are delivering matches what is documented. This also prevents both scope creep and gold plating.
4. It is important that a project manager be given a level of delegated authority to make decisions about whether to approve or decline change requests received to ensure that progress on the project can continue rather than being held up and having to wait for a meeting of the change control board. This delegated authority given to the project manager will usually relate to relatively minor changes.
5. The process of allocating a unique number to each change request on your change log is an example of your configuration management system.

Task 10: Plan risk management by developing a risk management plan, and identifying, analyzing, and prior to rising project risks in the risk register and defining risk response strategies, in order to manage uncertainty throughout the project life cycle.

1. The document that includes an analysis of the organizations risk tolerance and how this will affect your particular project's approach to risk is the risk management plan.
2. When a stakeholder raises an issue, it is recorded on the issues log and tracked. If the issue escalates, it can be placed on either the risk register or the watch list. The risk register records all identified risks on the project, assesses those risks for probability and impact, and develops risk response strategies for each identified risk. The watch list provides a place in which low-level risks are documented and regularly monitored to see whether they warrant escalation to the risk register.
3. Quantitative risk analysis seeks to assign a financial or time number to risk assessment.
4. The project manager should take responsibility for ensuring that the risk register is regularly monitored and updated.

5. If you decide to take out insurance to deal with an identified negative risk, you have chosen to use a transfer risk response strategy.

Task 11: Present the project plan to the key stakeholders (if required), in order to obtain approval to execute the project.

1. The role of the project sponsor is to provide financial and political support for the project, sign the project charter, and provide senior-level advice to the project manager.
2. The project manager should take responsibility for ensuring that the correct approval to proceed to project execution is obtained.
3. The five process groups of project management are initiating, planning, executing, monitoring and controlling, and closing.
4. The role a PMO will play in approving a project plan varies depending on the level of organizational project management maturity. An organization with a high degree of project management maturity might have a PMO that takes responsibility for approving a project plan prior to project execution beginning.
5. The OPM3 model, which stands for organizational project management maturity model, measures organizational project management maturity levels and provides guidance on how to increase the level of project management maturity.

Task 12: Conduct a kick-off meeting with all stakeholders, in order to announce the start of the project, to indicate the project milestones, and share other relevant information.

1. The project manager should organize a kick off meeting and take a lead role in participating in the kick-off meeting because stakeholders will be looking to the project manager to show leadership.
2. All stakeholders with a high level of interest in the project should be invited to the kick-off meeting
3. The kick-off meeting should be carried out where the project is to be completed whenever possible.
4. After the completion of the kick-off meeting, minutes and action log should be circulated, and the project manager should ensure that any agreed-upon actions are followed up on and completed.
5. A kick-off meeting should be scheduled for immediately prior to project execution, which could mean the end of project planning or when enough project planning has been completed to begin project execution, depending on how the project is being completed.

CHAPTER 3

Executing the project

The Executing the Project performance domain covers approximately 30 percent of the questions in the Project Management Professional (PMP®) exam. The tasks contained in the Executing the Project domain focus on those activities and processes required to perform and complete the work defined in the project management plan. It is the role of the project manager to use the relevant plans and baselines to coordinate resources, manage stakeholder expectations, and communicate effectively in order to produce the project deliverables. As a result of executing the planned work, changes are made that flow through the monitoring and control tasks and then back to the planning tasks in an iterative cycle. It is during the execution of the project processes that the majority of the project work is performed and the largest portion of the project budget is spent.

All executing work follows some sort of plan or description of the work to be done. For example, work to be done as part of scope, time, and cost is contained in their respective management plans and baselines. Work to be done as part of communications, procurement, and stakeholder management is also included in their respective management plans.

The work done as part of quality tasks is described in the quality management plan and, more specifically, in the quality assurance plan that is a specific executing task. The risk management plan and the risk register, specifically the planned risk responses, direct risk execution tasks. The human resource management plan guides the tasks involved in acquiring, developing, and managing project team members. The other source of executing task to be performed comes from the approved change requests that represents a description of work to be done on the project after it completes the approved change control process and its status is approved.

This chapter covers the following tasks:

- Task 1: Obtain and manage project resources including outsourced deliverables by following the procurement plan, in order to ensure successful project execution.
- Task 2: Execute the tasks as defined in the project plan, in order to achieve the project deliverables within budget and schedule.

- Task 3: Implement the quality management plan using the appropriate tools and techniques, in order to ensure that work is being performed according to required quality standards.
- Task 4: Implement approved changes according to the change management plan, in order to meet project requirements.
- Task 5: Implement approved actions, and follow the risk management plan and risk register, in order to minimize the impact of negative risk events on the project.
- Task 6: Maximize team performance through leading, mentoring, training, and motivating team members.

Task 1: Obtain and manage project resources including outsourced deliverables by following the procurement plan, in order to ensure successful project execution.

This task focuses on obtaining the resources required to carry out the work of the project. Resources refer to people, machinery, equipment, supplies, and budgets require to complete the project work. The individual plans prepared for each resource will guide which resources are required, the level of resources required, when they are required, and how they are obtained. If external resources are required, the procurement plan determines how these resources are obtained.

MORE INFO You can find out more about managing project resources by reading the chapters on Cost Management, Human Resource Management and Procurement Management in the PMBOK® Guide, 5th edition. You can also read the same chapters in the PMP Training Kit.

Exam need to know...

- Resources

  For example: What types of resources are used to produce project deliverables?
- Human resource management plan

  For example: What document is used to obtain and manage project human resources?
- Preassignment

  For example: How are most human resources obtained?
- Acquisition

  For example: What is the name of the technique for which a project manager advertises externally the human resources to work on the project?
- Virtual teams

  For example: What are some of the potential difficulties working with virtual teams?

- Staff assignments

  For example: How should individual roles and responsibilities be documented?
- Resource calendars

  For example: What is the best way to document when resources are and are not available?
- Cost management plan

  For example: What document is used to define how financial resources are obtained for the project?
- Procurement management plan

  For example: When carrying out external procurements, which document tells the project manager how the process should be carried out?
- Source selection criteria

  For example: In addition to price, what other criteria can be used to assess sellers wanting to provide external goods or services?
- Seller proposals

  For example: What is expected of sellers in response to procurement documents?
- Bidder conference

  For example: How does the project manager ensure that all potential sellers are given the same information and treated fairly during the procurement process?
- Proposal evaluation techniques

  For example: When evaluating all seller proposals received in response to procurement documents issued, what is the best way to determine which of the potential sellers should be selected to supply the required goods and services?
- Independent estimates

  For example: How does the project manager ensure that seller proposals are within an expected cost range?
- Procurement negotiations

  For example: Which tool and technique is used to produce signed project contracts?

Resources

Project work is completed by resources or by using resources. Resources include the skilled human resources that are responsible for completing the work as individuals or as part of a team. Resources also include the equipment, services, supplies, materials, and budgets required to complete the project work. Many resources are internal to the project and supplied by the performing organization. In relation to obtaining internal resources, the cost management plan and the human resource management plan guide the activities and tasks.

Through make or buy analysis, however, the decision can be made to procure resources externally via a formal procurement process. In that case, the procurement plan guides the way these resources are obtained. Make or buy analysis considers all the costs and benefits of making or supplying the goods or services within the organization compared with procuring it from an external organization.

True or false? Resources used on a project can include people, materials, or finances.

Answer: *True.* Project work is completed by using project resources, so they include the people responsible for completing the work, the materials used to complete the work, and the finances used to obtain people and materials.

For employment of project staff, the project manager has to take into account enterprise environmental factors such as market conditions and employment conditions because they might affect the ability to obtain staff.

> ***EXAM TIP*** **In the exam, you should look for any reference to resources. And first seek to determine whether it refers to human, materials, or financial resources. You should then determine whether these resources are procured internally or externally. If they are procured externally, they are subject to a formal procurement process.**

> ***MORE INFO*** **You can find out more about resources by reading Chapter 7 on cost management, Chapter 9 on human resource management, and Chapter 12 on project procurement management in the PMBOK® Guide, 5th edition.**

Preassignment

When you use the human resource management plan to acquire the human resources required for a project, there are a number of tools and techniques that are useful. Preassignment of project team members is very common; they are usually selected in advance by the organization, relevant functional managers, and the project manager. The project manager might not have much input into this process, depending on the type of organizational structure and the amount of power that the job has within it.

The project manager might have to engage in negotiation with functional managers to get the staff he wants preassigned to the project. The outcomes of these negotiations reflect both the amount of power between project manager and functional manager and the priority given to the project.

True or false? All staff members are preassigned to a project.

Answer: *False.* It is not a catch-all situation in which all staff are preassigned to a project. For any given project, there might be a mix of preassigned and external recruitment of staff.

> ***EXAM TIP*** **In the exam, you should carefully examine the scenario presented to determine how human resources have been obtained for the project and be able to distinguish between preassignment and external procurement of human resources because the processes are different for obtaining each one.**

MORE INFO You can find out more about preassignment in the Acquire Project Team process of the PMBOK® Guide, 5th edition.

Acquisition

For employees who cannot be obtained internally via preassignment, the performing organization and the project manager might need to acquire the required services and personnel from outside sources. This can be achieved by advertising, head hunting identified individuals, using recruitment consultants, subcontracting work to another organization, and employing a robust interview and appointment process. Where possible, project managers should be involved in this process because they have a clear understanding of not only the skills and experience required but also the organizational culture and team culture they are seeking to develop within the project.

Project managers also rely on established organizational process assets and the human resources department of the organization to assist with the process of external acquisition of project team members.

True or false? All team members working on the project are assigned to it from within the organization.

Answer: *False.* The organization might not have all the required staff or skills required, so it goes through a process of external acquisition and recruitment of project team members.

EXAM TIP In the exam, if you see any reference in a question scenario to acquiring project team members from outside the organization, it refers to the process of acquisition.

Virtual teams

The increasing prevalence of information technology is enabling many project teams to be formed virtually. Separate project team members might be geographically isolated from one another—whether in a different part of the building, another city, or a different part of the world. These virtual teams might be the best solution for obtaining project staff given existing constraints. Where possible, the best solution is always face-to-face or location project team members. But where this is not possible, virtual teams should seek to use as much technology as possible to increase and enhance effective communication.

The project manager faces unique challenges when managing virtual teams, including general work efficiency, effective communication, cultural differences, and the development of an effective team culture.

True or false? Whenever possible, all project team members should be seated so that they can see each other.

Answer: *True.* Although virtual teams are an increasing reality and the use of technology can overcome some of the limitations of locating project team members remotely, the best solution is always to have project team members co-located together.

> ***EXAM TIP*** **If the exam offers you a choice between face-to-face co-location of team members and the establishment of a virtual team, you should always choose face-to-face co-location.**

Staff assignments

As a result of acquiring project team members internally or externally, the project manager has documentation for individual people who have been assigned to the team. The project staff assignment is documentation of these assignments and can include a project team directory and organizational charts, such as the organizational breakdown structure.

True or false? It is valuable for all project team members to have an understanding of their role, responsibility, and place within the project and organization.

Answer: *True.* The project staff assignment documentation helps staff members know exactly what their roles are and how they fit with other team members.

Resource calendars

As result of acquiring the human resources required to complete the project, the project manager also creates resource calendars that show when all the project resources are available to do the work on the project. Resource calendars are an important input into activities around planning project time because resource availability directly affects the project schedule.

True or false? Resource calendars document when people and machinery are available to work on the project.

Answer: *True.* A resource calendar outlines the days and shifts that project resources can and cannot work, which is important input for project-scheduling activities.

> ***EXAM TIP*** **In the exam, look out for resource calendars as important input for project scheduling activities because they affect when tasks and activities can be completed.**

Cost management plan

The cost management plan is a component of the project management plan that describes how the project financial resources are planned, structured, and controlled. As such, it is an important plan to obtain and manage project financial resources. The cost management plan can help to establish the units of measure being used, the level of precision and accuracy in the activity cost estimates, any links to existing organizational process assets around financing for the project and rules performance measurement, and tracking actual cost performance against planned cost performance.

True or false? The cost management plan relates only to how accurate the cost estimates are on the project.

Answer: *False*. The cost management plan focuses on all aspects of project costs, including how they are estimated and planned, how funding for the project is structured, and how variances between what is planned and what is actually occurring are monitored and controlled.

> ***EXAM TIP*** **In the exam, look to use the cost management plan to obtain and manage the project financial resources that are required to complete the project work.**

Procurement management plan

For those goods or services that cannot be obtained from within the performing organization, a procurement management plan is useful for determining how goods and services are procured externally. The procurement management plan, which is a component of the project management plan, describes how the project manager acquires goods and services from outside the performing organization and can include guidance on the types of contracts to be used, how to manage multiple potential suppliers, how successful sellers of goods and services are selected, and how the procurement process is evaluated.

The types of resources that can be obtained externally generally refer to people, supplies, materials, and equipment. The procurement management plan does not refer to the external procurement of financial resources.

True or false? The procurement management plan guides the project manager and project team and addresses how to obtain goods and services that cannot be sourced from within the performing organization due to lack or unavailability of resources.

Answer: *True*. The procurement management plan is one part of the overall project management plan that specifically addresses how external procurements are conducted and how the procurement management process is evaluated.

> ***EXAM TIP*** **In any exam scenario that deals with external procurement, you should ensure that you have a procurement management plan and that you are fully aware of any organizational process assets that might affect the procurement process.**

> ***NOTE*** **It is very important for a project manager to follow any organizational process assets that relate to how procurement of goods and services is managed for an organization. In addition to the consequences of a lack of procurement planning, there are often other consequences for not following established internal procedures, including breaches of insurance and indemnity contracts that can expose the project manager to personal liability for any procurement decisions taken.**

Source selection criteria

Before going to external sources to obtain resources, the procurement management plan should outline the selection criteria that are used to select successful providers of goods and services. The most typical source selection criterion used in procurement activities is price, but there can be many others: experience, financial stability, health and safety record, and innovation. The particular mix of source selection criteria used reflects the procuring organization's emphasis.

It is also common for each of the source selection criteria used to be given a particular weighting so that different emphases can be placed on different criteria. For example, price usually has the greatest weighting, but other criteria to be given significant weighting as well. Table 3-1 shows a range of source selection criteria and the weighting given to each one to enable a more accurate selection of suppliers.

TABLE 3-1 Source selection criteria and weighting

CRITERIA	WEIGHTING
Price	5
Quality	3
Experience	3
Personnel	2
Health and safety	2

True or false? Source selection criteria should make it clear to potential service providers that the proposal is evaluated on price alone.

Answer: *False.* Source selection criteria can include price and any other attribute that the performing organization considers important when deciding which potential sellers should be awarded procurement.

> ***EXAM TIP*** **Whenever source selection criteria are mentioned in the exam, assume that they are used in conjunction with some form of weighted attribute and that the selection of successful sellers involves more than consideration of just price, except where the work involved as simple and short term.**

Seller proposals

When carrying out procurement management processes to obtain and manage project resources externally, the performing organization receives seller proposals from people and organizations interested in providing goods and services to the project. The seller proposals are prepared in response to the particular procurement document package issued by the performing organization and the project manager.

Typical forms of procurement documents include the request for information (RFI), invitation for bid (IFB), request for proposal (RFP), request for quotation (RFQ), and tender notice. The type of procurement document chosen to solicit seller proposals reflects the amount of information available in the procurement statement of work. The more detailed the procurement statement of work, the greater the level of detail required in seller proposals.

True or false? Seller proposals should contain enough information to enable the project manager to assess whether the seller is able to complete the required work.

Answer: *True.* In addition to responding to specific information contained in the project documents being used, any seller proposal should also make clear that the seller can complete the required work.

> ***EXAM TIP*** **In the exam, seek to understand in the scenario put forward what level of detail is known about the procurement statement of work because it directly influences the project document and the depth of response received from sellers.**

> ***MORE INFO*** **You can find out more about procurement documents, source selection criteria, and seller proposals in Chapter 12 of the PMBOK® Guide, 5th edition and Chapter 10 of the PMP Training Kit.**

Bidder conference

During the process of following the procurement plan to obtain and manage object resources externally, bidder conferences can be used to enable all potential sellers to meet, ask questions, and clarify information prior to submission of a seller response. Bidder conferences can be held either with all parties physically present or virtually, where everyone has access to the information electronically.

Bidder conferences are used to ensure that between the buyer and all prospective sellers there is a clear and common understanding of the procurement requirements, no bidders receive preferential treatment, and the procurement process is carried out on a level playing field. For example, if one party asks a question of the buyer, the buyer should provide the answer to all prospective sellers unless it is commercially sensitive information.

True or false? Bidder conferences are used by the project manager to ensure that the lowest price is received for the requested work.

Answer: *False.* Bidder conferences are used to ensure that all prospective sellers get the information they require to prepare seller proposals.

> ***EXAM TIP*** **You should always run your procurement processes fairly and transparently, without favoring any one potential seller over another. If a question in the exam poses a situation in which a potential seller attempts to gain an advantage by getting information from you that is not available to other sellers, you should ensure that it does not occur and make sure that all sellers are given the same information. If necessary, be prepared to exclude any unethical sellers from the procurement process.**

Proposal evaluation techniques

After the seller proposals are received, the project manager and project team use a variety of proposal evaluation techniques that consider the source selection criteria in the procurement management plan and go through a formal evaluation review process, which is generally defined by the buyer's procurement policies and organizational process assets. Proposal evaluation is often completed by a proposal evaluation committee headed by the project manager; it reviews all seller proposals received and makes its recommendation of seller choice to the project sponsor.

True or false? The proposal evaluation committee should make decisions during the evaluation of seller proposals about which criteria should be used and the weighting given to each of the criteria.

Answer: *False.* The source selection criteria that are used and the weighting of each of these criteria should be decided during the procurement planning activities and documented in the procurement management plan.

> ***NOTE*** **Be aware that in certain circumstances the decisions made during the proposal evaluation process can be challenged by unsuccessful sellers, particularly if it is a public organization conducting the procurement. As such, it is extremely important that you carry your procurement processes out in accordance with any relevant organizational process assets and with relevant statutes and legislations of the country in which you are working.**

Independent estimates

As part of using a procurement plan to obtain and manage project resources from external sellers, the project manager should consider using independent estimates to verify that seller proposals are within an expected range. Doing so ensures that sellers are not presenting proposals that are wildly inaccurate. Independent estimates enable a project manager to determine whether the procurement statement of work has been detailed enough to enable prospective sellers to develop an accurate seller proposal; whether there is collusion and price fixing among sellers; and whether the sellers' pricing is too low, which could indicate a lack of understanding of the work to be done.

Independent estimates are best carried out by professionals with relevant experience in the area in which the procurement statement of work is focused.

True or false? Independent estimates should be used by the project manager to determine whether the sellers fully understood the work to be done.

Answer: *True.* Independent estimates provide a date by which the project manager can determine whether prospective sellers understood the level of work required and whether there is anything suspicious about the pricing contained in seller proposals.

Procurement negotiations

After successful sellers are chosen, both the buyer and seller enter procurement negotiations to achieve mutual agreement prior to signing any contracts or agreements. Procurement negotiations conclude with a signed contract that is executed by both buyer and seller.

Procurement negotiations can be both simple and straightforward; or they can be complex, lengthy, and subject to a completely separate process. The type of procurement negotiations that occur reflects the depth and complexity of the procurement statement of work required. If the procurement negotiations are lengthy and complex, they can be treated as a completely separate process.

True or false? Procurement negotiations should be carried out after the procurement statement of work has been issued to all prospective sellers.

Answer: *False.* Procurement negotiations should be carried out after the selected seller has been chosen through the procurement process and proposal evaluation techniques because negotiations are conducted only with the preferred seller, not all prospective sellers.

> ***NOTE*** **Given that procurement negotiations result in a legally binding contract or agreement for both buyer and seller, it is always advisable to involve legal specialists in both negotiations and drafting of the contract.**

> ***MORE INFO*** **You can find out more about procurement negotiations in Chapter 12 of the PMBOK® Guide, 5th edition and Chapter 10 of the PMP Training Kit.**

Can you answer these questions?

You can find the answers to these questions at the end of this chapter.

1. What are the three documents most useful when seeking to obtain and manage project resources?
2. What is the name of the process by which most project team members are acquired?
3. During a bidder conference, if a prospective seller asks a question and requests that you do not share the information with other prospective sellers, what is your best course of action?
4. In addition to project price, what other criteria should be used when evaluating seller proposals?
5. What is the intended end result of procurement negotiations?

Task 2: Execute the tasks as defined in the project plan, in order to achieve the project deliverables within budget and schedule.

This task is very broad; it takes all the work that has been planned as part of the project management plan, its subsidiary plans, project baselines, and other documents, and uses them to execute all the project work to deliver the project deliverables with a particular focus on delivering the work within budget and on schedule.

Exam need to know...

- Project plan

  For example: What documents and baselines are contained in the project plan?
- Deliverables

  For example: What is the main focus of the executing tasks and activities in the project?
- Work performance data

  For example: During project execution, raw observations and measurements are collected and become known as what?
- Performance reporting

  For example: Why is performance reporting considered an effective communication and stakeholder management tool?

Project plan

The project plan, or project management plan, is the document or collection of documents that describes how the project is executed, monitored, and controlled. It can be a single document, but more often it integrates and consolidates a number of subsidiary documents that include project baselines and subsidiary plans. The baselines that it does include are the scope baseline, which is made up of the scope statement, work breakdown schedule (WBS), and WBS dictionary; schedule baseline; and cost baseline.

The subsidiary plans that make up the project plan include the following:

- Scope management plan
- Configuration management plan
- Requirements management plan
- Schedule management plan
- Cost management plan
- Quality management plan
- Process improvement plan
- Human resource management plan
- Staffing management plan
- Communications management plan
- Risk management plan

- Procurement management plan
- Stakeholder management plan
- Change management plan

Each of these plans specifies a different range of tasks to be done as part of the project work. Given the broad-ranging contents of the project plan, it is essential that enough planning has been done prior to beginning any execution activities. The project manager uses the project plan to guide executing activities and to measure actual performance against planned performance. The main focus of this task is to use the project plan to guide executing activities.

It is the responsibility of the project manager to ensure that the correct plan is used and that the plan is detailed enough to enable execution of tasks to proceed. It is also the responsibility of the project manager to ensure that all changes to project plans are managed in accordance with the documented and approved change control process. Use of the configuration management plan ensures that the project manager always uses the most accurate and latest iteration of any relevant plan. Approved changes to any of the baselines contained in the project plan alter the baseline.

> ***EXAM TIP*** **Remember that a project baseline is the original baseline plus any approved changes.**

True or false? The project plan is a single document that focuses on how the scope of the project is delivered and managed.

Answer: *False*. The project plan is the collection of documents and baselines that set out how all elements, not just the project scope, are delivered and managed.

> ***EXAM TIP*** **In the exam, when you see a reference to the project plan or project management plan, you should immediately know that it is a composite document made up of all the various subsidiary plans and the three key baselines. It is also important to know that you cannot proceed to any executing activities or tasks until sufficient planning has been done and documented in the project plan.**

Deliverables

Deliverables, which are the main tangible output of the project execution tasks, are defined by the project scope statement that incorporates customer requirements and specifications. A deliverable is a unique and verifiable product, result, or capability to perform a service that is required to be produced to complete a phase or project. It can be either the deliverable the customer has requested or a deliverable from another part of the project, such as project communications from the communications management processes.

True or false? A "deliverable" refers only to a physical product requested by the customer.

Answer: *False*. The term "deliverable" does refer to whatever it is the customer requested, but it also refers to many other products, services, or results produced by the work being done on the project. It is important that a deliverable is measurable in some way so that you can ensure it fulfills its intended purpose.

> ***EXAM TIP*** **Deliverables go through a series of steps before they are finally completed. The first step is the process of quality control checking, in which they are checked, or verified, against internal standards and specifications. If they pass these steps, they are presented to the customer for validation; if validated, they become accepted deliverables.**

Work performance data

As a result of executing the tasks defined in the project plan, work performance data is produced. Work performance data includes the raw observations and measurements that are gathered as work is being performed. Examples of work performance data include actual costs, actual start and finish dates, technical performance measurements, and number of change requests made.

> ***EXAM TIP*** **Work performance data becomes work performance information after it has been analyzed. Work performance information is then used in work performance reports.**

True or false? Work performance data includes observations and measurements about all aspects of project performance, not just project deliverables.

Answer: *True*. Work performance data can relate to any executing task and is often raw information and metrics about how the task is progressing, which is then used to measure against what was planned to look for variance. If variance is discovered, it is acted upon via the approved change control process.

Performance reporting

As the project tasks are executed, and work performance data is gathered, a key element of the communications management executing tasks is effective reporting of project performance. The communications management plan provides guidance on how project performance is to be reported, which in turn reflects the communication needs of individual stakeholders. Appropriate reporting of project performance is a key element in the successful management of stakeholder expectations.

The project manager can use a variety of performance reporting templates to provide the correct information in the correct format to satisfy stakeholder expectations. Content included in performance reporting can be presented in text, numerical, pictorial, graphical, summary, or detailed form depending on the identified needs of stakeholders.

True or false? Work performance reports should report progress only in relation to cost and time because they are the most important metrics for all stakeholders.

Answer: *False*. Different stakeholders have different interests in the project: Some stakeholders are certainly interested in cost and time progress; but other stakeholders require different information perhaps in relation to numbers of change requests, quality standards being met, or other similar metrics.

> ***MORE INFO*** **You can find out more about the tools and techniques involved in executing the tasks as defined in the project plan in the Direct and Manage Project Work process topic in Section 4.3 of the PMBOK® Guide, 5th edition.**

Can you answer these questions?

You can find the answers to these questions at the end of this chapter.

1. What are the three baselines contained in the project plan?
2. Which of the subsidiary plans of the project plan is most useful in guiding how stakeholder expectations are successfully managed?
3. What document guides show a project manager how to format the content of their performance reports?
4. Can you place work performance reports, work performance data, and work performance information in the order in which they are naturally developed?
5. What is the name given to any unique and verifiable product, result, or capability to perform a service that is required to be produced to complete a process, phase, or project?

Task 3: Implement the quality management plan using the appropriate tools and techniques, in order to ensure that work is being performed according to required quality standards.

This task focuses on the part of the quality management plan that focuses on quality assurance rather than quality control. Quality control tasks are completed during the monitoring and controlling domain tasks. Quality assurance involves ensuring that all the quality processes are being implemented and used appropriately so the work being performed meets the required quality standards. This is different from quality control, in which the project deliverables are inspected to see whether they conform to the required quality standards in the quality management plan.

The project manager must take responsibility for ensuring that the quality management plan is detailed enough to provide sufficient guidance on which quality management tools and techniques are to be used throughout the project. These tools and techniques are used on more than just the project deliverables; they determine whether all aspects of the project work are completed to the expected quality standards.

> ***MORE INFO*** **You can find out more about this particular domain task in the Perform Quality Assurance process in Section 8.2 in the PMBOK® Guide, 5th edition and in Chapter 6 of the PMP Training Kit.**

Exam need to know...

- Quality management plan

  For example: Which document is used to guide the execution of quality management tasks during the project?
- Process improvement plan

  For example: Where does the project manager turn to for guidance on how to ensure that continuous improvement is occurring on processes and procedures used in the project?
- Quality assurance

  For example: What is the difference between quality assurance and quality control activities?
- Ishikawa seven quality tools

  For example: What is the best way to graphically display the numerical results gathered from quality management monitoring and controlling?

Quality management plan

The quality management plan is an essential component required in order to carry out this particular domain task. The quality management plan is a subsidiary plan of the project plan that describes how an organization's quality policies are implemented, and how the project management team and project manager plan to meet the quality requirements for the project. Within the quality management plan are guidelines for carrying out quality assurance and continuous process improvement approaches for the project.

The content and depth of the quality management plan reflect the complexity, size, and industry of the project and any information gathered; completing this particular domain task can be used to update the quality management plan.

Specific information contained in the quality management plan are the type and frequency of quality audits, the specific quality management and control tools to be used, and a description of the quality metrics and quality checklists that are used.

True or false? The quality management plan contains guidance on all aspects of project quality, including both quality assurance and quality control.

Answer: *True*. The quality management plan is the subsidiary plan of the project plan focused on how all aspects of quality, both assurance and control, are carried out on the project.

EXAM TIP **All executing tasks must be based on the work done in a relevant plan. As such, if a question in the exam asks you about how you to execute particular tasks, your first point of reference should always be the relevant plan. This is very true of quality planning, which starts in the initial project conceptual stages.**

MORE INFO **You can find out more about the Perform Quality Assurance process by reading Chapter 8.2 of the PMBOK® Guide, 5th edition.**

Process improvement plan

The process improvement plan is a specific subsidiary of the project plan that details the processes and steps, analyzing all project management and product development processes in place to establish how they are carried out and to specify how continuous improvement of the processes can occur.

Continuous improvement is a very important concept of quality management. Quality improvement initiatives such as total quality management(TQM), Six Sigma, and process improvement models such as the organizational project management maturity model (OPM3) and capability maturity model integrated (CMMI) can be used as parts of an organization's commitment to continuous improvement and process improvement. It is the responsibility of the project manager to ensure that there is a commitment from the project team and the organization to continuous improvement.

Process analysis takes the steps outlined in the process improvement plan to determine whether there are opportunities for continuous improvement and examines all aspects of processes being used to determine the root cause of any issue not contributing to add value.

True or false? The process improvement plan guides the activities of the project manager and project team in determining which quality processes provide value and how to continuously improve these processes.

Answer: *True*. The purpose of the process improvement plan is to guide project manager and project team members to determine which processes to use in all aspects of quality management throughout the project and how to engage in continuous improvement of these processes.

Quality assurance

Quality assurance is the part of the quality management activities that focuses on ensuring that appropriate quality processes are in place and that they are being used in accordance with the quality management plan. It also involves a commitment to continuous improvement of all processes. Some of the processes are in relation to power quality control of the product is carried out while the rest of the processes are focused on making sure that things like that project management methodology is being followed, projects are being selected as per the agreed project selection process, and that the change control processes are being followed.

Whether quality processes are being followed is determined by using quality audits and process analysis. A quality audit is a structured independent process to check whether project activities are in compliance with both organizational and project processes and procedures. Quality audits are best done by an independent person who can comment objectively and should be regularly scheduled as part of the project work.

True or false? Quality audits are used to determine whether the product or deliverable is meeting the expected quality standards.

Answer: *False*. Quality audits are part of quality assurance process that is not focused on the quality of the product or deliverable, but instead focuses on the quality of the processes, policies and procedures being used in the project.

MORE INFO There are external standards, such as the ISO 9000 series of standards that focus on quality assurance. If you want to know more about quality assurance, please visit the ISO website: *www.iso.org*.

EXAM TIP For the exam, you need to know the difference between quality assurance and quality control. Here's an easy way to remember: Quality assurance is focused on processes and uses audits to check compliance, whereas quality control is based on the product and uses inspection. Both quality assurance and quality control use Ishikawa seven quality tools to record and interpret the results.

Ishikawa's seven quality tools

There are many different ways to represent data gathered when both quality assurance and quality control tasks are being carried out. The most common of these tools, Ishikawa's seven quality tools, are all graphical representations of information to enable easier understanding of the results.

The seven quality tools are these:

- Cause-and-effect diagram, which is also called the *"Ishikawa"* or *"fishbone diagram"*
- *Flowchart or run chart*
- *Check sheet*
- *Pareto diagram*
- *Histogram or bar chart*
- *Control chart*
- *Scatter diagram*

The cause-and-effect diagram, which is also called the *"Ishikawa"* or *"fishbone diagram,"* is used to describe a known defect and assess the variety of possible root causes. It enables you to consider multiple causes for a single problem. Figure 3-1 shows a cause-and-effect diagram with one level of analysis done.

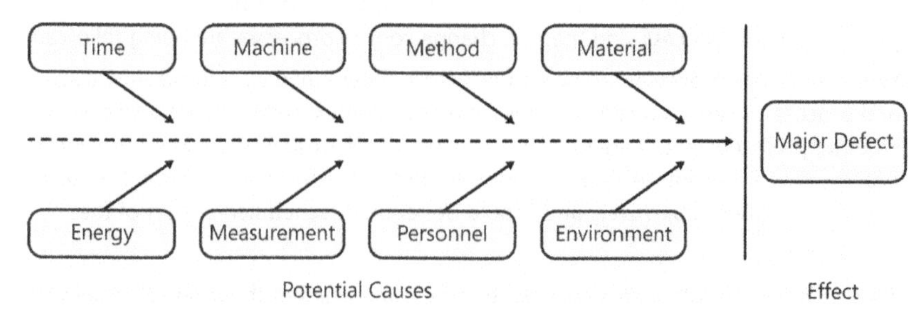

FIGURE 3-1 A diagram showing a cause-and-effect (Ishikawa or fishbone) diagram

Flowcharts are a convenient way to show the flow of information or the sequence of steps in a particular process. Figure 3-2 shows an example of a flowchart.

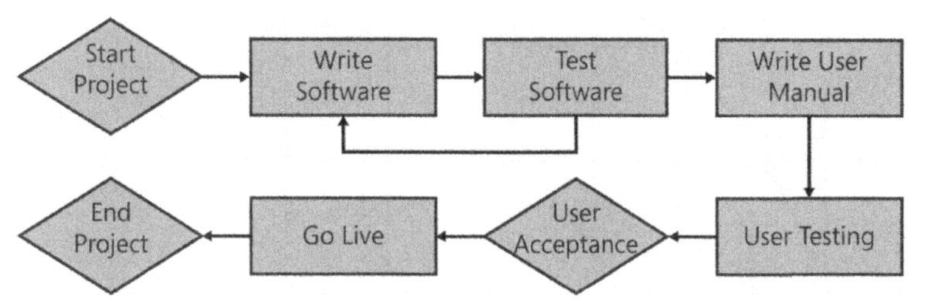

FIGURE 3-2 Flowchart showing quality process flow from beginning of project to end

EXAM TIP **In the exam, you might see the acronym *SIPOC*. It stands for *suppliers, inputs, process, outputs, and customers*; and refers to a particular type of flowchart used to document the flow of goods and information between customers.**

Checksheets are a convenient way to document the activities that must be done and provide a way of checking that they have been done. Checksheets are sometimes called tally sheets. Figure 3-3 shows an example of a checksheet.

Activity	Activity	Due date
Produce the first draft of the quality management plan	Completed	4/4/14
Receive feedback from team on first draft	In Progress	5/5/14
Finalize Quality Management plan	Not yet started	6/6/16

FIGURE 3-3 Example of a checksheet

EXAM TIP **The difference between a checksheet and a checklist is that a checksheet documents what is to be done, whereas a checklist documents what has been done.**

A *Pareto diagram* is a way of using a histogram, or bar chart, to document the frequency of particular events in descending order and then adding up the cumulative percentage of the quality defects to assess which subset of defects causes the greatest amount of problems. The purpose of the Pareto analysis shown in Figure 3-4 is to focus your attention and energy on those 20 percent of problems that are causing 80 percent of the issues.

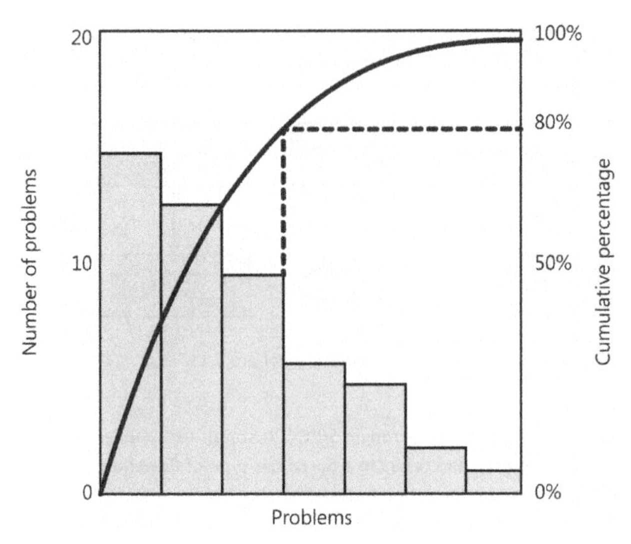

FIGURE 3-4 Example of a Pareto diagram

Histograms, or bar charts, are a simple way of representing frequency, or occurrence, of particular events. Figure 3-5 shows an example of a histogram.

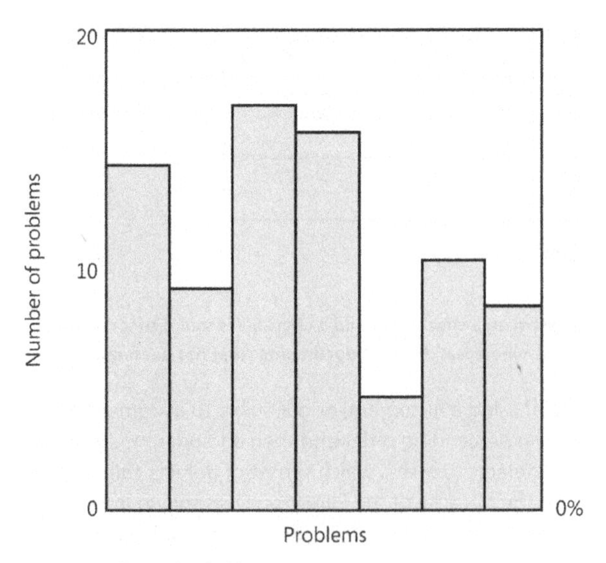

FIGURE 3-5 Example of a histogram

Control charts are an effective way of recording data and determining whether a manufacturing process is still in control or is about to go out of control. Information is gathered and plotted on the control chart around an expected average, or mean. You then set the upper and lower control limits, three standard deviations either side of the mean. Beyond these *control limits*, the upper and lower *specification limit* is set. Any data point that appears outside of the specification limit will not be accepted by the customer. Any data point that appears outside of the control limit but within a specification limit indicates that the process is out of control and investigation of the cause should commence immediately. Any information or data gathered within the control limits is acceptable.

The exception to this rule is when seven consecutive data points appear on either side of the mean. This is called the *rule of seven,* and it is statistically improbable that to get seven consecutive points on either side of the mean. If you do note seven consecutive data points above or below the mean, it signals that you should investigate the cause because the process might be about to go out of control. Figure 3-6 shows an example of a control chart. Note the appearance of seven consecutive data points above the mean, indicating the rule of seven.

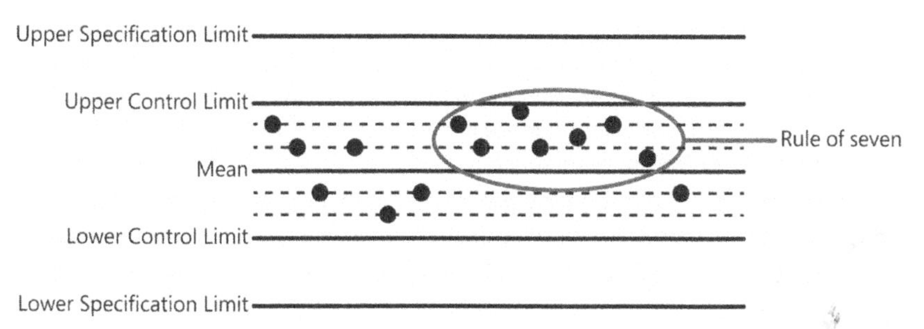

FIGURE 3-6 Example of a control chart

Scatter diagrams simply record the relationship between two variables in graphical form. Figure 3-7 shows an example of a *scatter diagram.*

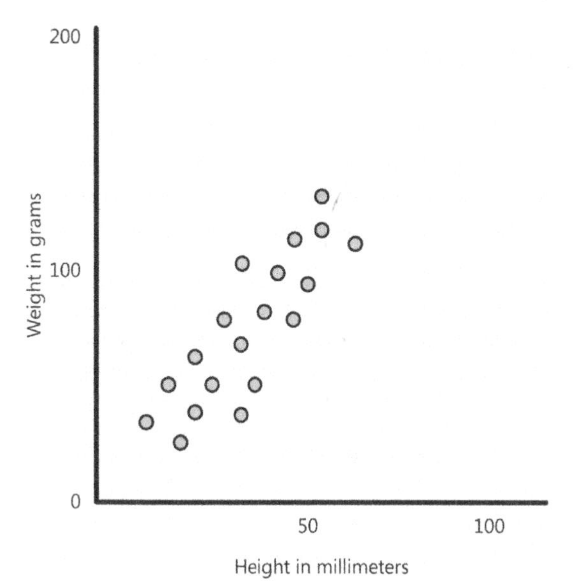

FIGURE 3-7 Example of a scatter diagram

In addition to the seven graphical tools developed by Ishikawa, there are several other tools that can be used both during the quality assurance processes and quality control processes to determine quality levels, obtain quality metrics, and present quality data in easy-to-understand formats.

These additional tools include the following:

- **Benchmarking** The process of comparing your quality practices to those of other projects or other organizations and seeing how you compare.
- **Design of experiments** A tool to assist with developing useful and reliable experiments to test quality. Key considerations in the design of experiments include identifying and controlling variables and understanding how the testing process can affect observed outcomes. A well-designed experiment can independently control different variables to determine which ones are causing problems.
- **Statistical sampling** Used when there are either too many quality checks to do or quality checks involve destructive testing. One constraint of statistical sampling is the assumption that the result from a small population is representative of the entire population.

There are also additional quality planning tools that can be used, including brainstorming and nominal group techniques, force field analysis, affinity diagrams, process decision program charts, interrelationship diagrams, tree diagrams, prioritization matrices, activity network diagrams, and matrix diagrams.

> ***EXAM TIP*** **For the exam, it is important to know the difference between each of these tools and under what circumstances each is best used for. Study each of them and ensure that you can identify them and know the circumstances under which each is best used.**

True or false? A control chart is best used to record the data gathered via a random sample taken from a large population.

Answer: *False.* A control chart is best used to record a data series, usually over time, and record the results against an expected mean and standard deviation to determine whether the process is in or out of control. Statistical sampling is best used to record data gathered via a random sample taken from a large population.

> ***NOTE*** **Most of the profession of modern quality management is based on the work of W. E. Deming and his colleagues and students. The foundational concepts of earnings approach to quality management are also used as the foundational concepts of the modern profession of project management. As such, it is important for any project manager to have a sound understanding of quality management to fully appreciate the profession of project management. If you are interested in finding out more about quality management tools, techniques and processes, it is recommended that you read about the work of W. E. Deming.**

Can you answer these questions?

You can find the answers to these questions at the end of this chapter.

1. How does the process of quality assurance differ from the process of quality control?
2. What is the best way to determine whether quality processes are being implemented and followed per the quality management plan?
3. Which of the Ishikawa seven quality tools can best determine the 20 percent of problems that are causing 80 percent of quality issues?
4. Whose responsibility is it to ensure that quality processes are being followed and implemented per the quality management plan?
5. Which document should a project manager use to ensure that the project is following the processes required to obtain continuous improvement in the quality processes?

Task 4: Implement approved changes according to the change management plan, in order to meet project requirements.

As part of carrying out the tasks associated with executing the project, the primary guidelines for the work to be completed are contained in the various plans and baselines. Of these, the scope baseline that comprises the scope statement, WBS, and WBS dictionary gives the best description of the work to be done as part of the executing tasks. A secondary description of work to be done on the project comes in the form of approved change requests. Approved change requests constitute requests for work to be done and can relate to any area of the project.

It is the responsibility of the project manager to ensure that all change requests go through the appropriate and approved change control process. If they are approved, they become a description of work to be done and are checked for completeness.

Exam need to know...

- Change management plan

  For example: What document provides guidance on how all changes to the project are to be documented and evaluated, and how decisions are made?
- Approved change requests

  For example: Why are approved change requests important to have to successfully execute project tasks?

Change management plan

The particular subsidiary document of the project plan that is most useful to the project manager to ensuring the tasks associated with implementing approved changes in order to meet project requirements is the change management plan. The change management plan sets out how variances are detected, how change requests are made, and how change requests are assessed and decisions made. The change management plan should be detailed enough to guide the project manager and the project team; and assess how all changes, no matter how large or small, are documented, assessed, and implemented.

It is common for a change request to be first considered by the project manager. Using whatever delegated authority project managers have, they can make decisions about whether it can be approved, rejected, or escalated to another step in the change control assessment process. If escalated, it can then go to the change control board, which assesses the impacts of the change and decides whether it should be approved.

True or false? After a project manager receives a request for a change, all change requests should be referred to the change control board.

Answer: *False.* Project managers should consult the change management plan and if they have delegated authority, they might be able to approve or decline the change request without submitting it to the change control board.

> ***EXAM TIP*** **The change management plan spells out exactly how all changes to the project should be documented and how the change control process should work. If you are presented with a scenario that asks where to find out how changes are processed, first refer to the change management plan.**

Approved change requests

Change requests that have been through the approved change control process and are approved represent additional work to be done on the project. As such, all approved change requests become work that must be executed and monitored for completeness. To successfully execute the tasks as defined in the project plan, there must be a record of the documented and approved change requests so the approved work can be carried out.

Approved change requests can include corrective actions, preventive actions, requests for defect repair, and updates to project documents and plans to reflect modified or additional content required of the project.

After a change request is approved, the work required of the change request should be immediately incorporated into the work breakdown structure and scope baseline. By doing this, the project manager can account for and estimate time and costs associated with the work required by the approved change request. The scope baseline includes what was originally included plus any and all approved changes.

> ***EXAM TIP*** **Whenever extra work is added to the project, either by approved change requests or in such areas as risk response strategies, it should immediately be added to the scope baseline, particularly the WBS. Time and cost estimates can be made for the work and they can be included in the project schedule and budget.**

True or false? All change requests represent additional work to be done on the project.

Answer: *False*. Change requests must be approved before they become additional work to be done on the project. Requested change requests do not represent additional work until they have been through the approved change control process and been approved.

EXAM TIP **All changes on a project must be documented and assessed via the documented and approved change control process. If you are given a scenario in which a change request is made, your first step is to assess it via your documented and approved change control process.**

Can you answer these questions?

You can find the answers to these questions at the end of this chapter.

1. Which document guides the project manager in how approved changes are to be implemented?
2. Who should take responsibility for ensuring that all approved changes are incorporated into existing plans and baselines?
3. How do approved change requests add extra work to the project?
4. What is the relationship between approved change requests and the work breakdown structure?
5. How is the work required by approved change requests monitored and controlled?

Task 5: Implement approved actions, and follow the risk management plan and risk register, in order to minimize the impact of negative risk events on the project.

As part of the executing tasks that are completed on a project, the risk register provides a documented source of risk-related tasks that must be completed. The information contained in the risk register includes the risk categories; individual identified risks; anticipated consequences of the risk events; qualitative and quantitative analyses of the risk events; and, most importantly for the execution of the project, the plan risk responses. Each of the plan risk responses, whether they are proactive or reactive, represents work to be done on the project. They are an incredibly useful guide to ensure that all the required executing tasks associated with risk management are completed as planned.

EXAM TIP **The key word is "approved." No action is taken on any requested change requests until they have been assessed and approved via the change control process.**

Exam need to know...

- Risk management plan

  For example: What document guides the project manager during the execution of risk management tasks?

- Risk register

  For example: Where can the project manager find a description of both proactive and reactive risk responses?
- Trigger conditions

  For example: What is the term used to describe an identified event or situation that indicates that a risk is about to occur?
- Workaround

  For example: If a risk event occurs that was completely unforeseen, what is the best course of action for the project manager to undertake?

MORE INFO **For more information about risk management processes, tasks, and activities, see the international standard ISO31000:2009 on risk management.**

Risk management plan

The risk management plan is the document that guides the project manager through all risk management activities. It is initially developed during the planning phases of a project and is used to guide the remaining planning work, the executing work to be done, and risk monitoring and controlling. It is the responsibility of the project manager to make sure that the risk management plan has been followed and to ensure that the executing tasks are sufficiently defined that the risk register has been completed to a satisfactory level.

The risk management plan is a component of the project management plan that describes how risk management activities are performed throughout the life of the project. These risk management activities and tasks refer to both the proactive and reactive risk responses to both positive and negative identified risks, and also to the agreed risk responses to an identifiable risk such as contingency plans and workarounds.

The risk register contains specific information relating to identifiable risks, whereas the risk management plan presents broader information, including the work to be done to deal with unidentifiable risks.

True or false? All potential risks on a project are negative.

Answer: *False.* Risk simply means uncertainty, and there is both negative and positive uncertainty on a project.

Negative uncertainty or risk relates to those events that could adversely affect the project, whereas positive uncertainty or risk represents opportunities for the project. For example, there could be a positive risk that a new technology might lower costs on your project, in which case you should seek to maximize the probability or impact of this risk occurring.

EXAM TIP **For the exam, assume that a risk event is negative unless the question or scenario specifically presents it as a positive risk or opportunity.**

MORE INFO **You can find out more about the project risk management knowledge area in Chapter 11 of the PMBOK® Guide, 5th edition and Chapter 9 of the PMP Training Kit.**

Risk register

The risk register is the document that contains the following: a description of the identified risk categories, a description of the individual identified risk events, a description of the consequences of each of the risk events, a qualitative analysis of the risk events, a quantitative analysis of the risk events, and a description of the plan risk responses. Plan risk responses can be either proactive or reactive in nature. If they are proactive, they represent work to be done prior to the risk management to either minimize the probability and impact of negative risks, or maximize the probability and impact of positive risks. If the plan risk responses are reactive, they represent work to be done on the project after the risk has occurred.

Regardless of whether the risk is a positive or negative or the planned risk response is proactive or reactive, the documented risk response represents work to be done on the project. Obviously, if the work is proactive, it is work that can definitely be done on the project; if it is reactive, it is work that can be done on the project.

It is the responsibility of the project manager to constantly monitor the risk register, particularly the plan risk responses, to ensure that the work of identified has been completed. The identified risks and the plan risk responses can form part of a checksheet that the project manager can use to ensure that the work has been done at the proper time.

True or false? Planned risk responses only represent work to be done on the project if the identified risks occur.

Answer: *False.* Plan risk responses that represent work to be done on the project if the identified risk occurs are necessarily reactive in nature. They are certainly identified and documented in the risk register. However, there are also proactive risk responses, which represent work to be done on the project before a potential risk occurs.

EXAM TIP **Whenever a risk response identifies work that is going to be done on the project it is the responsibility of the project manager to ensure that this work is reflected in the appropriate plans and baselines. For example, if a risk response task is about to be enacted in response to a risk events occurring the work involved should be included in the work breakdown structure for the project.**

Trigger conditions

As part of identifying plan risk responses, the risk register identifies a list of tasks to be completed to address identified risks if a particular event or situation arises. This is what is known as a trigger condition, which identifies a particular event or situation that indicates that a risk is about to occur. For example, a trigger condition could be a key staff member resigning from the project, which triggers a risk response for dealing with the handover of intellectual property and recruitment of a replacement.

After a trigger condition occurs, the risk it is associated with is no longer uncertain and is now an identified piece of work that needs to be completed. It is important that the project manager keep a very close watch on all trigger conditions because if they occur they represent additional work to be done as part of project executing tasks.

True or false? The appearance of a trigger condition means that either a positive or negative risk is about to occur.

Answer: *True*. Trigger conditions are specifically identified as ways to get an early warning that a particular identified risk, either positive or negative, is about to occur and give the project manager and opportunity to put in place and complete proactive work.

Workaround

Despite the best efforts of a competent project manager, project team members, and identified experts, it is highly possible to not be able to identify all risks that could occur on your project and document them in the risk register. If this situation occurs, there is no point looking to the risk register free guide about what work must be completed because there is no information in relation to an unidentified risk that occurred. Instead, the accepted course of action for a project manager is to undertake a workaround, which is a response to a negative risk or threat that has occurred for which no prior response has been planned and documented in the risk register.

The risk management plan should have information about how a workaround is completed, including information about who has which roles and responsibilities for organizing the workaround and making the required decisions. The project manager takes responsibility for ensuring that the risk management plan is followed in this respect.

The objective of a workaround is to develop a temporary solution to enable the project work to continue. The work required to complete the workaround represents executing tasks that must be performed on the project. Given the urgency of unplanned risks, it is often not possible for the project manager to have the time to incorporate the work required by the workaround back into the relevant baselines for the project. As such, there should be some form of contingency or management reserve is available to the project manager to use if a workaround is required.

True or false? The work to be performed as part of a workaround is identified and documented in the part of the risk register that deals with planned risk responses.

Answer: *False*. The nature of the workaround is that it is a response to unplanned and unidentified risks occurring on the project. It is not possible to document the work required as part of the workaround in the risk register at all.

Although it is not possible to document the work required for a workaround proactively in the risk register, it is possible to develop broad strategies, including communication lines, delegated authority, and reporting actions for a workaround if it needs to be used. The best place to record these strategies is the risk management plan.

EXAM TIP **If the exam question presents a scenario in which a risk has occurred, and you have consulted your risk register and found no record of the risk being identified or a planned risk response being developed, your first course of action should be to refer to the risk management plan on how a workaround is to be completed.**

Can you answer these questions?

You can find the answers to these questions at the end of this chapter.

1. What document provides guidance to the project manager about how all risk management planning, executing, and monitoring and controlling activities are completed?
2. Although the risk register contains a lot of information as a result of planning activities, it is the information contained in it relating to executing activities that is most important to the project manager during project execution. Which part of the risk register identifies work to be done on the project?
3. If you are a project manager working on a project and a negative risk suddenly occurs that you have no planned response for, what is your best course of action?
4. You are the project manager managing a large complex construction project and you have noticed a newspaper report forecasting that the price of cement will rise 5 percent in the next two months. You begin your planned response to procure cement materials early and store them to avoid the price increase. What does the forecast price rise in cement represent?
5. After a risk event has occurred, what does it represent for the project?

Task 6: Maximize team performance through leading, mentoring, training, and motivating team members.

Of all the executing tasks the project manager must take responsibility for performing on a project, perhaps the most important are focused on leading, mentoring, training, and motivating team members. Project team members complete the project work, so a project manager must lead them effectively to ensure that the work is completed. There is probably nothing more important than being able to effectively lead, mentor, train, and motivate team members to achieve maximum performance.

A great deal of a project manager's time is spent on leading and developing individuals and turning a group of individuals into a high-performing team. All these tasks and activities associated with team leadership, mentoring, training, and motivating represent work to be done during the executing stages of a project.

A lot of this work can be broken down, documented, and included in the project scope statement as work that can be estimated for time and cost. However, a lot of this work is just part of the expected activities, tasks and effort that a project manager should perform as leader of a project team.

> ***NOTE*** **One of the easiest ways to remember what must occur during the human resource management processes is to use the seven *Rs* of human resource management. The first step is to *recognize* the *roles* and *responsibilities* required on the project; and then *recruit* the people. A project manager must then determine how to *retain*, *reward*, and finally *release* team members.**

Exam need to know...

- Human resource management plan

  For example: What is the document that guides the project manager's efforts to maximize team performance on the project?
- Interpersonal skills

  For example: What are the key skills that a project manager must display to effectively maximize team performance through leading, mentoring, training, and motivation?
- Training

  For example: How can a project manager develop greater capability of individual project team members?
- Team-building activities

  For example: How can a project manager assist a group of individuals toward becoming a high-performing team?
- Recognition and rewards

  For example: What is the best way to provide recognition and rewards to motivate technical professionals working on the project?
- Personnel and team assessment tools

  For example: How does the project manager review, assess, and provide feedback to individuals and teams working on the project?
- Observation and conversation

  For example: What tool can be used by the project manager to help stay in touch with the work and attitudes of project team members?

Human resource management plan

As they do with all other executing activities and tasks, project managers should look to reference a documented guide to assist when completing activities and tasks associated with project human resource management. To successfully carry out the tasks of leading, mentoring, training, and motivating team members, the project manager relies on the human resource management plan, which describes how this work is achieved. The human resource management plan is a subsidiary plan of the overall project management plan and is developed iteratively during the planning work completed on the project.

The human resource management plan provides guidance to the project manager on how all project human resources should be defined, staffed, managed, and eventually released when the work on the project is complete. The human resource management plan can include information about specific roles, responsibilities, and experience required on the project; project organizational charts to present reporting lines; and a staffing management plan.

True or false? The human resource management plan sets out how project staff are identified, recruited, trained, rewarded, and released.

Answer: *True*. The purpose of the human resource management plan is to provide a project manager with clear guidance on how to identify and recruit project staff, reward and train them, and release them from the project after the work is complete.

> ***NOTE*** **All this work involved in maximizing team performance through leading, mentoring, training, and motivating team members should be included in the project scope statement, which includes the WBS for the project and time and cost estimates.**

Interpersonal skills

To successfully lead and manage the human resources on a project, a project manager must display a wide range of interpersonal skills. The appropriate use of these interpersonal skills assists the project manager to effectively manage the project successfully. There is a wide range of interpersonal skills that a project manager must develop and learn to use at the appropriate time. They include the following 11 key interpersonal skills:

- **Leadership** Project managers are responsible for developing their own leadership abilities and must realize that different situations call for different leadership styles or the demonstration of a different set of leadership competencies. Leadership is situational, so the type of leadership required over the life of the project will change. Figure 3-8 shows how different leadership styles can change from a more autocratic style at the beginning of a project to a more participatory, or supporting, style of leadership toward the end of the project.

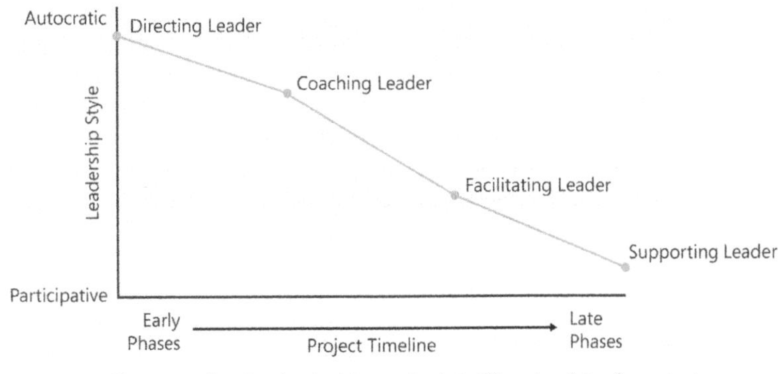

FIGURE 3-8 The types of project leadership required at different points of a project

In addition to this situational representation of leadership throughout the life of a project, Fielder's Contingency theory states that a leader's effectiveness is contingent, or dependent, on two sets of factors: whether the leader is task-oriented or relationship-oriented and whether the environment is stressful or calm. A task-oriented leader is more effective in stressful situations, and a relationship-oriented leader is more effective in calm situations.

There are five forms of power that a project manager can use to assist in leadership of and negotiation for the project team:

- Formal or legitimate power, which is based on the position that you hold as a manager. It should be viewed as an interim form of power as people might respect you initially because of the fact that you are the manager, but your subsequent actions could cause this form of power to become invalid; therefore, it is not the best form of power to use.
- The power to reward people, which is a good form of power to use because you are using it to incentivize good performance and discourage poor performance. It should not be used to blackmail or manipulate people.
- The power to impose penalties or punishment upon people, which is never the best form of power to use because it always generates negative feedback in both explicit and subtle ways.
- Expert power, which is an excellent form of power to use because it is one that is ascribed to you by others because of your respected position as a technical expert. You are viewed as the expert in a particular area, so people look up to you.
- Referent power, which is a result of your own personality and whether you are liked and respected by other people.

- **Team building** The ability to build teams is a key interpersonal skill for any project manager and leader. Team-building activities go together with good leadership to build a high-performing team.
- **Motivation** The ability to motivate people and understand what motivates different people is a key interpersonal skill for a project manager to have. The following are the most popular motivation theories that a project manager should be aware of:
  - Maslow's hierarchy of needs describes a situation in which people perform at their best when they have the opportunity to be what Maslow refers to as "self-actualized." This is the top of the needs pyramid he describes. People cannot fulfill higher-level needs until lower-level ones are fulfilled, however, and the current need always takes precedence. Figure 3-9 shows the levels in Maslow's hierarchy of needs.

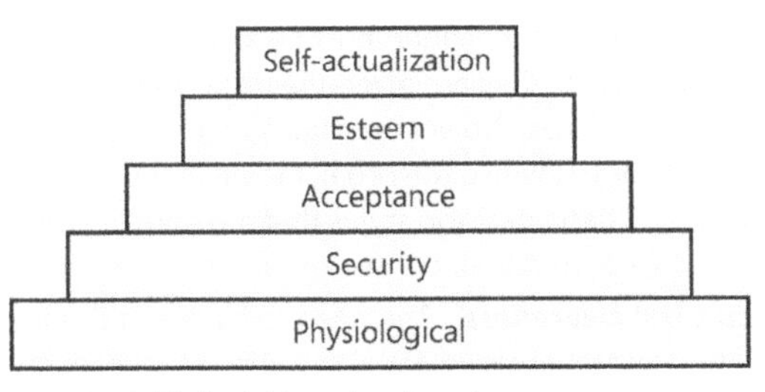

FIGURE 3-9 Maslow's hierarchy of needs

- Vroom's Expectancy Theory states that the expectation of receiving a reward for a certain accomplishment motivates people to work harder, but it works only if the accomplishment is perceived to be achievable.
- Herzberg's Motivation-Hygiene Theory states that hygiene factors (such as company policies, good supervision, and safe and pleasant working conditions) do not motivate, but their absence makes staff unsatisfied. Motivation factors (such as achievement, work, responsibility, and advancement) do motivate, but only if hygiene factors are in place. McClelland's Human Motivation, Achievement, or Three Needs Theory states that people work not for more money but instead for achievement, power, and affiliation; and a manager should use these three needs to motivate employees.
- McGregor's Theory X and Theory Y describe a manager's attitude toward staff or team members. A theory X manager believes that team members are inherently unmotivated to work, require constant supervision, and can't be trusted. A theory Y manager believes that people want to work, can be trusted, and are naturally ambitious and self-motivated.
- *Ouchi's Theory Z*, proposes that organizations should increase worker loyalty and raise worker productivity by offering a job for life and providing support for the employee both in and out of the workplace.

MORE INFO **You can find out more about all the theories of human motivation mentioned here by using the Bing search engine to search the Internet for reputable sites.**

- **Communication** The ability of a project manager to communicate with team members is a critical factor in whether the project is a success or failure. Openness in communication is a foundational concept that assists the project manager in developing a high-performing team and creating a culture of mutual trust. To communicate effectively, a competent project manager is aware of the need to use a variety of different communication styles and also be aware of some of the obstacles to good and effective communication.
- **Influencing** A key interpersonal skill for a project manager to demonstrate in order to effectively lead and manage project team is the ability to influence and get project human resources to align themselves with the project goals and objectives.

- **Decision making** A project manager must be able to demonstrate the ability to make a decision as they are given the responsibility and the authority to do so in many instances. Project managers might choose to make decisions individually or to involve the project team in the decision-making process. There are four basic decision styles that are normally used by project managers: command, consultation, consensus, and the coin flip.
- **Political and cultural awareness** The need to have a sophisticated level of political and culture awareness is essential to a project manager to manage a project team. This is increasingly important as more and more teams are made up either virtually with team members and different geographic locations, or team members from different cultural backgrounds.
- **Negotiation** A key interpersonal skill for the project manager is the ability to negotiate, particularly for obtaining and keeping project resources in the face of competition from the functional manager.
- **Trust building** Successfully leading and managing object team members build on a culture of mutual trust, and they are critical and effective. Team leadership without trust it is extremely difficult for the project manager.
- **Conflict management** Although conflict can at times be a positive and beneficial tool for soliciting lateral thinking, in most instances conflict is perceived as a negative influence on team performance and needs to be addressed promptly, openly, and with a view to resolving the core issues to ensure that it does not adversely affect team performance. The most common causes of conflict between project team members are time constraints, project priorities, resource availability, differences in technical opinions, administrative processes, project cost and budget, and individual personalities. It is the role of the project manager to take responsibility for setting in place ground rules for the accepted and expected behaviors in working with the team. If conflict does arise, the project manager must take responsibility for dealing with the conflict. There are six main ways of dealing with conflict, each with a different outcome, as follows:
  - Withdrawal or avoiding simply avoids dealing with conflict.
  - Forcing involves one party to the conflict pushing his or her viewpoint on another person and trying to have that person adopt it through the use of various forms of power.
  - Smoothing or accommodating tries to resolve conflict by getting parties to agree to disagree and put work ahead of conflict.
  - Collaboration as a conflict resolution technique seeks input from all parties to the conflict and seeks to find some form of compromise between the parties involved in the conflict in order to resolve it.
  - Compromise is a conflict resolution technique in which each party gives something up in order to resolve the conflict. Instead of being a win-win solution, the result can thus often be a lose-lose situation.
  - Confronting or problem solving is the best option for dealing with any conflict because it seeks to deal with the conflict in a permanent manner and resolve it openly.

- **Coaching** A project manager uses coaching of the project team and individuals within it as a way to develop higher levels of performance.

True or false? A project manager needs to display a wide variety and high level of understanding, of interpersonal skills to effectively lead and manage the project team.

Answer: *True.* Project team members respond better individually and collectively to a project manager who displays a high level of interpersonal skills.

Training

To fully develop team members and achieve the goal of a high-performing team, a project manager has to offer training in technical, nontechnical, and soft skills. Training, which can use internal or external trainers, can occur in a classroom environment; on the job; or, increasingly, via remote or online means. Training needs can be agreed upon with team members at regular intervals such as during their performance appraisals, or training can be provided reactively in response to observed needs.

> ***EXAM TIP*** **You should always assume that you have to provide training to team members. This is particularly important if you come across a question in the exam in which a team member does not have the right skills to complete an activity. Your first option is always to get them the required training.**

Team-building activities

One of the primary goals of leading, mentoring, training, and motivating team members is to establish a high-performing team. One of the best ways to achieve this goal is with team-building activities. Team-building activities should be done continuously throughout the life of the project and can take a variety of forms from a small and informal agenda items through to off-site activities.

The Tuckman five-stage model, or ladder, is a convenient way to describe the stages a team of people goes through: forming, storming, norming, performing, and adjourning. Teams can cycle between and within an area, and providing awareness of the model and stages to team members can help propel your team to the performing stage faster. The key point about the model is that your goal is to get your team to the performing stage and keep them there with proactive team management.

Forming behaviors are displayed when team members first meet each other and realize they are part of a group; they are characterized by excitement and anticipation of the work ahead. The next stage the team members go through is the storming phase, in which there can be arguments and political movements as team members determine the hierarchy and their place within it. After the team has completed storming behaviors, it then moves into the norming phase, in which expected and accepted behaviors of the team are established as the team begins to work together. If the team has successfully gone through forming, storming, and norming behaviors, it might reach a performing stage&performing phase and become a well-organized and high-performing team. The project manager needs to keep in mind that a team member leaving or a new team member joining can cause the team to go back to forming and storming behaviors. The final stage in the process is the release of staff from the team as the project is ending.

Figure 3-10 shows the different stages of the Tuckman five-stage model, or ladder, against performance and time. Although the diagram might seem to indicate a straightforward linear progression, the reality is that team dynamics can be highly unstable, and teams are always in danger of slipping backward into storming behaviors.

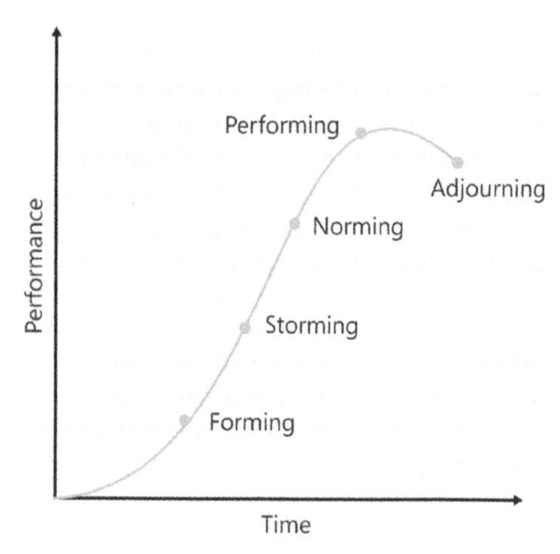

FIGURE 3-10 The Tuckman five-stage model of team development

True or false? After a team has completed storming behaviors, it becomes a high-performing team.

Answer: *False.* Teams first move through forming behaviors, then storming behaviors, and then norming behaviors on the way to becoming a high-performing team.

Recognition and rewards

The human resource management plan sets out ways in which individual team members and the team itself are rewarded. How you choose to recognize and reward your team members directly affects individual levels of motivation and a sense of being part of the team and wider organization. Although money is often seen as an effective reward, research is increasingly telling us that most project team members are motivated by other factors such as the ability to undertake new challenges, have greater autonomy, and develop a sense of purpose about their work.

In addition to tangible rewards and recognition, there are many other ways a project manager can recognize individual and group achievements and contributions. For example, by using public appreciation, handwritten notes, formal written recommendations, and appraisals, a project manager can provide effective recognition to team members.

It is the job of the project manager to ensure that an appropriate recognition and rewards system is in place.

True or false? The best way to reward individual achievement is to give a pay increase.

Answer: *False.* Financial rewards work only on certain occupations; generally, the pool working in the professional sphere of project management responds better to opportunities for professional development, challenge, autonomy, and recognition than they do to financial rewards. It is the role of the project manager to determine the most appropriate recognition and rewards system.

Personnel and team assessment tools

As part of completing the work to maximize team performance, project managers can undertake personnel assessment to give insights to themselves and individual project team members into areas of strength, weakness, and opportunities for improvement. There are a variety of tools that can be used by the project manager, such as surveys, proprietary personnel assessments, structured interviews, and 360° reviews.

One of the goals and objectives of personnel assessment is to carry out project performance appraisals, which can include clarification of an individual's roles and responsibilities, constructive feedback, resolution of issues, and development of individual professional training plans.

Team performance assessments contain information about performance of individuals and the whole project team. They can include an assessment of how well the team is performing as a whole and also individual assessments, such as key performance indicators (KPIs) from a person's job description, an assessment of interpersonal skills, and an assessment of contribution to the organization's goals. They can identify future training needs and contribute to professional development while the team members are on the project and also after they leave.

True or false? Any assessment of an individual or team should be carried out only in a regularly scheduled formal setting.

Answer: *False.* Although individual and team assessments are often carried out in a regularly scheduled formal setting, they can also be carried out on an informal basis.

Observation and conversation

Two of the easiest tools to use when attempting to maximize team performance through leading, mentoring, training, and motivating team members are the skills of observation and conversation. Both of these skills are used by the project manager to stay in close proximity to the work being completed and to the project team culture and attitudes. Most of the other work involved in maximizing team performance can be documented within the project scope, time, and cost baselines. Observation and conversation are notoriously difficult to break down into individual work packages, however, so they should be seen as some of the essential skills that a project manager can use in order to stay in touch with individual project team members and the project team.

True or false? A project manager should be able to use observation of team behaviors to determine whether the team is developing into a high-performing one.

Answer: *True.* By keeping a watchful eye on individual and team behaviors, the project manager should be able to determine whether the team is performing well.

Can you answer these questions?

You can find the answers to these questions at the end of this chapter.

1. You are the project manager on a project that is experiencing some uncertainty about which tools and techniques are most effective for maximizing team performance. Which document should you refer to in order to understand the approach you have chosen to take to maximize team performance?
2. Leadership, communication, negotiation, and motivation are all examples of what sort of skills a project manager should be able to display?
3. You are trying to resolve a conflict between several team members who just met and appear to be arguing for no good reason other than to establish who the senior technician is on the project. According to the Tuckman model of team development, what sort of behaviors are they displaying?
4. What is the best and most effective method of resolving conflict?
5. As a project manager, you have discovered that one of your team members does not have the required skills to complete the project work. Your project sponsor gives you the option to get training for the team member or release the member from the project. What should you do first?

Answers

This section contains the answers to the "Can you answer these questions?" sections in this chapter.

Task 1: Obtain and manage project resources including outsourced deliverables by following the procurement plan, in order to ensure successful project execution.

1. Project resources refer to human resource, equipment, and financial resources required to complete the project work, so the human resource management plan, the cost management plan, and the procurement management plan are the most useful when seeking to obtain and manage project resources.
2. Most project team members are appointed to the project via preassignment.
3. A bidder conference should always be carried out fairly and transparently and offer a level playing field to all prospective sellers. Therefore, in the first instance you should clearly explain to this potential seller that any information is given to all prospective sellers. You might want to escalate the matter and exclude this potential seller from the process entirely.
4. There are many forms of source selection criteria besides price, including technical capability, risk, management approach, financial stability, past performance and experience, and intellectual property rights.
5. The intended end result of procurement negotiations is a contract and agreement signed by both buyer and seller.

Task 2: Execute the tasks as defined in the project plan, in order to achieve the project deliverables within budget and schedule.

1. The three baselines contained in the project plan are the cost, scope, and time baselines.
2. The stakeholder management plan is most useful for guiding a stakeholder expectation to be successfully managed.
3. The communications management plan provides guidance for communications executing tasks and activities, including content and format of project performance reports.
4. The order in which they are naturally developed begins with a collection of work performance data that is then turned into work performance information. It is then used in work performance reports.
5. A unique and verifiable, product, result, or capability to perform the services required to be produced to complete a process, phase, or project is called a deliverable.

Task 3: Implement the quality management plan using the appropriate tools and techniques, in order to ensure that work is being performed according to required quality standards.

1. The process of quality assurance differs from the process of quality control in that quality assurance is focused on the quality processes within the project; quality control is focused on the product being delivered.
2. The best way to determine whether quality processes are being implemented and followed per the quality management plan is through the use of independent and regularly scheduled quality audits.
3. The best tool to be able to determine the 20 percent of problems that are causing 80 percent of quality issues is the Pareto chart.
4. It is the responsibility of the project manager to ensure the quality processes are being followed and implemented per the quality management plan.
5. The process improvement plan is the best document to turn to for guidance to ensure that the project manager and project team are following processes required to obtain continuous improvement and quality processes.

Task 4: Implement approved changes according to the change management plan, in order to meet project requirements.

1. The change management plan guides the project manager in how approved changes are to be implemented.
2. The project manager has responsibility for ensuring that all approved changes are incorporated into existing plans and baselines.
3. Approved change requests involve changes to the work to be performed into the project. Most require extra work to be done, and this work should be immediately reflected in the relevant management plans and baselines.
4. Approved change requests represent a change to the work required on the project, so these changes should be reflected in the WBS for the project.
5. After the work changes required by the approved change requests are incorporated into the relevant project plans and baselines, progress on executing the required work is tracked in the same way that other work in the project is tracked.

Task 5: Implement approved actions, and follow the risk management plan and risk register, in order to minimize the impact of negative risk events on the project.

1. The risk management plan provides guidance to the project manager on how all risk management planning, executing, and monitoring and controlling activities are completed.
2. Work to be done as part of executing activities and tasks on the project is identified and the planned risk responses, whether proactive or reactive, in the risk register.
3. Your best course of action in this case is to consult your risk management plan and follow any guidelines for completing a workaround.
4. The forecast price rise in this example represents a trigger condition that sets off predetermined work to be completed to mitigate the negative risk.
5. After a risk event has occurred, it is no longer uncertain and it represents work to be done on the project.

Task 6: Maximize team performance through leading, mentoring, training, and motivating team members.

1. To understand the particular approach you have chosen to take maximizing team performance, you should consult the human resource management plan.
2. Leadership, communication, negotiation, and motivation are all examples of interpersonal skills.
3. Arguing and conflict are typical storming behaviors.
4. The best and most effective method of resolving conflict is confronting and problem-solving.
5. You should always attempt to get training project team members in the first instance.

CHAPTER 4

Monitoring and controlling the project

The Monitoring and Controlling the Project performance domain covers approximately 25 percent of the Project Management Professional (PMP®) exam. It includes all the activities required to track actual progress against planned progress, detect variances, and manage the change control process. Monitoring and controlling activities and tasks are performed throughout the whole life of the project from project conception to project closure, and it is by completing monitoring and controlling tasks that the project manager and project team can gain insight into how well the project is performing.

This chapter covers the following tasks:

- Task 1: Measure project performance using appropriate tools and techniques, in order to identify and quantify any variances, perform approved corrective actions, and communicate with relevant stakeholders.
- Task 2: Manage changes to the project scope, schedule, and costs by updating the project plan and communicating approved changes to the team, in order to ensure that revised project goals are met.
- Task 3: Ensure that project deliverables conform to the quality standards established on the quality management plan by using appropriate tools and techniques, e.g. testing, inspection, control charts, in order to satisfy customer requirements.
- Task 4: Update the risk register and risk response plan by identifying any new risks, assessing old risks, and determining and implementing appropriate response strategies, in order to manage the impact of risks on the project.
- Task 5: Assess corrective actions on the issue register and determine next steps for unresolved issues by using appropriate tools and techniques, in order to minimize the impact on project schedule, cost, and resources.
- Task 6: Communicate project status to stakeholders for their feedback, in order to ensure the project aligns with business needs.

Task 1: Measure project performance using appropriate tools and techniques, in order to identify and quantify any variances, perform approved corrective actions, and communicate with relevant stakeholders.

The key activities to be completed in this domain task involve using a range of tools and techniques to compare actual project performance versus planned project performance; to discover and analyze any variance between the two; and if variance is discovered, to act on it.

Nearly all the monitoring and controlling work done on a project requires three distinct elements to be performed. The first is to have a description of the work that was planned and a description of the work that is actually occurring. It will take the form of a component of the project management plan or a baseline to describe the work that was planned, and work performance data and information to describe the work that is actually occurring.

Second, there should be tools for detecting and analyzing variances between the work that was planned and the work that is occurring. These tools take many forms depending on the type of work they analyze.

The third element, which is generated by the analysis of the planned versus actual work, takes the form of work performance information and change requests. All change requests are processed according to the documented change control process, and all approved changes are incorporated into the relevant plans and baselines via updates to the project management plan.

Table 4-1 shows each of the project management knowledge areas and the primary inputs relating to planned and actual work, the tools and techniques used for variance analysis, and the primary outputs generated as a result of performing monitoring and controlling tasks.

TABLE 4-1 A description of the primary planned and actual work, variance analysis tools and techniques, and outputs of each of the project management monitoring and controlling knowledge areas

KNOWLEDGE AREA	DESCRIPTION OF PLANNED AND ACTUAL WORK	VARIANCE ANALYSIS TOOLS AND TECHNIQUES	OUTPUTS
Scope management	■ Project management plan ■ Requirements documentation ■ Requirements traceability matrix ■ Work performance data	■ Variance analysis	■ Work performance information ■ Change requests ■ Project management plan updates

KNOWLEDGE AREA	DESCRIPTION OF PLANNED AND ACTUAL WORK	VARIANCE ANALYSIS TOOLS AND TECHNIQUES	OUTPUTS
Time management	■ Project management plan ■ Project schedule ■ Work performance data	■ Performance reviews ■ Project management software and scheduling tools ■ Modeling techniques	■ Work performance information ■ Schedule forecasts ■ Change requests ■ Project management plan updates
Cost management	■ Project management plan ■ Project funding requirements ■ Work performance data	■ Earned value management ■ Forecasting ■ Performance reviews ■ Project management software	■ Work performance information ■ Cost forecasts ■ Change requests ■ Project management plan updates
Quality management	■ Project management plan ■ Quality metrics ■ Quality checklists ■ Work performance data ■ Approved change request ■ Deliverables	■ Seven basic quality tools ■ Statistical sampling ■ Inspection ■ Approved change requests review	■ Quality control measurements ■ Validated changes ■ Verified deliverables ■ Work performance information ■ Change requests ■ Project management plan updates
Communications management	■ Project management plan ■ Project communications ■ Issue log ■ Work performance data	■ Information management systems ■ Expert judgment ■ Meetings	■ Work performance information ■ Change requests ■ Project management plan updates

KNOWLEDGE AREA	DESCRIPTION OF PLANNED AND ACTUAL WORK	VARIANCE ANALYSIS TOOLS AND TECHNIQUES	OUTPUTS
Risk management	■ Project management plan ■ Risk register ■ Work performance data ■ Work performance reports	■ Risk reassessment ■ Risk audits ■ Variance and trend analysis ■ Technical performance measurements ■ Reserve analysis ■ Meetings	■ Work performance information ■ Change request ■ Project management plan updates
Procurement management	■ Project management plan ■ Procurement documents ■ Agreements ■ Approved change requests ■ Work performance reports ■ Work performance data	■ Contract change control system ■ Procurement performance reviews ■ Inspections and audits ■ Performance reporting ■ Claims administration	■ Work performance information ■ Change request ■ Project management plan updates
Stakeholder management	■ Project management plan ■ Issue log ■ Work performance data	■ Information management systems ■ Expert judgment ■ Meetings	■ Work performance information ■ Change request ■ Project management plan updates

EXAM TIP **Note that the human resource management knowledge area does not have a specific monitoring and controlling tasks associated with it. This is because it is generally assumed that in a functional or matrix organization, it is the functional manager, not the project manager, who should take responsibility for monitoring and controlling project human resources. The project manager does a lot of acquiring, developing, and managing human resources during project execution domain tasks (as discussed in Chapter 3, "Executing the project").**

MORE INFO **You can find out more about monitoring and controlling work on a project by reading the Monitor and Control Project Work process in Chapter 4 of the PMBOK® Guide, 5th edition and in Chapter 2 of the PMP® Training Kit.**

Exam need to know...

- Project management plan

  For example: Where can the project manager find guidelines on how to complete the monitoring and controlling work to be done on the project?
- Schedule forecasts

  For example: What documents are used to measure actual project schedule progress against?
- Cost forecasts

  For example: What documents are used to measure actual project costs against in order to detect variance?
- Work performance data

  For example: What is the raw information gathered from observations, inspections, and testing better known as?
- Work performance information

  For example: After analyzing the raw work performance data a variety of analytical techniques can be applied to develop what?
- Work performance reports

  For example: How is work performance information presented to stakeholders to keep them informed about project progress?
- Analytical techniques

  For example: What tools and techniques can be applied to determine if a variance between actual and planned work is occurring?
- Meetings

  For example: What is the best way to involve project team members and other relevant stakeholders in the monitoring and controlling work that must be done on a project?
- Monitoring project procurements

  For example: How are project procurement checked to ensure they are being fulfilled per the agreements?
- Change requests

  For example: What is the best way to ensure that corrective or preventive action is recorded and assessed?
- Project management plan updates

  For example: What document can be updated as a result of variances discovered and acted upon during monitoring and controlling work?
- Issue log

  For example: Where is the best place to record issues that do not warrant inclusion on the watch list or risk register?

Project management plan

The project management plan and all its subsidiary plans, baselines, and other documents are essential for carrying out monitoring and controlling activities and tasks. These documents provide guidance to the project manager about what work is planned, and the project manager can use this description and check it against what is actually occurring to see whether any change control activities need to be performed. To successfully complete monitoring and controlling activities, it is absolutely essential that there is some form of documented and approved planning document.

The project management plan is the sum of the component plans, each of which relates to a particular area. The project management plan can include any of the following if appropriate to manage the project being completed:

- Scope management plan
- Configuration management plan
- Requirements management plan
- Schedule management plan
- Cost management plan
- Quality management plan
- Process improvement plan
- Human resource management plan
- Staffing management plan
- Communications management plan
- Risk management plan
- Procurement management plan
- Stakeholder management plan
- Change management plan
- Scope baseline
- Cost baseline or budget
- Time baseline or project schedule

The project manager chooses the appropriate plan, baseline, or document to carry out monitoring controlling activities and tasks.

True or false? It is possible to manage and assess project performance without a fully developed plan or baseline as long as the project manager is careful.

Answer: *False*. The only possible and professional way to manage and assess project performance is by comparing actual performance against planned performance. A description of the planned performance comes from a fully developed plan or baseline.

> ***EXAM TIP*** **In the exam, you should always look to have some sort of planning document to measure actual work against. If you don't have a detailed planning document, you can't accurately measure progress and variance.**

Schedule forecasts

Schedule forecasts, which are created by the work associated with planning of project time, are used to assess the planned schedule performance. They are then compared with actual schedule performance, and corrective or preventive change action is required if there is a variance between the two. Schedule forecasts are normally be represented by project network diagrams and Gantt charts. Figure 4-1 shows an example of a network diagram.

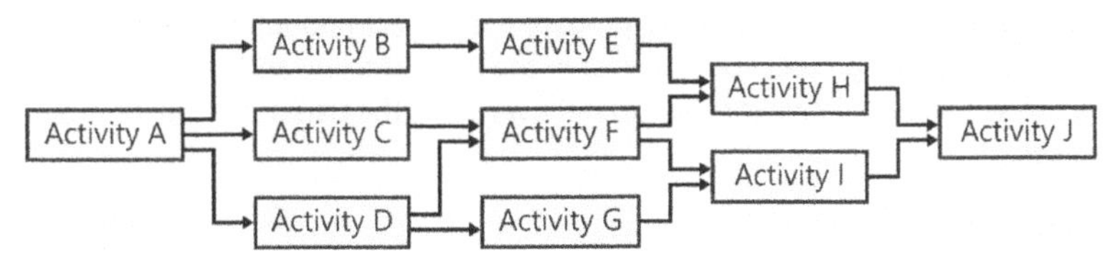

FIGURE 4-1 A network diagram showing the relationship among activities to be completed

Figure 4-2 shows an example of a Gantt chart.

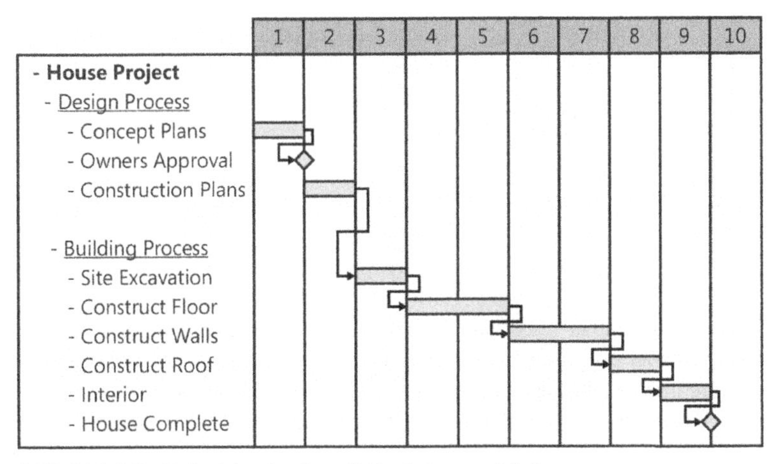

FIGURE 4-2 A Gantt chart showing the activities to be completed

True or false? To accurately assess whether the project is performing as forecast in relation to time, it is essential that the project manager has access to either the project network diagram or a Gantt chart.

Answer: *True.* Schedule forecasts set out what the expectations are for the project in terms of time performance, and they are used to compare work performance data and information relating to what is actually occurring in relation to time to determine whether there is a variance between the two.

> ***EXAM TIP*** **The two most common forms of schedule forecasts are represented by project network diagrams and Gantt charts. They are the results of project time management planning activities.**

MORE INFO **You can find out more about project time management planning activities by reading Chapter 6 of the PMBOK® Guide, 5th edition or Chapter 3 of the PMP Training Kit.**

Cost forecasts

Cost forecasts come in the form of both individual cost estimates and the approved project budget. The cost forecasts take individual cost estimates and use the time period in which they will be incurred to prepare the project budget. Figure 4-3 shows an example of a project cost forecast in the form of a line and bar graph. The line shows the cumulative forecast spend over time; the bars show the monthly forecast spend.

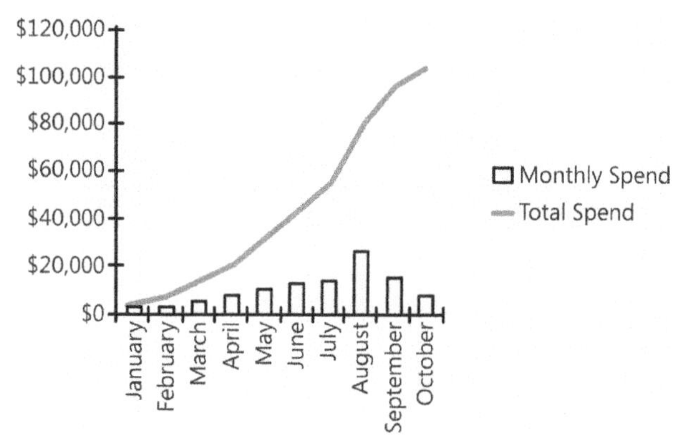

FIGURE 4-3 A chart showing both cumulative cost forecasts and cost forecasts per month

In determining whether the project is performing as expected in relation to cost, the project manager uses both individual cost estimates and the project budget and then compare them against actual work data and information in relation to cost. If a variance between the two is detected, the project manager can take some form of corrective, preventive, or other change action.

NOTE **The actual cost performance data and information is easily obtained from the cost accounting system that the project is using to track actual costs spent. A project manager should always have authority to monitor actual costs spent in real time and know how to use the organization's cost accounting system to extract the data needed.**

True or false? An approved project budget can be used by the project manager to determine whether the project is spending money as planned.

Answer: *True.* The project budget takes individual cost estimates and applies them to the time period in which the costs will be incurred to develop a project budget. This project budget can then be used to track whether the project is performing as expected in relation to cost.

EXAM TIP In the exam, remember the difference between the terms "cost" and budget." "Cost" refers to individual costs for specific activities or tasks, whereas "budget" is costs over time and reflects the time period in which the costs will be incurred.

MORE INFO You can find out more about the planning processes that produce the project budget by reading Chapter 7 of the PMBOK® Guide, 5th edition and Chapter 5 of the PMP® Training Kit.

Work performance data

Work performance data includes raw observations, measurements, and information gathered about project performance. It is most useful after it has been analyzed and has become work performance information. In relation to this particular monitoring and control task, having the correct work performance data and analyzing it correctly is essential to be able to accurately measure project performance.

Work performance data can be collected about any aspect of project performance, including how the project is performing in relation to scope, time, cost, quality, human resources, risk, procurement, communications, and stakeholder management.

Other tasks in the Monitoring and Controlling the Project domain deal with the specifics of managing changes to project scope, schedule, costs, quality standards, and the risk register (the specific forms of work performance data applicable to these areas will be discussed in more detail in the sections to follow).

True or false? Work performance data refers only to the scope, cost, and time baseline.

Answer: *False*. Work performance data can be gathered about any aspect of the project, not only the scope, time and cost baselines.

EXAM TIP For the exam, remember that work performance data about project performance is collected and then analyzed to become work performance information. This work performance information is included in work performance reports. Remember that work performance data becomes work performance information, which is included in work performance reports.

Work performance information

Work performance data becomes work performance information after it has been subject to a variety of appropriate analytical techniques. By analyzing work performance data and producing work performance information, a project manager can make sense of raw observations and measurements and use this work performance information to assist in determining whether the project is performing as expected. Work performance information can be generated about any aspect of the project.

NOTE Project management software is a widely used tool that can greatly assist a project manager and project team members. It can be used to gather work performance data, analyze it, and turn it into work performance information; it can also produce work performance reports. There are many examples of project management software, including Microsoft Project.

True or false? Work performance information includes raw observations, data, and measurements collected about project performance.

Answer: *False*. Work performance data includes raw observations, data, and measurements collected about project performance. Work performance data becomes work performance information after it has been subjected to analytical techniques.

EXAM TIP To successfully complete any monitoring and controlling task, you need some sort of work performance information to be able to compare against approved plans, baselines, and forecasts to detect variance. In the exam, if you are presented with a scenario that requires you to undertake any form of monitoring and controlling activities, you should first ensure that you have the correct work performance information to enable you to detect variance.

Work performance reports

Work performance reports are the text, graphical, physical, or electronic representation of work performance information that is sent to stakeholders to communicate project progress, decisions, or actions. Work performance reports are in the form that best suits both the information contained within them and the stakeholders' communication requirements. They enable the project manager to tell stakeholders, including project team members, how the project is progressing, whether variances have been detected, and about any actions taken as a result of the variances that were detected.

Common forms of work performance reports include weekly updates to the project team and project sponsor in the form of text; numbers; graphs; pictures; or more specific forms such as traffic lights or red, amber, green (RAG) analysis.

True or false? Work performance reports can be used by the project manager to keep stakeholders informed about how well the project is performing in a number of ways.

Answer: *True*. The main focus of work performance reports is to take work performance information and present it to be used to communicate project performance to stakeholders. By effectively communicating relevant project performance information to stakeholders, the project manager can proactively influence and manage project expectations.

Analytical techniques

There is a wide variety of analytical techniques that can be applied to work performance information to determine how the project is progressing. Each of the analytical techniques determines whether a variance is occurring between what was planned and what is actually occurring on the project. This variance analysis aids the project manager in gaining an early understanding of potential changes to the project.

It is up to the project manager to choose the appropriate analytical technique and apply it to the correct work performance information to get meaningful results. If the use of analytical techniques reveals that the project is not performing as forecast, the project manager must take action.

The most common forms of analytical techniques are these:

- Regression analysis
- Grouping methods
- Causal analysis
- Root cause analysis
- Failure mode and effect analysis (FMEA)
- Fault tree analysis (FTA)
- Reserve analysis
- Trend analysis
- Earned value management and forecasting methods
- Variance analysis

MORE INFO **You can find out more about each of these analytical techniques by using the Bing Internet search engine.**

Of these analytical techniques, the most commonly used are root cause analysis, FMEA, trend analysis, earned value management, and variance analysis (covered in more detail in the following sections).

True or false? Analytical techniques are used by the project manager to determine whether there is any variance between the work that was planned to be completed on the project and the work that is actually being performed on the project.

Answer: *True.* There is a wide variety of analytical techniques that are available to the project manager to determine whether there is any variance between the work that was planned to be completed on the project and the work that is actually being performed on the project. It is the responsibility of the project manager to choose the appropriate analytical technique.

EXAM TIP **In the exam, it is important to understand that analytical techniques are used to determine whether there is any variance between what you planned to do, which is described in the various plans and baselines, and what is actually occurring on the project, which is revealed by collecting work performance data and analyzing it to produce work performance information..**

Root cause analysis

Root cause analysis is a technique used in many areas of project management to determine the actual root cause (instead of the symptom) of an identified issue. It is more effective to determine the root cause of an issue and treat it than it is to treat the symptom that might reoccur if the root cause is not identified and treated. For project performance analysis, it is used to determine the root cause of an identified variance. The results of root cause analysis are displayed by using the cause and effect diagram, also known as the Ishikawa or fishbone diagram.

Figure 4-4 shows an example of a cause and effect diagram for an identified variance detected in the project transport costs.

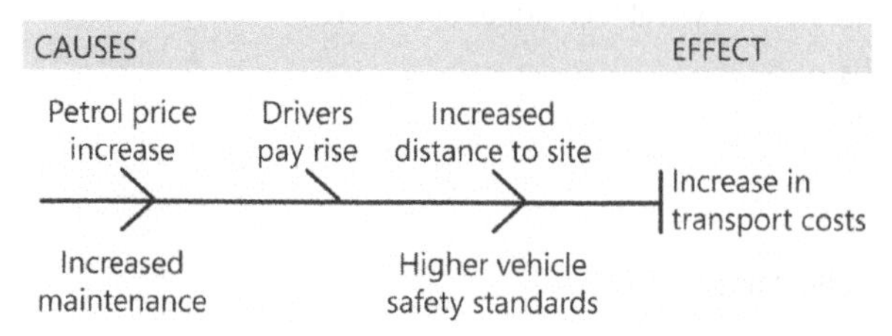

FIGURE 4-4 Identification of potential causes of increase in project transport costs

In addition to the cause and effect diagram, a popular and effective way of determining actual root cause is to apply the "five why's" technique. This technique seeks to ask the question "why" several times to determine why a particular cause occurred to get to the absolute actual cause. For the information shown in Figure 4-3, the five why's analysis could ask this question: "Why is there increase maintenance cost?" It could continue to ask the same question of each subsequent answer to get to the root cause.

MORE INFO **You can find out more about root cause analysis by using the Bing search engine.**

True or false? Root cause analysis tools and techniques can be used by the project manager to determine what is actually causing any variances between what was planned to be done on the project and what is actually occurring.

Answer: *True.* The main purpose of any root cause analysis is to enable the project manager to go beyond the visible symptoms of any variance detected between what was planned and what is actually occurring on the project, and then determine the root causes. By determining the root cause, any corrective or preventive actions can focus on the underlying cause rather than the visible symptom.

Failure mode and effect analysis (FMEA)

Failure mode and effect analysis (FMEA) is an analytical technique that identifies all potential failures in a process or product, and then determines what the effect of failure will be. It also looks at the effect of one identified failure on the chances of other failures occurring and the combined effect of multiple failures. If variances are detected during the assessment and analysis of project performance, the use of failure mode and effect analysis gives the project manager an understanding of the likely cause and impact of the variance.

Trend analysis

Trend analysis is a simple technique of using existing data about the difference between what was planned on the project and what was actually occurring, and then extrapolating from the data a likely future scenario based on the observed trends. In this way, a project manager can use work performance information and data to determine what a likely future scenario will be if the trend continues. For example, if a variance of the project budget is observed, trend analysis can forecast what the likely final impact on the project will be if this particular trend continues to occur.

Earned value management

The earned value management system provides a project manager with an effective way to establish what has occurred in the past in relation to both project cost and time. This information can be used to forecast likely future cost and time performance scenarios by using a range of mathematical equations. Earned value management takes the original project cost baseline, the planned value of the work you had expected to have completed by now, the earned value of the work you have completed by now, and the actual cost of delivering that value to determine what the project cost and schedule performance to date is. It can then forecast what the likely costs at completion will be by using the following formulas:

- **Budget at completion (BAC)** The original forecast budget for the project.
- **Planned value (PV)** The amount of value that you should have earned by this time in the project. Because the total planned value (PV) for a project equals the BAC, you can determine the planned value by simply determining how far through the project you are in relation to time and then mapping this back to the approved cost baseline to establish the PV. Figure 4-5 demonstrates how to determine the PV from the BAC.

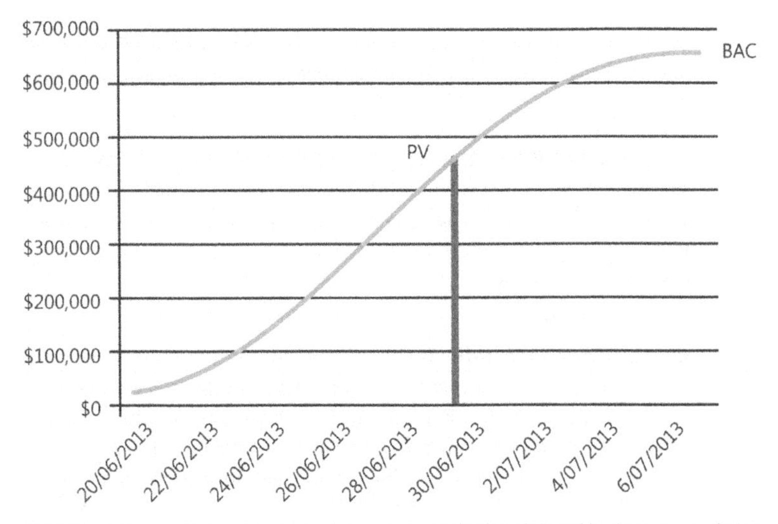

FIGURE 4-5 The project cost baseline showing planned value (PV) and budget at completion (BAC)

- **Earned value (EV)** The value of the work that has been completed. This is not the actual cost of the work that has been completed; it is the original ascribed value from the approved cost baseline for the value of the work.
- **Actual cost (AC)** The actual realized cost you incurred for the work that you have done to date. You can get a record of this from your accounts system.

  Figure 4-6 shows the planned value (PV), earned value (EV), and actual cost (AC) on a single graph. Incidentally, it shows a project in trouble in terms of both time and cost because the AC is above the PV, and the EV is less than the PV. Don't forget that the total PV equals the BAC.

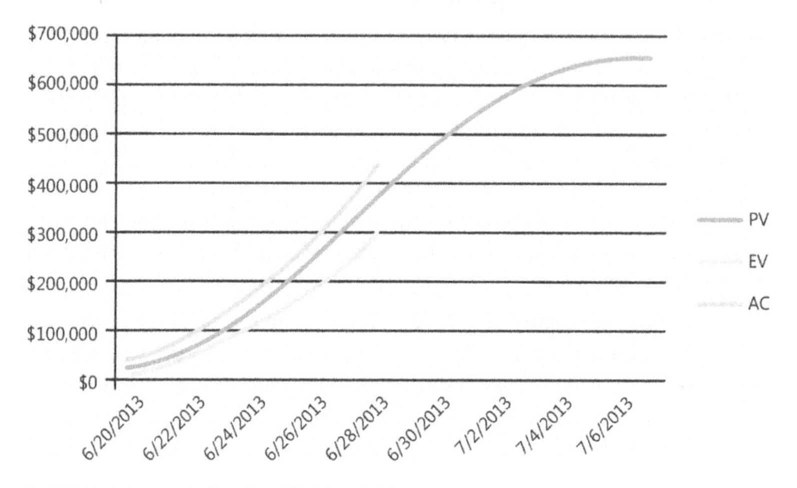

FIGURE 4-6 A record of project PV, EV, and AC

EXAM TIP **On most questions, you will be challenged to extract the BAC, PV, EV, and AC from the scenario given. Take your time to ensure that you are extracting the correct figures.**

- **Cost variance (CV)** This is simply the difference between the value of what you expected to have earned (EV) and the actual cost (AC) at this point. A positive cost variance is good and shows that the project is under budget; a negative cost variance is bad and shows that the project is over budget. The formula is as follows:

  $CV = EV - AC$
- **Cost performance index (CPI)** One of the limitations of the CV equation is that it gives you a simple gross figure. You cannot tell whether a $10,000 cost variance is significant in your project. If you are working on a $50,000 project, it would be significant; if you are working on a $10 million contract, it might not be so significant. The CPI calculation tells you the magnitude of the variance. A CPI of more than 1 is good because it means that the project is under budget; a CPI of less than 1 is bad because it means that the project is over budget. For example, if you have a CPI of 1.1, it means that for every

dollar you spend on the project, you get a $1.10 return. The formula is the following:

$CPI = EV/AC$

- **Schedule variance (SV)** This tells you whether you are ahead or behind your planned schedule. It is the difference between the EV and the PV. A positive SV is good because it means that you are ahead of schedule; a negative SV is bad because it means that you are behind schedule. The formula is the following:

  $SV = EV-PV$

- **Schedule performance index (SPI)** This is a ratio of the EV and PV that enables you to better determine the magnitude of any variance. An SPI of more than 1 is good because it means that the project is ahead of time; an SPI of less than 1 is bad because it means that the project is behind schedule. For example, if you have an SPI of 0.95, it means that every day you spend working on the project, you are getting a 0.95 day return. The formula is the following:

  $SPI = EV/PV$

EXAM TIP **A quick and easy way to remember the formula for CV, CPI, SP, and SPI is that each of the formulas starts with EV. If it is a formula relating to variance, CV or SV, the next symbol is a minus sign. If it is a formula relating to a performance index, CPI or SPI, the next symbol is a divide sign. If the formula is in relation to cost, CV or CPI, the final part of the formula is AC. If the formula is in relation to schedule, SV or SPI, the final part of the formula is PV.**

True or false? It is correct to report that a project is doing well in terms of both cost and time when the CPI is calculated to be .95 and the SPI is calculated to be 1.06.

Answer: *False*. In this example, the project is doing well in relation to time because the SPI is greater than 1, but it is not performing well in terms of cost because the CPI is less than 1.

Forecasting methods are the process of taking time and cost performance to date and using this information to forecast a likely future scenario. The time and cost performance measurements are CV, SV, CPI, and SPI. You can use these measurements and the following formulas to forecast a likely project cost at completion, the amount of money required to complete the project, and the difference between what you originally thought it would cost and what you now think it will cost.

- **Estimate at completion (EAC)** There are many ways to calculate a forecast estimate at completion (EAC). Keep in mind that in order to forecast a likely future cost or time frame for the project, you use historical information. Therefore, the quality of your EAC calculation will depend entirely on the quality of the historical information that you are using. The following four formulas use different inputs to calculate the EAC. Each one gives a different answer for the same project:

- **EAC = BAC/CPI** This is perhaps the simplest of the EAC calculations because it simply takes the original BAC and divides it by the CPI. Obviously, this is a useful calculation if your cost performance to date is indicative of your likely cost performance going forward. By the same measure, it is not a good calculation to use if your cost performance to date is not indicative of your cost performance in the future.
- **EAC = AC + ETC** Simply adding your ETC to your actual cost AC spent to date is an effective way to determine your EAC. However, the method by which you determine your ETC calculation will have a great effect on whether this formula is accurate.
- **EAC = AC + (BAC–EV)** This formula takes the AC spent to date and adds the total BAC with the current EV subtracted.
- **EAC = AC + ((BAC–EV)/(CPI × SPI))** This formula takes into account both the CPI and SPI and applies them to the value of the work left to complete.

EXAM TIP **You will definitely be asked questions relating to earned value management in the exam. Memorize these formulas and write them all down on a piece of scratch paper as soon as you start the exam.**

- **Estimate to complete (ETC)** The ETC calculation is simply the forecast of the remaining costs to be incurred on the project. The easiest way to calculate this is simply to subtract the AC spent to date from the EAC. The formula is the following:

  ETC = EAC – AC

- **Variance at completion (VAC)** The VAC calculation is simply the difference between what you originally thought the project was going to cost (BAC) and what you now think it will cost (EAC). A negative variance is bad; a positive variance is good. The formula is the following:

  VAC = BAC – EAC

EXAM TIP **In the exam, you will often be presented with a scenario that requires you to work out one set of figures before you can work out another set of figures. For example, you might be required to work out the EAC by using either CPI or SPI, but will not be given the CPI figures or SPI figures. You will instead be given figures for EC, AC, and PV, and be expected to work out either the CPI or the SPI first.**

- **To-complete performance index (TCPI)** The TCPI tells you the rate at which you have to work to achieve either the EAC or BAC, depending on which one you are targeting. A TCPI of less than 1 is good; a TCPI of more than 1 is bad. If you are using the original budget at completion as your target, the formula is the following:

  TCPI = (BAC-EV)/ (BAC-AC)

  If you are using the estimate at completion as the target, the formula for TCPI is the following:

  TCPI = (BAC-EV)/ (EAC-AC)

EXAM TIP **When doing any calculations in the exam, round your answer to two decimal places, but be prepared for an answer that is slightly different due to slight differences in the approach to rounding of decimal places.**

MORE INFO **You can find out more about the earned value management system by reading the Practice Standard for Earned Value Management, 2nd edition (Project Management Institute, 2011).**

NOTE **The earned value management is the default method used by many project managers to determine how well the project is performing in relation to both cost and time, and to use this performance information to forecast what the likely end cost or time will be for the project. If you don't already use the earned value management system on your project, it is recommended that you undertake training in this area and begin to use it. There are several software products available (including Microsoft Project), which can automatically calculate earned value management on a project.**

Meetings

As a tool and technique used to discover and analyze project performance and variance, meetings enable a project manager to involve the immediate project team members, wider project team members, and other selected stakeholders. Although the project manager should take ultimate responsibility for monitoring project performance and acting on any variances, all these monitoring and controlling tasks are better carried out with the input and oversight of other project team members and stakeholders with relevant experience.

To derive benefits from meetings, it is important that they are run professionally. Here are some tips for running effective meetings:

- Send out an agenda.
- Set ground rules about meeting attendance, preparation, start time, participation, and finish time.
- Leave nonagenda items for last or for outside of the meeting.
- Start on time and finish on time.
- Include only the people who need to be there only for the time they need to be there.
- Don't let people talk over each other.
- Have someone take concise minutes and circulate them after the meeting.
- Follow up on action points to ensure that they are being completed.

True or false? Meetings are primarily used as a team building technique.

Answer: *False*. Meetings serve many purposes, including as a team building tool. Project meetings can also be a very valuable communications tool that enable the team to get together to share technical information and make decisions that enable the project to proceed and succeed. Beyond enabling decision making, meetings are also useful forums to establish and maintain interpersonal relationships and define the expected team culture.

Monitoring project procurements

Some analytical techniques are used specifically for certain aspects of the project management plan; others can be used in many project management areas. Other domain tasks in this chapter focus on most of them, but three tools and techniques are associated with procurement management and are discussed here:

- **Procurement performance review** Usually carried out by the buyer of goods or services. The buyer conducts a structured review of how well the supplier is delivering the product, service, or result. The buyer uses product inspections and audits of the contractual terms to determine whether the seller is meeting the obligations.
- **Contract change control system** Defines how any changes will be made to contracts used on the project. It is part of the integrated change control systems of the project, and because contracts are formal legal documents, any changes to them need to be formal and legal. Both buyer and seller should ensure that all contractual changes are recorded and agreed to.
- **Claims administration** A technique for recording any disputes and disagreement about variances in the contracts the project is using. As part of the work involved in monitoring progress of contractual performance, claims might arise by either the buyer or seller, and they need to be monitored, recorded, and resolved. The preferred method of resolving contract claims is by negotiation, and a well-written contract should spell out exactly how claims will be monitored and resolved. Both buyer and seller will be actively involved in the settlement of any claims.

EXAM TIP **Remember that in the exam the word "claim" means dispute, disagreement, or appeal of a contract. This might differ from your normal use of the word.**

True or false? Monitoring of project procurement activities is done by both buyer and seller.

Answer: *True.* A contract is between a buyer and seller, so when it comes to monitoring performance of the agreed-upon contractual terms, it is up to both buyer and seller to take responsibility. Both want to ensure the other party is meeting the agreed-upon expectations and take action if not.

MORE INFO **You can find out more about managing project contracts by reading Chapter 12 of the PMBOK® Guide, 5th edition or Chapter 10 of the PMP Training Kit.**

Change requests

As a result of completing monitoring and controlling tasks and measuring project performance using appropriate tools and techniques, a project manager and project team can identify variances between the work that was planned to occur and the work that is actually occurring. If variances are detected, they need to be dealt with in an appropriate manner. The best way to deal with identified variances is for the project manager to treat them as a potential change to the project and issue a change request that requires a corrective, preventive, or other action to eliminate the variance or change project documents, plans, and baselines to reflect and accept the variance.

A change request can take many forms; it can be a simple email record, a change request template of a few pages, or a new business case if it is a significant change to the project. All change requests should be noted on the change register or log, and their status should be tracked. If a change request is approved, the actions and the work required by should be incorporated into the relevant project plans, baseline, and document.

All change requests should be processed in accordance with the documented change control process. This process generally involves the project manager having some delegated authority to consider change requests and make decisions on some of the smaller changes. It also requires the project manager to submit more significant changes to a change control board, which takes responsibility for evaluating the impact of the change and making a decision about whether it should be approved or declined.

True or false? Documented change requests should be raised only for significant project changes.

Answer: *False.* All changes to a project should be documented in some way. The level of documentation can reflect the size of the change request. Smaller changes can be documented in simple and straightforward documents; more significant changes can use a change control template or a business case.

> ***EXAM TIP*** **In the exam, if presented with the scenario that a change request is to be considered, the default scenario to assume is that your project has a documented change control process that has given delegated authority to some degree to the project manager, and that there is a change control board that meets during change control meetings to consider more significant change requests.**

Project management plan updates

Any change requests that are approved will be reflected in the relevant project management plans and baselines. As such, some of the more important outputs of this particular monitoring and controlling task are updates to the project management plan. These updates can affect any part of the project management plan, including any of the plans, baselines, or other documents.

> ***NOTE*** **In any project, it is important to have an appropriate configuration management system that enables a project manager to record and track the most important aspects of the project. These aspects can be versions of changes, issues, plans, documents, parts being used on the project, or iterations of deliverables. All these individual components of the project plan should have unique identifiers so that their status and whereabouts are known.**

True or false? The original project management plan should never be changed. Instead, any changes should be recorded separately so that they can easily be identified.

Answer: *False*. You should keep records of previous versions of any part of the project management plan, but the active version of the plan should always include all approved changes and project management plan updates.

> ***EXAM TIP*** **Keep in mind that the project scope, time, and cost baselines are made up of where you originally started plus any and all approved changes. As soon as a change is approved in relation to scope, time, or cost, it is immediately incorporated into the baseline and the baseline changes.**

Issue log

The issue log is a place to record any issues that stakeholders raise during monitoring and controlling tasks. Any issues that are discovered that do not justify escalation to the watch list, risk register, or having a change request raised can be recorded in the issue log.

True or false? If an issue becomes large enough, it is escalated to the risk register.

Answer: *True*. The issue log is the place to record issues. If they become serious enough for full consideration of impact and development of risk-response strategies, they are escalated to the risk register.

Can you answer these questions?

You can find the answers to these questions at the end of this chapter.

1. Can you describe the elements that all monitoring and controlling work includes?
2. If you have applied analytical techniques to work performance data, what will the result be?
3. What are the two main benefits of holding meetings as part of monitoring and controlling work?
4. If you have an AC of $4,500, a PV of $5,000, and an SPI of 1.1, what is your CPI?
5. Who should take responsibility for monitoring project procurements?

Task 2: Manage changes to the project scope, schedule, and costs by updating the project plan and communicating approved changes to the team, in order to ensure that revised project goals are met.

This domain task encompasses all the activities and work required to document, assess, and make decisions about possible changes to the project scope, schedule, or cost baselines. It is similar to other monitoring and controlling tasks in that it uses a description of the work to be done and compares it with the actual work being performed in relation to project scope, schedule, or costs. If variances are detected, change requests are assessed.

> ***MORE INFO*** **You can find out more about this domain task by reading about the Perform Integrated Change Control, Control Scope, Control Schedule, and Control Costs processes in the PMBOK® Guide, 5th edition; or the respective parts of the PMP® Training Kit.**

Exam need to know...

- Project management plan

  For example: What document provides guidance on how scope, time, and cost are to be managed?
- Baselines

  For example: What documents provide the information against which actual project progress is measured?
- Change requests

  For example: If a variance is detected between the scope baseline and work performance information about the scope of work being completed, what should a project manager do?
- Change control process

  For example: How are all potential changes to a project assessed?
- Change control tools

  For example: How are change requests evaluated and decisions made about whether they should be approved?
- Meetings

  For example: What is the best forum for project team members to use to exchange technical information about project time performance?

Project management plan

The project management plan is essential for managing changes to the project scope, schedule, and costs. The project management plan contains the scope management plan, the schedule management plan, and the cost management plan; as well as the respective scope, schedule, and cost baselines of the project.

The project management plan also contains the change management plan that will describe how changes to the project are documented, evaluated, and processed. It is by using these plans and baselines that variances can be detected and assessed in any of these areas.

If any variances are detected, the project manager can raise a change request that requires corrective or preventive actions, or an update to a plan or baseline. If a change request is raised, it should be documented on the change register or log and then assessed via the approved change control process for the project. After a change is approved, it becomes a part of the plan or baseline.

True or false? The project management plan describes only high-level work to be done on the project; the project manager cannot use it to guide specific work.

Answer: *False*. The project management plan is made up of all the other planning outputs that include plans, baselines, and documents that refer to specific areas on the project. The project management plan will guide the project manager on all aspects of the project.

Baselines

Project baselines provide a description of the planned work to be done on the project in relation to cost, time, or scope. By comparing actual work performed against a baseline, any variance can be detected and acted on.

The scope baseline is made up of the scope statement, work breakdown structure (WBS), and work breakdown structure dictionary (WBS dictionary). The cost baseline is the approved project budget that represents costs over time. The schedule or time baseline is the approved project schedule. Each of these individual baselines provides a solid metric against which actual performance can be compared.

True or false? Any baseline must always represent both what was originally approved and all approved changes to it.

Answer: *True*. A baseline incorporates the original agreed-upon scope, time, and cost, plus any and all approved changes to it.

> ***EXAM TIP*** **Remember during the exam that if you approve any changes to a baseline, these changes must be incorporated into the baseline.**

Change requests

After comparing the actual work being performed in relation to scope, time, or cost against the planned work to be performed in these areas, a change request should be raised if a variance is detected. Variance can be detected using any one or more of the tools discussed in the previous domain task. For detecting changes in scope, time, or cost, the main variance tools are these:

- Variance analysis
- Performance reviews
- Project management software and scheduling tools
- Modeling techniques
- Earned value management
- Forecasting
- Performance reviews
- Project management software

A change request can take many forms, depending on the agreed-upon change management plan. A change request can be initiated verbally, but must always be documented. If it is a small change, the change request documentation reflects it and is concise in nature. If it is a large change, the documentation is comprehensive and describes the change and impacts that it might have on any part of the project. All change requests should be given a unique number as part of the configuration management system.

After a change request is approved, it becomes a description of work to be performed on the project and should be used as an input into executing domain tasks. It is also important to monitor and control the change request to ensure that the work it requires is completed as expected.

EXAM TIP **It is very important that you remember that an approved change request becomes a description of work to be done on the project and becomes part of the project scope, so it is used as an input into the executing tasks. As with other descriptions of work to be performed on the project, there needs to be an element of checking to ensure that the work is done is expected.**

True or false? All change requests, no matter how small, must be documented.

Answer: *True*. To keep track of all changes to the project, it is important that all changes, no matter how small, are documented to ensure that scope creep does not occur. Scope creep happens when there are undocumented small changes made to the project so what is being delivered does not match what is documented on the project.

A project manager should ensure that all change requests are documented to avoid gold plating. Gold plating occurs when there is an opportunity to deliver more than the customer expects, and this work is undertaken without documenting it. A project manager and project team should always look for ways to exceed customer expectations, but if additional work is identified, it should be subject to a documented change request.

EXAM TIP **In the exam, you should keep a close eye on any question that presents a scenario in which you have the opportunity to carry on with small changes to a project without documenting them. Remember that all change requests must be documented and evaluated; then a decision is made.**

Change control process

The change management plan outlines the particular change control process that all potential changes to the project must go through. It is important that this is decided early on in the project, preferably during the planning stages. The change control process describes how all changes are to be documented and assessed, and how decisions are made about whether they are approved or declined.

NOTE **A typical change control process gives some delegated authority to the project manager to make decisions about whether the change has merit, and also some**

delegated authority to make a decision about whether the change should be approved or declined. This delegated authority enables the project manager to keep the project moving swiftly, as long as the changes are within the agreed-upon scope, time, and cost parameters of the project.

Larger changes that are outside the delegated authority of the project manager should go to a change control board at regularly scheduled change control meetings. The change control board comprises stakeholders with the skills, experience, and seniority to be able to make decisions about change requests. They should consider the impact of any change request on all other areas of the project. For example, a request to change the scope of the project will probably have an impact on both the time and cost of the project.

True or false? The change control process describes how changes will be identified.

Answer: *False*. Changes are identified by using a variety of variance analysis tools that compare planned work against actual work. After the change is identified, it is assessed via the change control process.

EXAM TIP **In the exam, you should assume that all projects have a documented and agreed-upon change control process. You should also assume that a project manager has some degree of delegated authority to assess the merits of individual change requests and to make decisions about whether small changes should be approved or declined.**

MORE INFO **You can find out more about the change control process for a project by reading about the Perform Integrated Change Control process in Chapter 4 of the PMBOK® Guide, 5th edition and Chapter 2 of the PMP® Training Kit.**

Change control tools

To assist the change control board members in their duties, there is a range of manual or automated tools that can be used, including these:

- Software to record changes.
- Electronic and physical tools to assess the impact of changes across multiple areas of the project.
- Tools to solicit feedback and expert input from relevant stakeholders.
- Tools to assist with decision making and communication of the decision to relevant stakeholders. The project manager and change control board members should make the decision about which tools are most useful and use them consistently.

Examples of change control tools are the change log, software to evaluate impacts across multiple areas of the project, communications techniques for soliciting feedback, and organizational process assets for ensuring that approved changes are implemented as expected.

True or false? Change control tools are used by the change control board during change control meetings to record, assess, and communicate decisions about change requests.

Answer: *True.* The purpose of change control tools is to enable the change control board to record, evaluate impacts of change, and communicate decisions about change requests.

> ***EXAM TIP*** **Change control tools are identified and documented as part of the agreed-upon change management plan; they originate from organizational process assets and enterprise environmental factors.**

Meetings

If any changes are approved, it is important that these changes are communicated to project team members to ensure that their expectations are proactively managed about the project. There are many effective ways to communicate with project team members, and the most effective way should be documented in the stakeholder management plan that should record individual stakeholders preferred communication methods.

> ***NOTE*** **There are several effective ways to communicate, including performance reports and the publication of the change log. This information can be made available via email distribution, which is a push form of communication because information is pushed to the recipients; or made available on a project intranet, which is a pull form of communication because the recipients must go and get the information.**

One of the best and most effective ways to communicate with project team members is in a meeting because it takes advantage of the power of face-to-face communication. Meetings should be run effectively to ensure that they add to the project. (Task 1 covered some suggestions for how to run an effective meeting.)

True or false? Communicating with project team members should be done only to distribute formal project information.

Answer: *False.* Any form of project communication is an excellent way to distribute formal project information, but effective communication is also an effective way to build a project team culture and improve morale within the team.

Can you answer these questions?

You can find the answers to these questions at the end of this chapter.

1. What are the elements of the scope baseline?
2. If a change is approved to the project scope, what is the first step a project manager should take?
3. If a project manager has received a change request and has declined to consider it any further, what is the project manager using to make this decision?
4. You are working on a project, and your approved change control process says that all potential changes to the project budget of more than 5 percent

must be considered by the change control board. A customer requests a change that will increase the budget by 7.5 percent and will pay for it, and don't want you to take the change to the change control board. What should you do?

5. Who should be on the project change control board?

Task 3: Ensure that project deliverables conform to the quality standards established in the quality management plan by using appropriate tools and techniques, e.g. testing, inspection, control charts, in order to satisfy customer requirements.

This particular domain task focuses on the process of quality control that seeks to confirm that the project deliverables conform to expected requirements and characteristics. There are many quality control tools that can assist the project manager and project team ensure that project deliverables do indeed conform to the defined quality standards established in the quality management plan. Many of these tools are also used during work associated with quality assurance covered in Chapter 3 of this book. It is the responsibility of the project manager to decide which tools are the most appropriate.

EXAM TIP **Make sure that you know the difference between quality assurance and quality control. Quality assurance is focused on checking that project processes are being followed and is performed during the executing domain tasks. Quality control is focused on checking that the project deliverables and products are correct and that they conform to expected requirements and specifications. It is performed during the monitoring and controlling of domain tasks.**

MORE INFO **You can find out more about quality control by reading about the Perform Quality Control process in Chapter 8 of the PMBOK® Guide, 5th edition and Chapter 6 of the PMP® Training Kit.**

Exam need to know...

- Quality management plan

  For example: What document guides the project manager during quality control tasks?

- Quality metrics

  For example: How will the project manager measure the quality of the project deliverables?

- Quality checklists

  For example: What document provides a list of activities to be completed as part of quality control work?

- Approved change requests

  For example: How is the work described in an approved change request checked for conformance to requirements?
- Work performance data

  For example: What information is gathered and analyzed to provide work performance information about the quality of project deliverables?
- Deliverables

  For example: What output from the project management work being completed must be checked for conformance to requirements?
- Seven basic quality tools

  For example: What are the most common ways of representing complex work performance data and quality metrics in a graphical form?
- Statistical sampling

  For example: What method should the project manager use when the sample size is too large or requires destructive testing?
- Inspection

  For example: How is the quality of the deliverable checked?
- Quality control measurements

  For example: What is produced as a result of carrying out quality control work on the project?
- Validated changes

  For example: What steps does a project deliverable go through before being presented to the customer for acceptance?
- Scope verification

  For example: What process is used by the project manager to gain acceptance of the project deliverable from the customer?

Quality management plan

The quality management plan guides the project manager and project team to carry out the quality control tasks on the project. It is developed during the quality planning processes and is a component of the project management plan. The quality management plan outlines how the project management team plans to meet the quality requirements set for the project relating to both quality assurance and quality control. It can be formal or informal, detailed or summary in nature, depending on the size and complexity of the project being undertaken.

NOTE **A subsidiary of the quality management plan is the process improvement plan that is primarily used to assess and analyze project management processes and identify opportunities for continuous improvement. This topic is covered in more detail in Chapter 3 of this book.**

True or false? The quality management plan describes how quality assurance and quality control requirements will be met.

Answer: *True*. The purpose of quality management plan is to proactively decide how all quality activities, including quality assurance and quality control activities, on the project will be undertaken.

> ***EXAM TIP*** **As with all other areas of project management, you should always ensure that your work is guided by some sort of plan. For quality management activities, you should look to the quality management plan to guide your work.**

Quality metrics

To ensure that the project deliverables conform to the required quality standards, a project manager requires quality metrics. Quality metrics provide a description of a project deliverable or product attribute and how it will be measured. Some typical examples of quality metrics include the following:

- On-time performance
- Cost control
- Defect frequency
- Failure rate
- Reliability
- Function points
- Mean time between failure
- Mean time to repair

The project manager and project team members are responsible for determining which quality metrics are the most appropriate to use depending on the particular deliverable or product being measured.

True or false? Quality metrics are used by the project manager and project team members to determine whether a project deliverable or product conforms to the expected requirements and specifications and will satisfy the customer.

Answer: *True*. The purpose of quality metrics is to enable the assessment of project deliverables or products against expected requirements and specifications.

Quality checklists

A quality checklist is a documented set of steps that a project manager can follow during quality control work. A quality checklist is used to outline the required quality steps and to ensure that a project manager does go through the required quality steps and can record that the required steps are completed.

True or false? A quality checklist records the information gathered from quality inspections.

Answer: *False*. The quality checklist sets out the steps that must be performed to gather information during quality inspections, but it does not record the information itself. The information will be recorded in some form of project management information system.

EXAM TIP **Checklists are a good idea, not just for completing quality-control activities but also for a range of other project initiating, planning, executing, monitoring and controlling, and closing activities.**

Approved change requests

As discussed in the previous domain task, approved change requests represent work to be completed on the project and should be used as an input into planning and then executing work. They also represent work that must be checked during quality control work, so they are a useful input into this monitoring and control domain task.

Any approved change requests should not only document the work to be done but also describe how it will be checked for correctness. After an approved change request has been implemented and checked, conformance then becomes a validated change.

True or false? Approved change requests represent a description of work to be done on the project, and all work to be done on the project must be checked for conformance to expected quality requirements and specifications.

Answer: *True.* Approved change requests represent a description of work to be done on the project and, like all other work to be done on the project, it must be checked for correctness and conformance to expected quality requirements and specifications besides being successfully executed.

Work performance data

To determine whether project deliverables conform to the quality standards established in the quality management plan, a project manager requires work performance data specifically about quality on the project. Gathering work performance data can be done by following the quality management plan and using quality checklists and quality metrics.

Work performance data includes a description of planned project work compared with actual technical performance, schedule performance, cost performance, and any differences between the expected quality metrics and the observed quality metrics.

True or false? Quality work performance data is used to develop work performance information, which provides an analysis of whether the project deliverables and products meet the required quality standards.

Answer: *True.* Work performance data on its own does not provide an analysis of quality issues on the project. The raw data needs to be analyzed and turned into work performance information before it becomes a useful tool for assessing project deliverables and products.

Deliverables

A deliverable is any unique or verifiable product, a result, or a capability required by the project. Before becoming a verified deliverable, it must be subject to quality control work to determine whether it meets the quality requirements. If it does meet the required quality control standards, it becomes verified and moves on to the scope verification work.

A key focus of this particular domain task is the assessment of project deliverables against expected quality standards. If they meet the standards, they then become verified deliverables that can be presented to the customer. If the customer is happy with the deliverables, the deliverables become accepted and used as an input into the closing processors and work of the project.

> ***EXAM TIP*** **Remember the flow of deliverables as an initial output from executing work; then as an input into quality control work where they are verified; then presented to the customer during scope validation work; and if accepted by the customer, they become accepted deliverables that are used as an input into closing processes and work.**

True or false? Deliverables relate only to products produced by the project.

Answer: *False.* A deliverable can be a product produced by the project, but it can also be a result of capability required by project scope.

Seven basic quality tools

The seven basic quality tools developed by Kaoru Ishikawa are very useful to help the project manager and project team members determine whether the project deliverables conform to the expected quality standards established on the quality management plan. Each of the seven tools takes complex work performance data and presents it graphically for easy interpretation. The seven quality tools are the following:

- Cause and effect diagram, also known as a fishbone or Ishikawa diagram
- Flowcharts and process maps
- Checksheets, also known as tally sheets
- Pareto diagrams
- Histograms or bar charts
- Control charts
- Scatter diagrams

> ***MORE INFO*** **Each of these seven basic quality tools is covered in more detail in Chapter 3 of this book.**

True or false? Each of the seven basic quality tools enables a project manager to interpret work performance data about quality.

Answer: *True*. Each of the seven basic quality tools is a graphical representation of work performance data gathered using quality metrics.

> ***EXAM TIP*** **If you are carrying out any sort of quality management activities, you will find the seven quality tools very useful. If you see a reference to any of these tools during the exam, you should immediately know that you are carrying out quality management activities. Remember that the tools are used during both quality assurance and quality control.**

> ***MORE INFO*** **You can find out more about and examples of the seven basic quality tools by using the Bing search engine to search the Internet.**

Statistical sampling

In addition to the seven basic quality tools, other tools can be used during quality control. Statistical sampling involves choosing a small part of a large population for inspection, and extrapolating the results of testing the small population to the entire population. This is a very useful technique to use when testing the entire population would not be feasible due to its large size or when testing involves destructive tests.

> ***EXAM TIP*** **The exam requires you to have a basic knowledge and understanding of statistical processes. Fortunately, they are all covered in this book. You do not need to have an in-depth knowledge of statistical processes and analysis.**

True or false? Statistical sampling is a tool that should be used if testing of a project deliverable or product involves destructive testing.

Answer: *True*. Statistical sampling is an excellent tool to use when testing a project deliverable or product that involves destroying it to determine whether it meets the required quality standards. Obviously, testing the entire population would result in the destruction of all the deliverables, so statistical sampling is a much better option.

Inspections

An inspection is an examination of the project deliverable or product to determine whether it meets the documented quality standards. An inspection produces work performance data about the project deliverable or product, and this work performance data can be analyzed and turned into work performance information to help the project manager determine whether the product or deliverable is meeting the required quality standards.

True or false? Inspections can be used to determine whether the processes for quality management are being followed.

Answer: *False*. Inspections are a tool used during quality control activities that seek to determine whether products or deliverables meet the expected quality requirements. Audits are used during quality assurance work to determine whether the processes of quality management are being followed.

EXAM TIP **Remember that inspection is a tool for quality control work, and audits are tools used in quality assurance work. Quality assurance work is covered in the executing domain tasks; quality control is a monitoring and control task.**

Quality control measurements

Quality control measurements are the documented results of the control quality activities that have been carried out, and they are used to record and communicate these results to the relevant stakeholders. The quality management plan specifies which format and content are included in quality control measurements.

Verified deliverables

If, as a result of carrying out quality control work and testing whether the project deliverables conform to the quality standards established in the quality management plan, the deliverables are found to be in accordance with the quality standards, they become verified deliverables. A verified deliverable has been determined to be correct and in accordance with the expected quality requirements and standards.

True or false? Deliverables produced by the project become verified after they have been determined to be correct and in accordance with the expected and documented project quality standards and requirements.

Answer: *True*. There are several steps that deliverables go through after they have been produced. The first of these is an internal quality control check to determine whether they meet the required quality standards; if they do; they become verified. These verified deliverables are used as an input into scope verification work and are presented to the customer for acceptance. If the customer agrees that they meet the requirements, they become accepted deliverables that are used as an input into the closing processes.

EXAM TIP **Remember that before being presented to the customer all deliverables must go through the quality control process to verify that they meet quality control requirements. Only after becoming verified deliverables can they be presented to the customer for acceptance.**

Scope validation

After a deliverable has been through the internal quality control processes and been verified as being correct and conforming to the required and documented quality control specifications, it becomes a verified deliverable. Verified deliverables are used as an input into the scope validation work to be done on the project, with the goal of obtaining acceptance of the deliverables from the customer.

The process of validating the deliverables uses inspection as a tool. Inspection includes examining and measuring the deliverable and comparing this work performance data and information against the customer requirements and product acceptance criteria to determine whether the product is acceptable to the customer.

If the customer confirms that the product meets the documented requirements and other acceptance criteria, the deliverables are formally signed off and approved by the project manager, sponsor, and customer. Proof of acceptance is then used as an important input into the work involved in closing the project.

True or false? Accepted deliverables occur when the customer formally acknowledges that the deliverables meet their requirements and specifications

Answer: *True.* A deliverable moves from the internal acceptance process of quality control to become a validated deliverable. It is then presented to the customer for inspection; if it meets the documented requirements, it becomes an accepted deliverable.

> ***EXAM TIP*** **Remember that verification is an internal process completed before validation. Verification is done by the project manager and project team. Validation is done by the project manager, project sponsor, and customer.**

> ***MORE INFO*** **You can find out more about the Validate Scope process by reading Chapter 5 of the PMBOK® Guide, 5th edition and Chapter 3 of the PMP® Training Kit.**

Can you answer these questions?

You can find the answers to these questions at the end of this chapter.

1. What is the key difference between quality control and quality assurance?
2. Under which circumstances would you choose to use statistical sampling?
3. What are the seven basic quality tools?
4. A customer is not happy with the deliverables and refuses to accept them. After checking all the written agreements, requirements, scope baseline, and other relevant project documents, you find that they are concise, accurate, and well written. Additionally, they clearly describe the requirements, characteristics, and criteria for acceptance for the deliverable, and the deliverable meets every one of them. You discover that the area of customer dissatisfaction relates to work that was not part of this project. What should you do?
5. What is the name of the document that provides guidance to the project manager on how all quality management activities on the project will be carried out?

Task 4: Update the risk register and risk response plan by identifying any new risks, assessing old risks, and determining and implementing appropriate response strategies, in order to manage the impact of risks on the project.

This domain task is focused on using the risk register and the documented planned risk responses to determine whether they are still correct and appropriate and whether there are any new risks that need to be added and assessed, and ensuring that risks are being monitored and controlled proactively. The risk management plan provides guidance on how and how frequently these activities are to be carried out. The project manager will take responsibility for determining the appropriate application of relevant tools and techniques.

MORE INFO **You can find out more about this domain task by reading about the Control Risks process in Chapter 11 of the PMBOK® Guide, 5th edition, Chapter 9 of the PMP® Training Kit, and the ISO31000 Risk Management standard available from the ISO website (*www.iso.org*).**

Exam need to know...

- Risk management plan

  For example: What document provides guidance to the project manager about how the risk management work will be carried out on the project?
- Risk register

  For example: What document describes and records the expected risks and planned responses on the project?
- Work performance data and reports

  For example: How will the project manager obtain information about the suitability of planned risk responses?
- Risk reassessment

  For example: What tool does the project manager use to see whether identified risks are still valid and determine whether new risks have manifested?
- Risk audits

  For example: How does the project manager determine whether the process for identifying risks is appropriate and robust?
- Variance and trend analysis

  For example: What tool or technique is used to determine whether there is a difference between forecast risks and actual risks that occur?
- Reserves analysis

  For example: How are quantifiable financial risks provided for in the project budget?
- Change requests

  For example: If a variance between forecast risk events and actual risks events is discovered, what should the project manager do?
- Risk response strategies

  For example: What proactive action should a project manager undertake to ensure that potential uncertainty on the project is appropriately mitigated?

Risk management plan

The risk management plan is a component of the project management plan that specifically deals with how project risks will be identified and managed, which particular risk methodology will be used, individual roles and responsibilities for managing risk on the project, and any associated budgets or time frames. The risk management plan can also determine risk categories, stakeholder tolerances, reporting formats, and risk tracking. The risk management plan is prepared during the planning stage of the project and is used in the executing, monitoring and controlling, and closing stages to guide how the work will be carried out.

Just like any of the other monitoring and control tasks, the risk management plan should be available to the project manager before this particular domain task begins.

True or false? The risk management plan is used by the project manager and project team members to guide how risks will be monitored and controlled.

Answer: *True*. The key purpose of the risk management plan is to guide the project manager and project team members for all aspects of risk management on the project, including how risks will be monitored and controlled.

Risk register

The risk register is a key input that enables the project manager to complete this particular domain task because it includes identified risk categories, individual risk events, and assessment of the risk if it occurs, qualitative or quantitative assessment of the risk, and a planned risk response. Monitoring and controlling the risk register involves checking the risks identified, assessing those risks, determining whether the planned responses are still appropriate and accurate, and determining whether risks need to be closed out or new risks have been identified that need to be added to the risk register.

A watch list is part of the risk register and provides a list of low-priority risks that do not warrant inclusion on the risk register at this stage, but should be monitored in case the probability or impact of the risk increases. In that case, they should be added to the risk register.

True or false? Among all the other data about project risks included in the risk register are the specific proactive and reactive responses planned to ensure that risks are appropriately managed.

Answer: *True*. The risk register is a very comprehensive document that includes a lot of information about identified risks on the project, including the specific proactive and reactive planned responses to each one.

> ***EXAM TIP*** **Remember that any risk responses that are identified represent work to be done on the project, so whenever a risk response is planned, it should be added to the WBS for the project as well as the time, cost, and resources allocated to it to ensure that it is completed.**

Work performance data and reports

As with other monitoring and controlling domain tasks, in order to successfully complete this work you require work performance data related to various performance results affected by risks. This data could include information about deliverables' status, schedule progress, costs incurred, and effectiveness of risk responses.

The work performance data is analyzed and becomes useful work performance information, which is subsequently included in work performance reports. The specific types of analytical techniques applied to work performance data to make them useful work performance information can include these:

- Variance analysis
- Earned value data
- Forecasting data

These specific work performance reports will be in the format specified by the risk management plan.

True or false? Work performance data enables a project manager to understand whether risks are eventuating as anticipated, and planned risk responses are working as planned.

Answer: *False.* Work performance data is raw information that does not provide any in-depth conclusion until it has been analyzed and becomes work performance information.

Risk reassessment

As a result of carrying out this domain task and updating the risk register and risk response plan, a continuous process of risk reassessment is carried out. This process involves checking that the current identified risks and their forecast impacts are still accurate, or whether any new information has been discovered that requires these assessments to change.

Risk reassessment also examines whether particular risks need to be closed as the time frame for the recurrence has passed. Risk reassessment also includes a general monitoring of the entire project to see whether any new risks have manifested and if they warrant inclusion on either the watch list or risk register.

How often a risk reassessment is carried out will depend on the stage and complexity of the project and the requirements of stakeholders.

EXAM TIP **It is always a good idea to keep risk reassessment at the forefront of your team's mind and keep it as a priority agenda item on any team status meetings.**

True or false? Risk reassessment involves many tasks, including checking whether already identified risks have had their potential impact accurately assessed.

Answer: *True.* The process of risk reassessment does include many tasks, all centered around checking and double-checking the risk assessment that was initially done to see whether it was done correctly, whether there is new information that would change the assessment, or whether there are any new risks identified that need to be documented.

> ***EXAM TIP*** **The risk register should be treated as a very live document and constantly referred to, checked for completeness and accuracy, and reassessed to ensure it is still an accurate document.**

Risk audits

Risk audits can have two purposes. Its first purpose is to enable the project manager to determine the effectiveness of the overall risk management processes being used on the project. This is done to ensure that the processes are appropriate to the project.

The second purpose of a risk audit is to examine whether a planned risk response has been effective in dealing with an identified risk. This is done to determine whether risk responses need to be amended for future risks.

The risk management plan will set out the frequency, objectives, and format for a risk audit in either category. A risk audit can be performed as part of routine project team meetings or as part of a separate, focused risk audit meeting.

True or false? A risk audit can be used to determine whether the risk register has been compiled according to the risk management plan.

Answer: *True.* One of the functions of a risk audit is to determine whether documented risk processes have been followed. It is these risk processes that will determine whether the risk register has been developed according to the risk management plan so it will be a useful tool to use.

> ***EXAM TIP*** **Remember that any sort of audit focuses on processes rather than products.**

Variance and trend analysis

As with other domain tasks focused on monitoring and control activities, there is a need to use variance analysis tools and techniques to determine whether there is a difference between the work that was planned and the work that is actually occurring. Variance and trend analysis tools such as earned value analysis and trend analysis can be useful to determine whether there is any difference between the identified risks and the risks that are manifesting, the forecast impacts and the observed impacts, and the efficacy of the planned risk responses compared with the efficacy of the actual risk responses.

Variance and trend analysis can also include technical performance measurement that compares the actual technical accomplishments achieved during project execution to the planned level of technical accomplishments. These technical performance measurements can include metrics such as weight, transaction times, and number of defects; and a variance between what was forecast in terms of technical accomplishment and what is being achieved in terms of technical achievement represents risk to the project.

The risk management plan will set out which particular variance and trend analysis tools and techniques will be used, and is the responsibility of the project manager to ensure that they are used appropriately.

True or false? A type of variance analysis that can be used to determine whether the planned cost of risk responses is equal to the actual cost of risk responses is the earned management technique.

Answer: *True.* The earned value management technique, with its assessment of project cost and time, is a valuable tool to use to determine whether there is a difference between the planned cost of risk responses and the actual cost of risk responses.

Reserves analysis

A contingency reserve for the project might have been developed during the process of developing the risk register and performing quantitative risk analysis. If so, it was built up using information and assumptions relevant at the time. An important part of completing the monitoring and controlling work associated with project risk management is to analyze whether the amounts calculated to be included in the contingency reserve are still accurate, whether some risks have passed without using the allocated contingency reserve, and whether there are new risks that should be quantitatively analyzed to determine any additional contingency reserve. If an allocated contingency reserve is not used because a forecast risk event did not eventuate, the amount of contingency allocated to it should be returned to the organization.

If any new or amended reserve amounts are identified, the risk register needs to be updated to reflect it, and a change request might need to be documented and assessed.

True or false? A contingency reserve can be built up using quantifiable data on the probability and impact of an identified risk.

Answer: *True.* To build up a contingency reserve, it is necessary to have quantifiable data about probability and impact of risks, and to translate this quantity of assessment into either money or time contingency.

> ***EXAM TIP*** **A contingency reserve is developed for the known risks on the project using qualitative risk analysis and should be under the control of the project manager. A management reserve is developed for unknown or unforeseeable risks on a project and is under the control of senior management.**

Change requests

As a result of carrying out the monitoring and control work to update the risk register and risk response plan, there might be a need to issue a change request to formally document and assess any changes. The risk management plan will set out the process of determining whether a change request needs to be raised, the delegated authority level of the project manager to make decisions about the change, and the process that changes need to go through to be evaluated and decisions made.

Change requests relating to monitoring and controlling of risks on the project can include either recommended corrective actions or recommended preventive actions. Recommended corrective actions can include contingency plans and workarounds to deal with changed risk conditions or unidentified risks that manifest. Recommended preventive actions can be used to ensure that future project work aligns itself with the risk management plan and other aspects of the project management plan.

> ***EXAM TIP*** **A workaround is a solution for a risk that arises that wasn't forecast. It is intended to be a temporary solution to enable to the project to continue.**

True or false? Any change requests raised in relation to risk need to comply only with the risk management plan, not the change management plan.

Answer: *False.* The risk management plan sets how changes are identified and the process of documenting them. It also describes how they will be assessed, and it will refer to the overall project change management plan that sets the way changes in the project will be documented and assessed.

Risk response strategies

As part of the work involved in planning your particular approach to risk and developing the risk register, consideration would have been given to appropriate risk responses for each of the identified risks. Risk responses represent work to be done as part of the project scope, and all work must be checked for completeness and accuracy. This is true for planned risk responses as well as for other work being completed. As part of monitoring and controlling the risk-related work being done, you should check that the proactive risk responses have been implemented as planned and that any reactive ones have had the desired effect. If any risk response has not worked as planned, changes should be made, and this information should also be captured in the lessons learned process.

When considering appropriate risk response, there are four accepted response types for negative risks, or threats; and four accepted response types for positive risks, or opportunities. Table 4-2 lists the responses.

TABLE 4-2 Risk responses

NEGATIVE RISKS, OR THREATS	POSITIVE RISKS, OR OPPORTUNITIES
Avoid	Enhance
Transfer	Share
Mitigate	Exploit
Accept	Accept

True or false? Taking out insurance to cover a possibility of your project being affected by adverse weather conditions is an example of risk mitigation.

Answer: *False*. Insurance is a form of transfer because it makes the risk someone else's problem if it occurs.

Can you answer these questions?

You can find the answers to these questions at the end of this chapter.

1. What element of the risk register will be most useful to the project manager during monitoring and controlling work on the project?
2. What is the key purpose of a risk audit?
3. If an approved contingency reserve is not used as a result of a forecast risk event not occurring, what should happen to the contingency reserve?
4. When should risk reassessment be carried out?
5. If an unanticipated risk occurs on a project, which risk response strategy should a project manager use?

Task 5: Assess corrective actions on the issue register and determine next steps for unresolved issues by using appropriate tools and techniques, in order to minimize the impact on project schedule, cost, and resources.

This domain task uses the issue register, or log, as a starting point and ensures that documented corrective actions are undertaken to resolve issues and stop them from escalating. If issues do escalate, they might involve recording them on the project watch list or risk register and developing specific risk responses for them.

Exam need to know...

- Issue register

  For example: What is the document that the project manager can use to record any issues that are raised by stakeholders on the project?
- Corrective and preventive actions

  For example: If a variance between actual and planned work is discovered, what actions can a project manager consider to rectify the variance?
- Communications tool

  For example: How can the issue log be used as a communications tool to influence stakeholder expectations?

Issue register

The issue register, or issue log, is the document that records all issues that have been identified in the project. An issue is any point in question or dispute, or is subject to discussion over which there are opposing points of view.

In addition to describing the identified issue, the issue register or log also documents the planned corrective or preventive action, the person who has responsibility for monitoring and addressing the issue, and any other information such as agreed-upon time frames for resolving the issue.

In addition to the technical information contained about the issues, the issue register or log is an effective communication tool for managing stakeholder expectations. It does this by enabling stakeholders to see that their issues are taken seriously by the project manager and that they have been recorded and are being dealt with. As such, the preparation and updating of an issue register or log can be an effective tool for managing project team members' and stakeholders' expectations.

> ***EXAM TIP*** **All issues on the issue register or log do not need to be resolved at the completion or closure of the project because some of the issues are so minor that they do not warrant effort to resolve them. This is in contrast to all risks identified on the risk register, which must be closed out so the project can be closed.**

True or false? The issue register or log, the watch list, and the risk register are all interrelated and represent a path of escalating identified issues, variances, and risks on the project.

Answer: *True.* The issue register or log is the best document to record minor issues on the project. If the issues become more than minor and become risks, they might be escalated to the watch list if they are low probability and impact risks, or escalated to the risk register if they warrant more detailed analysis of the probability and impact and the development of appropriate risk responses.

> ***EXAM TIP*** **In the exam you will see the document that records issues referred to as either the issue register or issue log. It is both a technical document for recording planned responses to address project issues and also a very effective communication and stakeholder management tool.**

Corrective and preventive actions

A corrective action is any action undertaken by the project manager and project team, in response to variance analysis, to bring future project performance in line with the forecast project performance captured in the project management plan and its subsidiary documents and baselines.

A project manager can use several tools and techniques to ensure that corrective and preventive actions are appropriate and adequately deal with the issues, including using accurate data gathering and analytical techniques.

To successfully implement corrective actions, a project manager must first have a well-developed set of baselines against which to measure actual work performance on the project. Without a well-defined set of documents that describe what is supposed to occur on the project, the project manager cannot determine variance. Corrective actions can only be defined and implemented only in response to variance between the planned and actual work on the project.

Corrective actions should be seen as the final step in a process that begins with having a defined plan and accurate work performance information to detect variance. With this information, variance can be detected that might require corrective action to be initiated, but before this step, it is important that the root cause of the variation is determined rather than the surface cause to ensure that the proposed corrective action deals with the variance. After the corrective action has been agreed upon and implemented, it is important to measure whether it has resulted in the expected change in project performance. If it has not resulted in the expected changes to project performance, the process might need to be repeated and further corrective action taken.

In addition to using corrective actions to eliminate variance between planned and actual project work, another option for the project manager is to take preventive actions. Implementing preventive actions is an attempt to ensure that a future variance will not occur; corrective actions seek to put a project back on track after a variance has occurred. An example of a preventive action can be additional resources allocated to a work package or activity to ensure that it meets the expected time frame.

True or false? Corrective actions are reactive, and preventive actions are proactive.

Answer: *True.* This is generally true because corrective actions are in response to detected variance and preventive actions are attempts to stop variance from occurring. They can get a little confusing, however, because some preventive actions are taken in response to detected variance to ensure that they don't happen again.

EXAM TIP **Remember that significant corrective actions need to be processed according to the agreed-upon and documented change control process.**

Communications tool

The issue log is a very important technical document for recording identified issues and planning corrective or preventive actions to deal with the issues, but it is also an important communication document. It communicates by enabling stakeholders to have their issues documented, and they can then see that their issues are being taken seriously and dealt with.

The project manager should make sure that the issue log is kept up to date and that stakeholders are regularly updated about progress in dealing with the issues. Input and feedback from stakeholders can also be obtained to improve the accuracy and validity of the issue log. By effectively using the issue log as a communication tool, the project manager can influence stakeholders' expectations to be more in favor of the project.

Can you answer these questions?

You can find the answers to these questions at the end of this chapter.

1. What type of information is usually recorded in the issue log or register?
2. What is the difference between corrective and preventive actions?

3. What information is essential to ensuring that the corrective action is done?
4. What tool or technique should a project manager use to ensure that the planned response to an issue addresses the root cause?
5. How does a project manager use the issue log or register as a communications tool to manage stakeholder expectations?

Task 6: Communicate project status to stakeholders for their feedback, in order to ensure the project aligns with business needs.

To ensure that stakeholders continue to support a project, or at least not oppose it, it is essential that they are communicated with regularly about the project status. This domain task is focused on communicating the status of the project to stakeholders based on what both the communications management plan and stakeholder management plan outline. The goal is to ensure that stakeholder engagement with the project is kept high, and that information flows freely and appropriately to the right stakeholders at the right time about the status of the project.

Exam need to know...

- Communication management plan

  For example: What document gives the project manager information about timing and format of project communications as well as key messages?
- Stakeholder management plan

  For example: What document provides the project manager with guidelines about identifying stakeholder expectations?
- Work performance reports

  For example: What is the most effective way to present work performance data and work performance information so that stakeholders can understand project status?

Communication management plan

The communication management plan, which is developed during communication management planning work, will guide the project manager on how all project communications will be carried out: frequency, type, and method of communications; and key messages and opportunities for feedback. It is needed to carry out this particular monitoring and control task because it provides a project manager with a clear guideline of how the project status will be communicated to stakeholders.

These guidelines include a reference to what information will be included and what will be excluded. It includes information about the format of the status reports, and whether they will be summary or detailed, electronic or physical, text or pictorial in nature. The communication management plan also outlines the frequency of project status reports and how feedback from stakeholders will be gathered.

The type of communication methods chosen can include formal, informal, written, verbal, push or pull, or any combination. The communications management plan provides guidance on which form of project communications is most appropriate.

The communications management plan also outlines how the communications processes and work being completed will be monitored and controlled to ensure that it is still valid and effective. The communications management plan also sets how feedback from stakeholders will be gathered, interpreted, and incorporated into future project performance reports and the communications management process.

True or false? The communication management plan sets how each and every project communication will be developed, produced, and transmitted.

Answer: *False*. The communications management plan is not that detailed. Instead, it provides guidelines and plans for how project communications will be carried out. It might provide additional detail on frequency and type of communications and key messages, but it will not go into that much detail.

> ***MORE INFO*** **You can find out more about the communication management plan by reading Chapter 10 of the PMBOK® Guide, 5th edition and Chapter 8 of the PMP® Training Kit.**

Stakeholder management plan

The stakeholder management plan identifies the management strategies required to manage stakeholder expectations of the project. The plan is essential for communicating effectively with stakeholders because it identifies the following:

- Stakeholder communication preferences
- Information to be distributed to stakeholders
- Expected stakeholder impact of communicating project status
- Time frame and frequency of preferred information
- Method for updating the stakeholder management plan

Distributing timely and appropriate project status reports is an effective way of managing stakeholder expectations of the project. It is up to the project manager to ensure that the content, format, and frequency of the project status reports align with what stakeholders require. There is no point in sending information to stakeholders about how the project is performing in relation to cost when all they care about is the impact it is having on them personally. The format is important as well because some stakeholders might prefer face-to-face meetings to receive project status updates; others might prefer email updates.

Relevant project stakeholders who might want to see project status reports include these:

- Project team members
- Consultants
- Project sponsor

- Steering committee members
- Senior managers within the organization
- Customer
- Suppliers

NOTE **The process of managing stakeholders' expectations involves proactive influencing by project managers as part of the interpersonal skills that they should possess. They should be expert influences of stakeholders based on building relationships, networking, reciprocity, and mutual benefit. The difference between influencing and manipulation is a fine one, but influencing is the ability to sway opinion and support based on prestige, power, and trust. Manipulation is influencing with devious intent.**

A key function of the stakeholder management plan is to guide the development of the stakeholder register. The stakeholder register provides valuable advice to the project manager trying to influence stakeholder expectations with appropriate project status reports because it contains information including the following:

- Stakeholder identification information
- Assessment of stakeholders' requirements, expectations, and influence on the project
- Classification of stakeholders by level of support, influence, or power

True or false? The stakeholder management plan provides guidance to the project manager and project team on how stakeholder expectations will be managed by the release of timely and appropriate project status reports.

Answer: *True*. The purpose of the stakeholder management plan is to define strategy for managing stakeholder expectations of the project. This includes providing guidance to the project manager and project team on how stakeholder expectations will be managed by the release of timely and appropriate project status reports.

MORE INFO **You can find out more about managing stakeholder engagement with project status reports by reading Chapter 13 of the PMBOK® Guide, 5th edition and Chapter 11 of the PMP® Training Kit.**

Work performance reports

The most effective way to provide stakeholders with project status update is with the preparation and distribution of work performance reports. Work performance reports are developed using work performance information.

The format, content, and frequency of work performance reports released to stakeholders will be determined by information in both the stakeholders' management plan and the communications management plan. Different stakeholders will require different information, in different formats, and at different times. For example, senior managers might want to view the project milestone list in a simple high-level project status report; project team members might want to get detailed project status reports that cover a lot of information.

Work performance reports and the work performance information they are based on are collected, stored, and distributed by project management information systems that can be electronic or physical in nature.

True or false? Work performance status reports need to be tailored to individual stakeholders' requirements.

Answer: *True*. Each stakeholder might have slightly different requirements for the format, content, and timing of project status reports.

Can you answer these questions?

You can find the answers to these questions at the end of this chapter.

1. Which two plans are most useful to a project manager seeking to use project status reports to manage stakeholder expectations?
2. What is the best format for work performance reports?
3. Who should take responsibility for ensuring that stakeholder expectations are proactively influenced?
4. How are work performance reports collected and stored?
5. Is it the communications management plan, stakeholder management plan, or stakeholder register that describes individual stakeholder communication preferences?

Answers

This section contains the answers to the "Can you answer these questions?" sections in this chapter.

Task 1: Measure project performance using appropriate tools and techniques, in order to identify and quantify any variances, perform approved corrective actions, and communicate with relevant stakeholders.

1. All monitoring and controlling work includes having a description of planned work usually captured in a plan or baseline; and a description of the work actually being performed, usually captured in some sort of work performance data. Monitoring and controlling work also includes some form of variance analysis to detect differences between planned and actual work. Finally, if a variance is detected, a change request is documented and analyzed, and a decision is made. As a result, there might be updates to the project management plan.

2. Applying analytical techniques to work performance data results in the creation of work performance information.
3. The two main benefits of holding meetings as part of monitoring and controlling work are the ease with which technical information is exchanged by people in a face-to-face setting and the benefit of a useful team building tool.
4. This question requires you to work out the EV by determining what EV will give an SPI of 1.1 if the PV is $5,000. To calculate this, divide the SPI by the PV, which results in an EV of $5,500. You can then calculate CPI by dividing EV by AC to arrive at 1.22.
5. Project procurements should be monitored by all parties who have entered into the agreements. It is not just the responsibility of the project manager for the buyer; it is the responsibility of both buyer and seller.

Task 2: Manage changes to the project scope, schedule, and costs by updating the project plan and communicating approved changes to the team, in order to ensure that revised project goals are met.

1. The scope baseline is made up of the project scope statement, WBS, and the WBS dictionary.
2. After a change is approved, it represents additional work to be performed on the project. This extra work should be incorporated into the scope baseline, which includes adding it to the WBS and assessing the cost, time, and resources associated with doing the work.
3. If a project manager has received a change request and has declined to consider it any further, he or she is using delegated authority.
4. If the approved change control process says that all changes to the project budget over 5 percent must go to the change control board, this change must go to the board. It would probably be considered favorably because the customer has agreed to pay the increased amount. Remember that at all times you should work within the existing rules and laws. If you disagree with them, you can seek to change them, but you must abide by them until they are changed.
5. The change control board should be made up of people who have the required level of skills, experience, and authority to assess and make decisions about change requests.

Task 3: Ensure that project deliverables conform to the quality standards established on the quality management plan by using appropriate tools and techniques, e.g. testing, inspection, control charts, in order to satisfy customer requirements.

1. Quality control is a monitoring and control activity that uses inspection as a tool to determine whether project deliverables meet quality requirements. Quality assurance is an executing process that uses audits to determine whether project processes are being followed and whether there are opportunities for continuous improvement.
2. You would use statistical sampling if the total population size was too large to make individual sampling feasible or if testing involved destructive testing.
3. The seven basic quality tools are these:
   - The cause and effect diagram, also known as a fishbone or Ishikawa diagram
   - Flowcharts and process maps
   - Check sheets, also known as tally sheets
   - Pareto diagrams
   - Histograms or bar charts
   - Control charts
   - Scatter diagrams
4. In this case, you should proceed with project closure; the deliverables would be considered accepted because they meet the documented and agreed-upon requirements. The customer might not be happy about this, but there is a carefully worded agreement. If there were any ambiguity in this case, you would decide in favor of the customer.
5. The quality management plan, which is part of the project management plan, provides guidance to the project manager about how all quality management activities on the project should be carried out.

Task 4: Update the risk register and risk response plan by identifying any new risks, assessing old risks, and determining and implementing appropriate response strategies, in order to manage the impact of risks on the project.

1. The entire risk register is useful to the project manager during monitoring and controlling work because it provides a description of risk categories, events, probability, impact, and planned risk responses—all of which need to be monitored and controlled.

2. The key purpose of a risk audit is to determine whether the risk management processes described in the risk management plan and relevant organizational process assets have been followed. A second purpose of the risk audit is to determine whether planned risk responses are appropriate.
3. Contingency reserve amounts that are not required should be returned to the performing organization.
4. Risk reassessment is a continuous process that should be carried out throughout the life of the project.
5. A workaround is an excellent response to an unanticipated risk occurring because it results in a temporary solution to enable the project to continue.

Task 5: Assess corrective actions on the issue register and determine next steps for unresolved issues by using appropriate tools and techniques, in order to minimize the impact on project schedule, cost, and resources.

1. The issue log records information about issues that are points in question or dispute, or subject to discussion over which there are opposing points of view.
2. The difference between corrective actions and preventive actions is that corrective actions are generally reactive in response to an issue that has already occurred; preventive actions are proactive to try and stop an issue from occurring.
3. It is essential to have accurate work performance data and information to ensure that issues are analyzed correctly before undertaking corrective action.
4. The best tool or technique to use to ensure that the planned response to an issue addresses the root cause is root cause analysis, the Ishikawa diagram, and the "five why's" analysis.
5. The issue log is an effective communication tool to manage stakeholder expectations because it enables stakeholders to see that their issues are being taken seriously enough to be recorded, and corrective or preventive action is being undertaken to resolve the issue.

Task 6: Communicate project status to stakeholders for their feedback, in order to ensure the project aligns with business needs.

1. The communications management plan and stakeholder management plan are the two plans most useful to a project manager seeking to use project status reports to manage stakeholder expectations.
2. The best format for any work performance report is defined by individual stakeholder requirements and preferences.
3. It is the role of the project manager to ensure that stakeholder expectations are proactively influenced.

4. Work performance reports are collected, stored in, and retrieved from the project management information systems being used by the project.
5. It is the stakeholder management plan that describes individual stakeholder communication preferences.

CHAPTER 5

Closing the project

The Closing the Project performance domain covers approximately 8 percent of the Project Management Professional (PMP®) exam. It covers the work involved in formally closing a project, which includes gaining formal acceptance, transferring ownership, completing documented closure procedures, gathering lessons learned, and measuring customer satisfaction. All projects must be closed either as a result of normal and expected conditions, or as a result of unexpected conditions; and the project manager should take responsibility for ensuring it is done correctly. The nature of the closure (either normal or abnormal) dictates what sorts of closure tasks are completed. The process of, and documented conditions for, project closure are usually prepared and approved early on in the project and can be recorded as a project closure checklist.

This chapter covers the following tasks:

- Task 5.1: Obtain final acceptance of the project deliverables by working with the sponsor and/or customer, in order to confirm that project scope and deliverables were met.
- Task 5.2: Transfer the ownership of deliverables to the assigned stakeholders in accordance with the project plan, in order to facilitate project closure.
- Task 5.3: Obtain financial, legal, and administrative closure using generally accepted practices, in order to communicate formal project closure and ensure no further liability.
- Task 5.4: Distribute the final project report including all project closure-related information, project variances, and any issues, in order to provide the final project status to all stakeholders.
- Task 5.5: Collate lessons learned through comprehensive project review, in order to create and/or update the organization's knowledge base.
- Task 5.6: Archive project documents and material in order to retain organizational knowledge, comply with statutory requirements, and ensure availability of data for potential use in future projects and internal/external audits.
- Task 5.7: Measure customer satisfaction at the end of the project by capturing customer feedback, in order to assist in project evaluation and enhance customer relationships.

Task 5.1: Obtain final acceptance of the project deliverables by working with the sponsor and/or customer, in order to confirm that project scope and deliverables were met.

This task focuses on the work that occurs after the deliverables of the project have been through internal quality control processes and the external process of validating them to become accepted deliverables. At this point, they have been accepted by all relevant stakeholders and are then used in project closure tasks.

Exam need to know...

- Accepted deliverables

  For example: What are accepted deliverables?
- Final acceptance

  For example: Which stakeholders are involved in final acceptance?

Accepted deliverables

All deliverables produced by the project go through a three-stage process. The first step is an internal monitoring and controlling quality control task in which the project manager takes responsibility for ensuring that the deliverables conform to the quality standards established on the quality management plan by using appropriate tools and techniques (for example, testing, inspection, and control charts) to satisfy customer requirements. After these quality control tasks are complete, the deliverables are now validated deliverables.

In the second step in the process, the validated deliverables are presented to the customer for acceptance. If accepted by the customer, they become accepted deliverables. The third step in the process sees these accepted deliverables used to formally initiate closing processes and activities. Figure 5-1 shows the three stages in consecutive order.

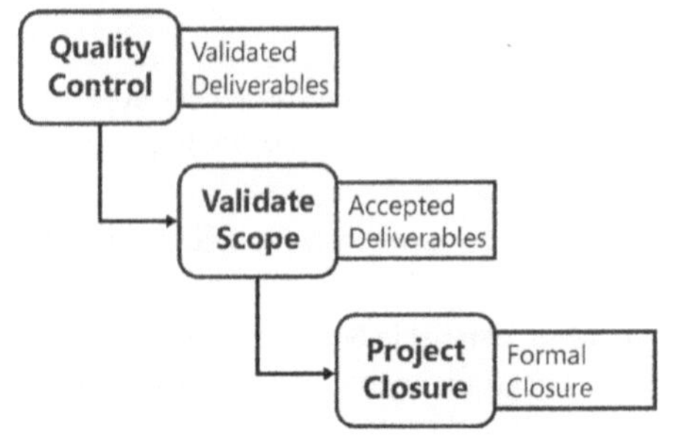

FIGURE 5-1 A diagram showing the process of project deliverables becoming validated, accepted, and then used as part of project closure

True or false? The project customer performs quality control procedures to ensure the project deliverables are validated.

Answer: *False*. The tasks involved in validating deliverables are an internal process and are completed by the relevant project team members under the responsibility of the project manager.

The customer is part of the activities involved in validating the scope and creating accepted deliverables. The project sponsor takes sole responsibility for accepting all other project deliverables on behalf of the performing organization that are not required to be accepted by the customer. They include all other work included in the project scope that doesn't refer to attributes of the product of the project.

> ***EXAM TIP*** **You should memorize and understand the process that deliverables go through before being used in project closing activities because a question in the exam will present a scenario that clearly indicates at which point in the three stages the deliverable is. You then know what work has been done and what is unfinished.**

> ***MORE INFO*** **You can find out more about the stages of project deliverables by referring to the description of activities involved in the Control Quality, Validate Scope, and Close Project or Phase processes in the PMBOK® Guide, 5th edition.**

Final acceptance

After the project deliverables have been through the necessary quality control and scope validation processes, they are formally accepted by the relevant stakeholders (usually the project sponsor and the customer). The project manager takes responsibility for ensuring that the closing activities are completed and the formal acceptance is gained and documented.

Final acceptance should always include formal documentation that is signed by the relevant parties such as the project manager, project sponsor and project customer. You cannot go on to complete any other tasks involved in project closure until you have documented proof that final acceptance has been gained.

True or false? Final acceptance means that the project is now formally closed.

Answer: *False*. Final acceptance is an important first task in the project closure process. There are still tasks focusing on transferring ownership, completing documented closure procedures, gathering lessons learned, and measuring customer satisfaction to be completed as part of full project closure.

> ***EXAM TIP*** **Remember the emphasis placed on formally initiating a project, and how important it was to document that initiation and approval? That same emphasis of formal acceptance of the deliverable and formal proof of it also applies to project closure activities. You should treat project closure just as seriously: Ensure that it follows an agreed-upon process and that acceptance from all relevant parties is put in writing.**

MORE INFO You can find out more about final acceptance by reading about the process called Close Project or Phase in the PMBOK® Guide, 5th edition or Chapter 2 of the PMP Training Kit.

Can you answer these questions?

You can find the answers to these questions at the end of this chapter.

1. Who takes responsibility for ensuring that final acceptance is gained?
2. Which stakeholder accepts the project deliverables on behalf of the performing organization?
3. How do accepted deliverables differ from validated deliverables?
4. What is the primary role of the customer in final acceptance?
5. Does final acceptance mean that the project is formally closed?

Task 5.2: Transfer the ownership of deliverables to the assigned stakeholders in accordance with the project plan, in order to facilitate project closure.

This task addresses the tasks focused on formal transfer of ownership of the project deliverables to the relevant stakeholder or stakeholders. This process is outlined in the approved project plan and has to be formally documented to provide proof that it has occurred.

Exam need to know...

- Transfer

  For example: How should transfer of ownership of the project deliverables be carried out and recorded?
- Customer

  For example: What is the role of the customer in project closure?

Transfer

Transference of ownership occurs for the project deliverables between the performing organization and the customer. Both parties require formal proof that this has occurred for future reference and to mark the point in the project where responsibility for the deliverable was transferred. As such, the process of transference of ownership should be a formal documented form of communication between the two parties, recording mutual agreement that it has occurred and the date. The terms, conditions, and process for transference is outlined in the project plan and can also be contained in any contracts used in the project. It is the responsibility of the project manager to be familiar with all the legal, administrative, and financial criteria that must be fulfilled to finalize transference of ownership.

True or false? Transfer of the project deliverable to the customer occurs as soon as the project manager approves the accepted deliverables.

Answer: *False*. Transfer of ownership is an agreement between at least two parties, so each party must formally agree for it to occur.

> **EXAM TIP** You need to understand the different roles involved in transference of ownership. The project manager takes responsibility for the tasks involved, but requires written approval of the project sponsor on behalf of the performing organization and the customer who accepts the deliverables.

Customer

The customer is one of the more important stakeholders involved in formal transference of ownership because it is usually a customer to whom the ownership of the project deliverable is made. The customer is the stakeholder who has requested the project deliverable and will also take ownership of it. This transfer of ownership between the performing organization and the customer must be formally documented and recorded because it is a legally binding agreement and record.

The project manager takes responsibility for overseeing the process of ownership transfer, but the customer must formally accept ownership. After the transfer is complete, all rights and responsibilities for the project deliverable also transfer.

> **NOTE** A customer can be either an external customer who has commissioned the performing organization to complete the project or an internal customer from the same organization.

True or false? After formal transfer of ownership is complete the project manager has no further legal rights to the project deliverable.

Answer: *True*. Final transference of ownership is carried out after all administrative, legal, and financial terms have been met; the customer now has full legal ownership of the project deliverable.

Can you answer these questions?

You can find the answers to these questions at the end of this chapter.

1. Who takes responsibility for ensuring that formal transfer of ownership of the project deliverable is completed correctly?
2. What is the role of the customer in the transfer of ownership of the project deliverable?
3. What are the three main components of formal documented transfer of ownership that all parties should ensure are met?
4. What form of communication is best for transfer of ownership of the project deliverable?
5. When should the process for formal transfer of ownership be documented?

Task 5.3: Obtain financial, legal, and administrative closure using generally accepted practices, in order to communicate formal project closure and ensure no further liability.

To be confident that the formal project closure has occurred, the project manager must ensure that all appropriate and required financial, legal, and administrative closure tasks have been performed and documented. This is an essential part of both the transfer of ownership of the deliverables and also of ensuring that the project manager and performing organization have no further liability. It is the responsibility of the project manager to ensure that these tasks are carried out in accordance with the project plan, but he or she has to consult with other relevant stakeholders such as the project sponsor and customer.

Successfully completing legal, financial, and administrative closure also requires procurement audits to assess the entire procurement process and might require the use of procurement negotiations to formally end disputed contracts. If you are doing a project in multiple phases, financial, legal, and administrative closure is done at the end of each phase; not just at the end of the overall project.

Exam need to know...

- Financial closure

  For example: Where do you find the information required to assist the project manager complete financial closure?
- Legal closure

  For example: What documents are required to complete legal closure?
- Administrative closure

  For example: Which activity is done last: financial closure or administrative closure?
- Procurement audits

  For example: How does a project manager determine whether the processes involved in procurement activities have been followed and if they are appropriate for the project?
- Procurement negotiations

  For example: What tool or technique is useful to ensure that disagreements or disputes about procurement contracts can be resolved?

Financial closure

Financial closure includes tasks associated with ensuring that all invoices owed have been paid, and all incoming cash flows have been received in accordance with the project budget and any contracts or other procurement documents that have been used as part of the project. Most of this information is obtained from the organization's cost accounting system, and the project manager must be able to reconcile all aspects of the information contained in the cost accounting system with the project budget. All variances must be resolved and accounted for before full financial closure can occur.

The process of financial closure can become complicated by such financial matters as contractual retention payments that are often held for months after practical completion of the project deliverable. The project plan should clearly state what the process and procedures are for dealing with financial closure under these conditions.

True or false? Financial closure requires all elements of the project budget and cost account to be reconciled.

Answer: *True*. In order for all elements of financial closure to be completed, you must be able to reconcile your approved project budget with the information recorded in the project cost accounting system.

If there is a variance between the project budget and the information contained in the project cost accounting system, it must be accounted for, dealt with according to approved change control processes, and documented.

> ***EXAM TIP*** **Remember that you cannot finish carrying out financial closure until you have successfully reconciled all the project cost accounts and documented all variances in accordance with your project plan.**

Legal closure

For legal closure to be completed successfully, the project manager must have access to any and all contracts used on the project. These contracts set the terms for full and final legal closure of the project. The role of the project manager is to ensure that all these terms and conditions have been met, and if they cannot be met, to ensure that any dispute-resolution procedures have been followed and completed.

If dispute resolution is required because the parties to a contract disagree over contractual terms or one party fails to satisfy agreed terms, the steps to go through, in order, are negotiation, then mediation, then arbitration, and finally litigation. Legal closure cannot be obtained until all steps have been successfully completed.

True or false? All contracts used on a project are successfully ended per the terms agreed in the contract.

Answer: *False*. Many contracts must end with a process of negotiated settlement because of poorly worded contracts and procurement documents, or a disagreement about interpretation between the parties.

> ***EXAM TIP*** **You should always keep records of any contracts used on the project and always abide by and follow the terms and conditions set out in the contract. Otherwise, you might be in breach of the contract.**

Administrative closure

Administrative closure includes all the tasks involved in ensuring that all the required internal processes relating to project closure have been completed per the project plan. It includes work generating, gathering, storing, archiving, and disseminating information to formalize closure of a phase or project. Administrative closure work includes collecting project records, ensuring that they reflect final specifications; analyzing project success, effectiveness, and lessons learned; and archiving such information for future use. It includes information about any aspect of the project, including reviews of project initiation, planning, executing and monitoring, and controlling work that has been done.

The project plan should clearly define what constitutes administrative closure, and this information is used by the project manager to complete the required work. This is important because the project manager needs to collect information throughout the project lifecycle to be used in these closing tasks, and it is difficult without an agreed-upon definition of what administrative closure is.

True or false? The work required to be done as part of administrative closure should be defined and documented during the project's planning stages.

Answer: *True.* Even though the work completed as part of administrative closure is done at the end of a project or phase, it should be defined and documented during the planning stages of a project.

> ***EXAM TIP*** **Administrative closure activities require that the financial and legal closure activities have been carried out and completed first.**

Procurement audits

A procurement audit is a defined and structured review of the procurement processes used throughout the project. It includes all the procurement work done, including planning procurements, carrying out the procurements, and monitoring and controlling the contracts used. The purpose of a procurement audit is to identify what went well and what did not go well, and then capturing this information in the lessons learned documentation.

True or false? A procurement audit examines the deliverables required by a contract to determine whether it is acceptable.

Answer: *False.* The procurement audit is focused on the procurement processes, not deliverables that have been used throughout the project.

> ***EXAM TIP*** **Remember that any time you see an exam reference to any kind of audit, it means examining a process of some sort.**

> ***MORE INFO*** **You can find out more about procurement audits by reading about the process called Close Procurements in the PMBOK® Guide, 5th edition.**

Procurement negotiations

As a result of carrying out closure of a project that has utilized contracts with other parties to deliver the goods or services required, the project manager must close all contracts used on the project in accordance with the agreed-upon terms of the contract. There are often disputes between parties to the contract about what constitutes closure due to poorly worded contracts, ambiguity, or misunderstanding, however. In this instance, the project manager has to facilitate procurement negotiation activities to reach a final settlement of all outstanding issues, claims, and disputes.

The steps taken in procurement negotiation follow four available options (in order of most favorable to least favorable): negotiation, mediation, arbitration, and finally litigation.

> ***NOTE*** **It is not uncommon for procurement documents and contracts to spell out exactly how disagreements will be handled and binds all parties to follow the agreed-upon escalation process. Therefore it is important that a project manager be acutely aware of the contents of all contracts being used in the project.**

True or false? Before resorting to litigation, a project manager should endeavor to resolve procurement disputes through negotiation, mediation, and arbitration.

Answer: *True*. You should not immediately resort to litigation because of the cost, time, and effort involved as well as the recognition of a full breakdown in the relationships between parties to the contract. Before resorting to litigation as an option of last resort, the project manager should endeavor to resolve procurement disputes through negotiation, mediation, and arbitration

> ***EXAM TIP*** **You should remember the four steps of procurement negotiation. If a question asks which one is best, choose the option that is most favorable from the options presented. Always consider litigation as final option only after the other options have been tried.**

> ***MORE INFO*** **You can find out more about procurement negotiations by reading about the process called Close Procurements in the PMBOK® Guide, 5th edition.**

Can you answer these questions?

You can find the answers to these questions at the end of this chapter.

1. What documents does a project manager require to complete legal closure of a project?
2. Where can a project manager obtain the financial information relating to project performance required to complete financial closure?
3. Why is administrative closure work carried out after legal and financial closure work?
4. What is the key purpose of carrying out a procurement audit?

5. What is the correct order from most-preferred to least-preferred of the methods for conducting procurement negotiations?

Task 5.4: Distribute the final project report including all project closure-related information, project variances, and any issues, in order to provide the final project status to all stakeholders

After procurement negotiations are complete; and financial, legal, and administrative closure is approved; the next step for the project manager to complete closure activities is to distribute the final project report to the relevant stakeholders. This final project report should comprehensively document that the project has been closed in accordance with the project plan, discuss any project variances, and deal with any identified issues whether resolved or not.

Exam need to know...

- Final project report distribution

  For example: What information should the final project report contain?
- Project variances

  For example: How are project variances detected?
- Issue log

  For example: Which document records issues raised by stakeholders?

Final project report distribution

The format, content, and distribution method of the final project report is in accordance with both the stakeholder management plan and the communications management plan, which are both part of the project management plan.

The stakeholder management plan identifies the relevant stakeholders who will receive the final project report; the communications management plan identifies identify the key messages and methods of distribution for the final project report.

The project manager takes responsibility for ensuring that the final project report has the required information and is distributed to the correct stakeholders via the appropriate communication methods.

The format of the final project report can be a template that is part of the organizational process assets of the performing organization. The format, content, and timing of distribution of the report should be agreed on in the planning stages of the project so the project manager can collect the relevant information during the project.

The content of the final project report includes documented evidence that the project has been closed and under what circumstances, reference to acceptance criteria, and verified stakeholder acceptance. The final project report also provides stakeholders with information about any significant variances that occurred during the project and how they were dealt with. It also refers to the issue log and any unresolved issues.

If the project closure report is being completed at the end of a phase, it contains information relating to how the project transitions to the next phase and what approvals are required.

True or false? The project closure report is done after legal, financial, and administrative closure activities have been performed.

Answer: *True*. The project closure report needs to include information confirming that legal, financial, and administrative closure activities have been performed and as such must be performed after they have been completed.

> ***EXAM TIP*** **In the exam, you should always assume that your project plan provides specific time and cost allowances to complete the work associated with the project closure activities and the project closure report. This might differ from your own experience.**

Project variances

The final project report contains a great deal of relevant information about the project. In addition to information confirming that the project deliverables were accepted; ownership is transferred; and legal, administrative, and financial closure tasks are complete; it also contains information about significant project variances—their impact and how they were dealt with during the project.

> ***NOTE*** **Detecting a project variance has three important elements. The first is a baseline from which any variance is measured. This baseline can be a scope, time, cost, or quality baseline prepared as part of project planning activities. Alternatively, the baseline can also be a particular part of the project management plan.**
>
> **The second element is a description of work being performed. This description can be in many forms depending on the work being performed, but is an appropriate metric to get meaningful information about the work being done.**
>
> **You then require the third element of a tool or technique focused on variance analysis that can detect any difference between the baseline, which represents the expected work, and the work performance information, which records what is actually occurring. Any difference between these two is a variance.**

The types of project variances referred to in the project closure report might include information about variances between planned and actual costs, scope, time, quality, human resource requirements, or identified and actual risks. In fact, any element of the project plan can result in a variance. It is important to record these variances in the final project closure report as both an acknowledgment of what occurred and as a record for future projects as part of capturing lessons learned.

True or false? Project variances include any information detailing a difference between a project baseline and work performance information.

Answer: *True*. A project variance can be defined only by comparing planned work against actual work.

Issues log

The issues log is produced to document issues raised by stakeholders, so its use is an important way of managing stakeholder expectations. The issues log records the particular issue raised by the stakeholder and what action, if any, is being taken to resolve the issue. Many of these issues are resolved as a result of the actions taken, but others will not be resolved at the time of project completion.

It is important to include information about significant issues that were encountered and resolved, and also information about significant unresolved issues to the stakeholders so that they can see what was addressed and what was not addressed during the project lifecycle. Information about issues is also a valuable input into any lessons-learned process for other current projects or for future projects.

> ***EXAM TIP*** **Unlike the risk register, in which all risks must be closed, not all the issues listed on the issues log need to be resolved at the completion of the project.**

True or false? Besides recording information about specific issues, the issues log is an excellent way to manage stakeholder engagement.

Answer: *True*. The issues log shows stakeholders that their issues are being taken seriously, so it is a great way to manage their expectations and level of engagement.

> ***MORE INFO*** **You can find out more about the project issues log by reading Chapter 13 of the PMBOK® Guide, 5th edition.**

Can you answer these questions?

You can find the answers to these questions at the end of this chapter.

1. Who should take responsibility for preparation and distribution of the project closure report?
2. Which two plans would the project manager find most useful when preparing and distributing the project closure report?
3. What are the three elements necessary for detecting variance on a project?
4. What information should be contained in an issues log?
5. What information is typically contained in a project closure report?

Task 5.5: Collate lessons learned through comprehensive project review, in order to create and/or update the organization's knowledge base.

The collection and storage of lessons learned is a very important part of both recording what went well and not so well on a project. The lessons learned are also an important contribution to future projects and the overall level of organizational project management maturity. It is the responsibility of the project manager to ensure that lessons learned are gathered at significant points in the project, particularly at project closure, and that the lessons learned document is added to the organization's lessons learned knowledge base for future reference.

Exam need to know...

- Lessons learned

  For example: What information is included in the lessons learned document?

- Organizational process asset updates

  For example: Which organizational process assets are updated by lessons learned?

Lessons learned

Lessons learned are a record of the knowledge gained addressing project events during initiating, planning, executing, monitoring and controlling, and closing a project. They are a useful record for the current project, other current projects, and future projects. They can record any significant information about the project from the selection process, tailoring project management methodologies, the depth and type of planning done, implementation and execution approach, and monitoring and controlling activities. They provide an opportunity to reflect on and record what went well and what did not go so well on the project.

Gathering lessons learned is done by several means. It can be done by collecting relevant information throughout the project, and can also be gathered by holding specific facilitated meetings or workshops with relevant stakeholders specifically to gather lessons learned. The process for gathering and recording lessons learned should be defined during project planning activities.

After collection, the lessons learned document should be stored for future retrieval in the organization's lessons learned knowledge base, which can be in electronic or hard copy form depending on the organization.

> ***NOTE*** **Each organization has its own particular way of gathering, storing, and retrieving lessons learned. Some use hard copies of documents and plans; others use electronic means or a mix of the two. The method is less important than ensuring that it is actually done.**

It is the responsibility of the project manager to ensure that the information contained in the lessons learned documentation is shared with the relevant team members.

True or false? Lessons learned should refer only to the scope, time, and cost elements of the project.

Answer: *False.* Although they are three very important elements of the project, the scope, time, and cost performance on a project are not the only areas that are reviewed and documented as part of collating the lessons learned. Lessons learned can examine and record information about any aspect of the project.

EXAM TIP **You should always assume two things in the exam. The first is that when beginning a new project, you have access to lessons learned documentation from previous projects. The second is that you always complete a lessons learned process yourself.**

MORE INFO **You can find out more about lessons learned in the PMBOK® Guide, 5th edition.**

Organizational process asset updates

As a result of gathering and documenting your projects lessons learned, you might want to update a variety of organization process assets to incorporate the lessons learned. Examples of the types of organizational process assets that can be updated as a result of lessons learned include the project selection and approval criteria, templates used for planning activities, and even project closure checklists. The type of lesson learned dictates which particular organization process asset is updated.

True or false? Organizational process assets include any templates and defined processes used to assist in completing projects.

Answer: *True*. Organizational process assets include plans, policies, processes, and procedures owned by the organization doing the project.

Can you answer these questions?

You can find the answers to these questions at the end of this chapter.

1. What sort of information should be included in the lessons learned documentation?
2. How should lessons learned be gathered?
3. What is a lessons learned knowledge base?
4. How does gathering lessons learned influence organizational process assets?
5. Who has responsibility for gathering and storing project lessons learned?

Task 5.6: Archive project documents and material in order to retain organizational knowledge, comply with statutory requirements, and ensure availability of data for potential use in future projects and internal/external audits.

At the completion of the project, a project manager has a wide variety of significant documents relating to project initiation, planning, execution, control, and closing. The information contained in these documents represents significant intellectual property for the organization to add to its organizational knowledge base. By archiving these documents so that they can be accessed easily for other projects, the organization can learn from past experience, increase the chances of project success, and increase its level of organizational project management maturity.

Exam need to know...

- Archiving techniques

  For example: What should occur to all significant project records, documents, plans, and communications at the completion of the project?
- Statutory requirements

  For example: Where should a project manager look to determine how long project records must be archived?

Archiving techniques

The process of archiving records involves storing the information gathered on the project for easy future retrieval. The method of archiving reflects the format of the original information. If there are a lot of hard copies of documents and plans, they can be archived in a protected storage facility in some sort of easy-to-understand filing system. Electronic forms of archiving are becoming increasingly popular because they take up less physical space, allow for full indexing and searching of stored material, and enable multiple team members in a virtual environment to access the information. Electronic archiving can be used for all electronic documents and copies of plans as well as for scanning hard copies of documents.

Each organization has its own processes, procedures, and policies for what is involved in archiving, the format it will take, and the length of time archived records are held. The project manager should take responsibility for ensuring that these rules are followed. In addition to the information being useful to other projects being undertaken, it must also be readily available for any future internal or external audits of the project or the organization's activities.

The organization's policies should also make clear what happens to the records at the end of the required archive period. This generally refers to the way in which the records are destroyed.

True or false? An organization's archives can be either physical storage of hard copies of documents or an electronic record of project documents and plans.

Answer: *True*. The archiving system can be either physical or electronic (or both), depending on the specific organizational policies on archiving and the future needs for retrieval.

> ***EXAM TIP*** **Although you might find these archiving tasks at the end of the project not as exciting as some of the other project work you have undertaken, you should always treat every question about it in the exam as important because the storage of project information for future retrieval by other projects is seen as an essential part of improving project management practices from initiation to completion on any project. You should assume that you will do this on all projects and that the project manager will take responsibility for ensuring that it is done.**

Statutory requirements

Although the organization performing the project has its own organizational process assets that set out how information will be stored and retrieved and the length of time it will be stored, many countries around the world also have legislation that requires organizations to keep information for a certain number of years. This is so documents and records that are required for an external audit for legal, financial, or tax reasons by the government can be retrieved.

The statutory requirements of the country in which the project is being undertaken override the organization's own policies, particularly concerning the length of time records must be stored. A project manager should always know what the relevant statutory requirements are for records storage and understand that overriding them is a breach of the law. As a result, the organization and the project manager might be subject to legal action.

True or false? A project manager should comply only with the organization's rules for storage of archived project material.

Answer: *False.* Although project managers should always comply with the relevant organizational rules relating to storage of archived project material, they must also align with government regulations about content; format; and the length of time that records are kept for legal, tax, and other purposes.

> ***EXAM TIP*** **A chain of custody tracks the location and control of evidence and is required to maintain the integrity of the evidence. If the chain of custody is not maintained, the evidence can be challenged in a court of law and thrown out as inadmissible.**

> ***MORE INFO*** **You can find out more about statutory requirements for archiving of organizational records by using the Bing search engine to search for your local government requirements.**

Can you answer these questions?

You can find the answers to these questions at the end of this chapter.

1. What does archiving mean?
2. What sorts of project records are archived?
3. Where should a project manager look for guidance on what sort of archiving technique to use and the length of time records need to be stored?
4. What is more important: an organization's own policies and procedures relating to archiving or government statutes and legislation relating to archiving?
5. Who should take responsibility for ensuring that project records are archived correctly?

Task 5.7: Measure customer satisfaction at the end of the project by capturing customer feedback, in order to assist in project evaluation and enhance customer relationships.

One of the last tasks that a project manager must take responsibility for is to measure customer satisfaction relating to the project deliverable and the processes used to deliver the project. Although completed at the end of a project, measuring customer satisfaction should be done throughout the project as well.

There are two main reasons for measuring customer satisfaction: to enable the organization to determine whether the project performed according to expectations and to learn ways to improve for future projects. The second reason is to enhance the relationship with the customer to increase the chances of repeat business.

Exam need to know...

- Customer satisfaction

  For example: Why is it important to gather information about customer satisfaction?
- Feedback techniques

  For example: What sort of data-gathering techniques can be used to get feedback from the customer?

Customer satisfaction

Among all the objectives a project can have, a high level of customer satisfaction is perhaps the most important. Customer satisfaction can be measured in a variety of ways, and the project manager should always consult with customers about which metrics are important to them in assessing their level of satisfaction. Common metrics for assessing customer satisfaction include satisfaction with the deliverable, the cost, the quality, project communications, the performance of the project manager and project team, how changes were managed, and the number of defects.

NOTE **The triple constraints on a project are usually described as cost, time, and quality (or scope) because these are the elements that usually define project success. Usually at least one of them, but often more than one, is an essential constraint on the project. It is often said that customer satisfaction is the next most important project constraint.**

Feedback from the customer assists the project sponsor, project manager, and project team assess whether the projected benefits the project was to deliver have been achieved. This process is known as benefits realization and it involves looking at the original benefits and outcomes the project was set up to achieve and measuring whether they were. This is different from producing a project deliverable; that is an output, not an outcome. Benefits realization is an important part of assessing the success or otherwise of any project, and customer feedback is an essential part of it.

True or false? Customer satisfaction is focused on whether the deliverable was produced per the terms of the agreed specifications.

Answer: *False.* There are many ways in which customer satisfaction can be measured, including whether the deliverable was produced per the terms of the agreed specifications and many other metrics.

> ***EXAM TIP*** **Measuring customer satisfaction is one of the last tasks that a project manager has responsibility for. If a question in the exam asks where you find information about how to complete this task, the best answer is a planning document, specifically one focused on project closure tasks prepared early in the project.**

Feedback techniques

Collecting data about customer satisfaction can be done with a variety of data-gathering techniques including interviewing, surveys, questionnaires, and product review. The particular method chosen will reflect how the customer wants to provide the information. All feedback information gathered should be documented and presented in a way that the information obtained can be easily understood and the data easily presented to other stakeholders for their information, review, and action.

The feedback obtained from the customer should be first reviewed to see whether any immediate actions are required and then archived with other project documents for future reference.

True or false? The customer should always provide feedback about levels of satisfaction in writing.

Answer: *False.* The customer might prefer to give verbal feedback about the level of satisfaction. However, the information should always end up in documented form so it can be stored.

Can you answer these questions?

You can find the answers to these questions at the end of this chapter.

1. Who should take responsibility for determining levels of customer satisfaction?
2. When should information about customer satisfaction be gathered?
3. What metrics can be used to measure customer satisfaction?
4. What are examples of common data-gathering techniques used to gather customer satisfaction information?
5. During the process of assessing benefits realization, is it the output or outcome that is more important?

Answers

This section contains the answers to the "Can you answer these questions?" sections in this chapter.

Task 5.1: Obtain final acceptance of the project deliverables by working with the sponsor and/or customer, in order to confirm that project scope and deliverables were met.

1. Responsibility for ensuring final acceptance lies with the project manager, who ensures that the correct stakeholders are consulted and their formal acceptance is noted.
2. The project sponsor is the stakeholder who accepts the project deliverables on behalf of the performing organization.
3. Accepted deliverables have been presented to the customer after becoming validated deliverables as a result of work carried out by the project team.
4. The primary role of the customer is to formally accept that part of the project scope of work that delivers the product the customer requested.
5. Final acceptance is the first step on the project closure tasks that must be completed. There are still tasks focused on transferring ownership, completing documented closure procedures, gathering lessons learned, and measuring customer satisfaction to be completed.

Task 5.2: Transfer the ownership of deliverables to the assigned stakeholders in accordance with the project plan, in order to facilitate project closure.

1. The project manager takes responsibility for ensuring that formal transfer of ownership of the project deliverable is completed correctly.
2. The customer is the stakeholder who takes final formal ownership of the project deliverable.
3. All parties should ensure that all required administrative, legal, and financial conditions of transfer of ownership are met.
4. Written and formal forms of communication are best to record transfer of ownership of the project deliverable.
5. The process for formal transfer of ownership should be in the approved project plan.

Task 5.3: Obtain financial, legal, and administrative closure using generally accepted practices, in order to communicate formal project closure and ensure no further liability.

1. A project manager requires all procurement documents such as contracts in order to check they have been completed per the agreed terms and complete legal closure of a project.

2. The financial information about project performance can be obtained from the project's cost accounting system.
3. Administrative closure work includes recording the outcome of the legal and financial closure work, so it must be done after everything is completed.
4. The key purpose of carrying out a procurement audit is to examine all procurement processes used on the project to discover what went well and what did not go so well and then record this information in the lessons learned documentation.
5. The order of procurement negotiation methods from most preferred to least preferred is negotiation, mediation, arbitration, and litigation.

Task 5.4: Distribute the final project report including all project closure-related information, project variances, and any issues, in order to provide the final project status to all stakeholders.

1. The project manager should take responsibility for preparation and distribution of the project closure report.
2. Two plans that the project manager finds most useful when preparing and distributing the project closure report are the stakeholder management plan that identifies the relevant stakeholders who will receive the final project report, and the communications management plan that identifies the key messages and methods of distribution for the final project report.
3. The three elements necessary for detecting variance on a project are a baseline of some sort, some relevant work performance information, and a tool or technique for variance analysis.
4. The issue log should contain information about the stakeholder who raised the issue, what the issue is, and any actions taken and outcomes achieved to resolve the issue.
5. The content of the final project report includes documented evidence that the project has been closed and under what circumstances, reference to acceptance criteria, and verified stakeholder acceptance. The final project report also provides stakeholders with information about any significant variances that occurred during the project and how they were dealt with. It also refers to the issue log and any unresolved issues.

Task 5.5: Collate lessons learned through comprehensive project review, in order to create and/or update the organization's knowledge base.

1. Lessons learned can examine and record information about any aspect of the project.
2. The process for gathering lessons learned should be planned at an early stage in the project and include data-gathering techniques and facilitated meetings and workshops with stakeholders.

3. The lessons learned knowledge base is the store of historical information and lessons learned about previously competed projects.
4. As a result of gathering lessons learned, there might be a lesson learned about the suitability of a particular organizational process asset. This is the time to update it to reflect the particular lesson learned.
5. The project manager has responsibility for gathering and storing project lessons learned.

Task 5.6: Archive project documents and material in order to retain organizational knowledge, comply with statutory requirements, and ensure availability of data for potential use in future projects and internal/external audits.

1. Archiving is the process of sorting, storing, and filing for future retrieval of relevant and significant documents, communications, reports, and plans used at any stage in the project.
2. All relevant and significant project records, documents, and plans relating to project initiation, planning, executing, monitoring, and controlling should be archived.
3. A project manager should look at any organizational process assets and any government statutory requirements.
4. Both are very important, but government statutes and legislation must take precedence because overriding them is a breach of the law.
5. The project manager should take responsibility for ensuring that project records are archived correctly.

Task 5.7: Measure customer satisfaction at the end of the project by capturing customer feedback, in order to assist in project evaluation and enhance customer relationships.

1. The project manager should take responsibility for determining the levels of customer satisfaction.
2. Information about customer satisfaction should be gathered throughout the project, but information about the final deliverable can be gathered only after it has been produced and handed over, so this is done at the end of the project.
3. Common metrics for assessing customer satisfaction include satisfaction with the deliverable, the cost, the quality, project communications, the performance of the project manager and project team, how changes were managed, and the number of defects.
4. There are several data-gathering techniques that can be used, including interviewing, surveys, questionnaires, and product review.
5. Although both are important, the outcomes are more important because they align with the reason why the project was done in the first place.

Index

A

B

C

D

E

F

G

H

I

K

L

M

N

O

P

Q

R

S

W

About the author

SEAN WHITAKER, BA, MSc, MBA, PMP, has a diverse project management background, having successfully managed complex projects in the construction, telecommunications, and IT industries. He brings this diversity of experience into sharp focus with his emphasis on professional and appropriate project management. Sean regularly teaches and speaks about project management, and has been a long-term volunteer with the Project Management Institute. He is also the cofounder and CEO of Falcon Training, one of the world's best project management training companies.

In addition to this book, he has written several books on project management, including the *PMP® Training Kit* and *The Practically Perfect Project Manager*.

When not writing about, speaking about, or teaching project management, Sean manages to find time to pursue his musical hobbies. He is always happy to answer questions about project management and can be reached at *sean@seanwhitaker.com*.

About the author

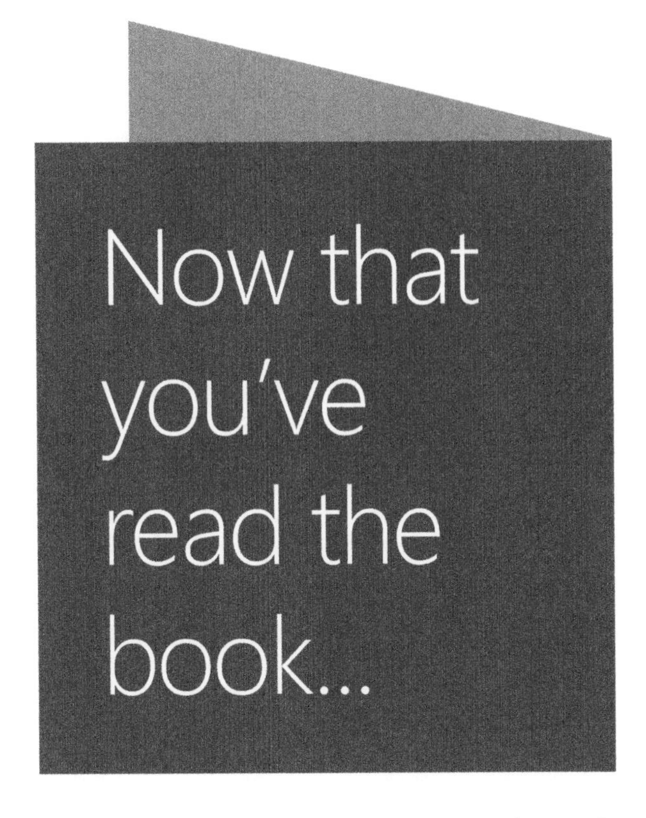

Tell us what you think!

Was it useful?
Did it teach you what you wanted to learn?
Was there room for improvement?

Let us know at http://aka.ms/tellpress

Your feedback goes directly to the staff at Microsoft Press, and we read every one of your responses. Thanks in advance!

CPSIA information can be obtained at www.ICGtesting.com
Printed in the USA
BVOW10s1654200813

328878BV00002B/2/P